CRIME AND CRIMINALS

OPPOSING VIEWPOINTS®

Other Books of Related Interest in the Opposing
Viewpoints Series:

America's Cities
America's Prisons
Chemical Dependency
Child Abuse
Criminal Justice
The Death Penalty
Drug Abuse
Mental Illness
Poverty
Racism in America
Suicide
Violence in America
War on Drugs

CRIME AND CRIMINALS

OPPOSING VIEWPOINTS®

David Bender & Bruno Leone, *Series Editors*

Paul A. Winters, *Book Editor*

OPPOSING
VIEWPOINTS
SERIES®

Greenhaven Press, Inc., San Diego, CA

Greenhaven Press, Inc.
PO Box 289009
San Diego, CA 92198-9009

Library of Congress Cataloging-in-Publication Data

Crime and criminals : opposing viewpoints / Paul A. Winters,
    book editor.
        p.   cm. — (Opposing viewpoints series)
    Includes bibliographical references (p.   ) and index.
    ISBN 1-56510-176-6 (lib. : acid-free paper) — ISBN 1-56510-
177-4 (pbk. : acid-free paper)
    1. Crime—United States. 2. Crime prevention—United States.
[1. Crime. 2. Crime prevention.] I. Winters, Paul A., 1965–   .
II. Series: Opposing viewpoints series (Unnumbered)
HV6791.W55   1995
364.973—dc20   94-4976
                                                                       CIP0
                                                                         AC

"Congress shall make no law . . .
abridging the freedom of speech,
or of the press."

First Amendment to the U.S. Constitution

The basic foundation of our democracy is the first amendment
guarantee of freedom of expression. The Opposing Viewpoints
Series is dedicated to the concept of this basic freedom and the
idea that it is more important to practice it than to enshrine it.

Contents

Why Consider Opposing Viewpoints?

"The only way in which a human being can make some approach to knowing the whole of a subject is by hearing what can be said about it by persons of every variety of opinion and studying all modes in which it can be looked at by every character of mind. No wise man ever acquired his wisdom in any mode but this."

John Stuart Mill

In our media-intensive culture it is not difficult to find differing opinions. Thousands of newspapers and magazines and dozens of radio and television talk shows resound with differing points of view. The difficulty lies in deciding which opinion to agree with and which "experts" seem the most credible. The more inundated we become with differing opinions and claims, the more essential it is to hone critical reading and thinking skills to evaluate these ideas. Opposing Viewpoints books address this problem directly by presenting stimulating debates that can be used to enhance and teach these skills. The varied opinions contained in each book examine many different aspects of a single issue. While examining these conveniently edited opposing views, readers can develop critical thinking skills such as the ability to compare and contrast authors' credibility, facts, argumentation styles, use of persuasive techniques, and other stylistic tools. In short, the Opposing Viewpoints Series is an ideal way to attain the higher-level thinking and reading skills so essential in a culture of diverse and contradictory opinions.

In addition to providing a tool for critical thinking, Opposing Viewpoints books challenge readers to question their own strongly held opinions and assumptions. Most people form their opinions on the basis of upbringing, peer pressure, and personal, cultural, or professional bias. By reading carefully balanced opposing views, readers must directly confront new ideas as well as the opinions of those with whom they disagree. This is not to simplistically argue that everyone who reads opposing views will—or should—change his or her opinion. Instead, the series enhances readers' depth of understanding of their own views by encouraging confrontation with opposing ideas. Careful examination of others' views can lead to the readers' understanding of the logical inconsistencies in their own opinions, perspective on why they hold an opinion, and the consideration of the possibility that their opinion requires further evaluation.

Evaluating Other Opinions

To ensure that this type of examination occurs, Opposing Viewpoints books present all types of opinions. Prominent spokespeople on different sides of each issue as well as well-known professionals from many disciplines challenge the reader. An additional goal of the series is to provide a forum for other, less known, or even unpopular viewpoints. The opinion of an ordinary person who has had to make the decision to cut off life support from a terminally ill relative, for example, may be just as valuable and provide just as much insight as a medical ethicist's professional opinion. The editors have two additional purposes in including these less known views. One, the editors encourage readers to respect others' opinions—even when not enhanced by professional credibility. It is only by reading or listening to and objectively evaluating others' ideas that one can determine whether they are worthy of consideration. Two, the inclusion of such viewpoints encourages the important critical thinking skill of objectively evaluating an author's credentials and bias. This evaluation will illuminate an author's reasons for taking a particular stance on an issue and will aid in readers' evaluation of the author's ideas.

As series editors of the Opposing Viewpoints Series, it is our hope that these books will give readers a deeper understanding of the issues debated and an appreciation of the complexity of even seemingly simple issues when good and honest people disagree. This awareness is particularly important in a democratic society such as ours in which people enter into public debate to determine the common good. Those with whom one disagrees should not be regarded as enemies but rather as people whose views deserve careful examination and may shed light on one's own.

Thomas Jefferson once said that "difference of opinion leads to inquiry, and inquiry to truth." Jefferson, a broadly educated man, argued that "if a nation expects to be ignorant and free . . . it expects what never was and never will be." As individuals and as a nation, it is imperative that we consider the opinions of others and examine them with skill and discernment. The Opposing Viewpoints Series is intended to help readers achieve this goal.

David L. Bender & Bruno Leone,
Series Editors

Introduction

"Violence . . . cannot be isolated by race or income or class. Fear stalks us all; suspicion saps us all. There is no exemption."

Jesse Jackson

Fear of crime affects all Americans in both obvious and subtle ways. Placing bars on windows and car steering wheels, carrying personal weapons, and refusing to venture out at night are obvious responses to fear. But when the government responds to the public's perception of danger with restrictions on liberty (such as curfews), increased taxes for police and prisons, and harsher, more punitive laws, even those who feel relatively safe from crime are affected. Fear of crime even affects criminals—especially the ones who get caught. For example, repeat offenders in California now find themselves subject to a new "three strikes, you're out" law. Advocated by President Bill Clinton and passed or being considered by a growing number of states, three strikes laws mandate greatly increased minimum prison terms or life sentences for those convicted of three felonies.

Three strikes laws and similar "get tough on crime" measures reflect a swing of the pendulum away from prison reform efforts that began about two centuries ago. Although prisons today are intended to serve four functions—retribution, incapacitation (removal from the opportunity to commit crimes), deterrence, and rehabilitation—the fourth is a relatively new requirement. The drive to make prisons a place where criminals could be reformed into honest, productive citizens began with a British movement in the late 1700s that established the first penitentiaries: prisons that were designed to make inmates feel sorry, or penitent, for their crimes. In America, around the same time, Pennsylvania Quakers formed the Philadelphia Society for Alleviating the Miseries of Public Prisons; they believed that some criminals could be reformed through meditation and hard work. If it worked, rehabilitation would not only restore these criminals to a productive life but also save money—the money lost due to crime itself as well as the costs of repeatedly apprehending, trying, and incarcerating the same offenders.

Over the next two hundred years, the relative balance among

the four functions of prisons gradually shifted toward rehabilitation. The moral and economic appeal of rehabilitation reached a peak in the 1960s and 1970s. In those decades, an emphasis on the rehabilitative function of prisons was reflected in the community correctional centers and halfway houses set up by federal and state governments. Overcrowded prisons, which forced the early release of many criminals, also contributed to the popularity of these alternative sentencing options.

But by the 1980s a variety of factors—such as high recidivism rates, a perceived increase in drug-related violence, and highly publicized incidents of "wilding" and other forms of random brutality—had begun to swing the pendulum of public opinion back to a demand for "law and order." Rehabilitation attempts had not been effective, according to some crime watchers. In the words of George Lardner, who reports on criminal justice for the *Washington Post*, "We like to think that rehabilitation works, but there is no evidence . . . that it does." Order could best be achieved, many now felt, by returning to principles of harsh punishment for criminals—such as three strikes laws.

The three strikes policy gained popularity and political momentum after the details of a particularly shocking murder were widely publicized. On October 1, 1993, in Petaluma, a small town in a rural area of northern California, twelve-year-old Polly Klaas was kidnapped from her bedroom during a slumber party, with her mother asleep nearby. The case was given national attention by the media, which closely followed the two-month search for the child until her accused kidnapper led police to her body on December 4.

The circumstances of the Klaas kidnapping fed a growing perception that no one was safe. Mike Reynolds, who started the drive for California's three strikes law following his own daughter's murder, gave voice to a growing concern: "What these crimes have done is show people that you can do all the right things [to avoid crime] and it doesn't matter." The disclosure that the man accused of the Klaas kidnapping had been convicted twice before of kidnapping and had only recently been paroled from prison added fuel to calls to put criminals in jail and keep them there.

Like Mike Reynolds, Mark Klaas—Polly Klaas's father—supports a three strikes law that would put violent felons in jail for life on their third strike, while requiring long sentences on the first strike for those who commit sex crimes against children. Klaas is among those who oppose the recent hastily adopted California three strikes law, however, because it also applies to nonviolent offenders and would be very costly. According to Klaas, "Three out of four of the crimes [the law] addresses aren't violent. We [will] pay for our mistake with high taxes to deal out cruel and unusual punishment to nonviolent offenders." Klaas, who fears that tax money will be taken from state spending on education to pay for new prisons, believes that a more carefully considered and crafted bill should be passed.

The rush to support and enact three strikes laws and similar harsh measures is at least in part the result of a public perception that there is increased reason to fear crime. Whether such fears are justified and whether tougher measures are appropriate and effective are among the topics debated in *Crime and Criminals: Opposing Viewpoints*, in these chapters: What Causes Crime? What Will Prevent Crime? Can Controlling Guns Control Crime? How Should America Deal with Young Offenders? How Is Fear of Crime Affecting America?

A December 1993 article in the *Los Angeles Times* expressed a popular sentiment with the title "Fear Is Starting to Run Our Lives." This anthology examines that proposition as it surveys current debates on effective responses to crime and criminals in American society.

What Causes Crime?

Chapter Preface

In the mid-1960s, President Lyndon Johnson launched what he called a "war on poverty," intended to fight poverty with government-created jobs and economic revitalization in urban and poverty-stricken areas. In the 1980s and early 1990s, with the public's attention focusing on crime, officials of the Bush administration asserted that the social programs of the war on poverty not only had failed to reduce poverty but were responsible for exacerbating crime. Disavowing government-run social programs, the Bush administration launched a "war on crime" designed to combat crime with the threat of harsh jail sentences for criminals. The war on crime was based on a much different view of the cause of crime from the one held by those who fought the war on poverty.

The officials of the Bush administration who originated the war on crime believed that crime is committed by people who lack a sense of personal responsibility. These officials blamed the social programs of the war on poverty for an increase of crime in the late 1980s. Echoing the Bush administration officials, commentator Midge Decter argues that the social programs of the sixties undermined personal responsibility by promoting a reliance on government to solve all problems. In Decter's words, "the efforts of government have done much to undermine [people's] capacity to take charge of their own lives. Yet taking charge of their own lives is the *only* thing that will save them."

A critic of the Bush administration and author of *Money, Murder, and the American Dream*, Charles Derber believes that crime is caused instead by a breakdown of social responsibility. He contends that the free market policies and the neglect of social programs of the Reagan and Bush administrations were responsible for an increase of crime beginning in the late 1980s. According to Derber, the Reagan/Bush economic policy loosening government control of business encouraged an everyone-for-himself, anything-goes attitude where responsibility to society did not matter. Derber argues that the neglect of social programs, coupled with this anything-goes attitude, not only left the poor to fend for themselves but left them infected with the same attitude. In Derber's words, "Just as insider trading and leveraged buy-outs symbolized the 'greed is good' credo in the corporate suites, dealing crack and grabbing handbags were signs of the times on ghetto streets."

The reasons people commit crimes—whether something internal for which they are personally responsible, or something in the social environment for which society is responsible—are debated in the following chapter.

"Genes can help determine the probability that an individual will turn to criminal behavior."

Genetic Factors Influence Criminal Behavior

James K. Hughes

In 1992, the National Institutes of Health withdrew funding for a proposed conference on genetic factors of criminality, due to opposition from groups that labeled such research racist. In the following viewpoint, James K. Hughes supports the funding of such research as a promising approach to reducing crime. He believes that heredity can predispose a person to criminality, and he criticizes liberal opposition to this research as stifling scientific enquiry.

As you read, consider the following questions:

1. In this author's view, what role does the social environment play in causing crime?
2. Does Hughes suggest what can be done for people who are "genetically" predisposed to criminal behavior?
3. Hughes states that "crime is a moral issue." Does this contradict his belief that research into the genetic basis for crime can be "promising"?

James K. Hughes, "Liberalism Thwarts Science," *Conservative Review*, October 1992. Reprinted with permission.

It is axiomatic that problems cannot be solved unless we understand them. Crime is a moral issue, but that does not mean to say that we should not look for the causes of criminal behavior in the hope of finding ways to alleviate it. Sound character training is one solution, but liberals have for long been telling us that environmental influences alone are responsible for criminal behavior. They hold that the criminal is not responsible for his actions, and that society is responsible, because society permits the environment that causes people to commit crimes.

Most Americans know in their hearts that the liberal explanation for crime is a partial truth, and is not the whole answer. Criminals are people who commit crimes where others would not. Character training, and an environment in which criminal temptations do not exist, are highly relevant. But a number of scientists are beginning to find evidence that criminal tendencies may be also to some extent hereditary.

As always, any reference to heredity upsets liberals and minorities deeply, and Leftist protests recently caused the National Institutes of Health to stifle further enquiry by scholars into the genetic basis behind crime by withdrawing funding for a conference on the subject.

Personality and Genetic Heritage

The idea that crime runs in families was well known to early Europeans. The Greeks believed that most personality tendencies were heritable, and believed that the tendency to be truthful and the tendency to lie were largely inherited qualities. Lowly people like slaves told lies, whereas well born people of respected ancestry did not tell lies. Early eugenicists in Britain and America pointed to the unavoidable evidence that crime tended to run in families. But the growing infiltration of liberals into the academic world led to a swing of "respected" opinion among social scientists, until it became a tenet of sociological opinion that social conditions created criminals. Talk about "the culture of poverty" became dominant, as though our forebears from the earliest of times had not been extremely poor as compared to modern welfare-supported ghetto dwellers, but had still in general lived very moral lives.

More recently, however, with advanced research into genetics and a small but creative and respected proportion of academic psychologists beginning to study the role of heredity in determining human character, psychologists are beginning to agree (with the exception of a vocal minority of hardline liberals and committed Leftists) that the individuals' personality is largely determined at birth by their genetic heritage. Identical twins have an identical genetic heritage, but siblings only share about 25% of their genes. Of course, where the parents belong to the

Genetic Factors in Crime: Findings, Uses & Implications

Researchers have already begun to study the genetic regulation of violent and impulsive behavior and to search for genetic markers associated with criminal conduct. Their work is motivated in part by the early successes of research on the genetics of behavioral and psychiatric conditions like alcoholism and schizophrenia. But genetic research also gains impetus from the apparent failure of environmental approaches to crime—deterrence, diversion, and rehabilitation—to affect the dramatic increases in crime, especially violent crime, that this country has experienced over the past 30 years. Genetic research holds out the prospect of identifying individuals who may be predisposed to certain kinds of criminal conduct, of isolating environmental features which trigger those predispositions, and of treating some predispositions with drugs and unintrusive therapies.

The Institute for Philosophy and Public Policy is sponsoring a conference to consider the implications of this research. We are bringing together researchers investigating the heritability and neurobiology of criminal conduct and of related behavioral and psychiatric disorders; historians, sociologists and philosophers who will put this research into cultural and intellectual context; criminal justice experts who will gauge the impact of this research on investigation and adjudication; legal scholars and ethicists who will discuss its impact on sentencing practices and conceptions of moral responsibility. This conference will integrate the concerns and findings of several disciplines on a range of topics, from the mathematical modeling of polygenic disorders to the courtroom use of genetic-predisposition evidence.

The goal of the conference will not be to achieve consensus: it would be naive to expect agreement among scholars and practitioners committed to different assumptions, methodologies and values. Rather, our goal will be to clarify and narrow their areas of disagreement: about the present state of research, e.g., whether specific findings are replicable; about the interpretation of that research, e.g., whether accepted findings are generalizable to other populations or other criminal offenses; and, finally, about moral and policy issues raised by the research, e.g., how does the capacity to predict and explain misconduct affect the appropriateness of blame and punishment? In sum, we hope to improve the ratio of light to heat in a debate that will only intensify as findings about the heritability and neurobiology of violent and antisocial behavior proliferate, and as proponents of genetic explanation become more ambitious.

Prospectus for proposed conference scheduled for October 1992 (later cancelled), sponsored by the Institute for Philosophy and Public Policy and the National Institutes of Health.

19

same race, children will tend to be similar, but all parents know that each child (other than an identical twin) has his or her own personality from the earliest days of childhood.

It does not take much reasoning to recognize that some personality traits will incline an individual toward socially acceptable behavior, while other personalities are likely to lead to trouble—and possibly to criminal behavior. Thus genes can help determine the probability that an individual will turn to criminal behavior.

Research in the 1970s

In the 1970s, two scholars of Harvard Medical School, Dr. Stanley Walzer (a psychiatrist) and Dr. Park Gerald (a geneticist) planned a program to explore already identifiable evidence that some "sociopaths" or persons with strong criminal tendencies actually possessed a chromosomal aberration.

Their theory went beyond the relation between heredity and overall personality. It sought to enquire whether there was a *direct* link between specific genetic aberrations and criminality. Because they were so harassed by liberal threats that they dropped their investigation, the research necessary to prove or disprove their theory was never carried out.

The normal pattern for human chromosomes is 23 pairs for each individual, of which the sex-determining ones are normally an XX pair in a female and an XY pair in a male. Some individuals, however, are born with either an extra female chromosome (XXY) or an extra male chromosome (XYY). The two doctors planned a long-term study to find out what effect this aberration might have on human health and behavior.

However, earlier studies had indicated, following investigations in several countries, that persons born with an extra male chromosome were ten to twenty times more frequent in homes for the criminally insane than in the general male population. Because a small group of Leftist activists (organized around a Marxist-connected group known as Science for the People) thought that the study proposed by Professors Walzer and Gerald would hurt the feelings of any individuals found to possess this genetic aberration, they started a campaign of harassment and organized protest which eventually forced Professors Walzer and Gerald to abandon their research. Thus, mankind must presumably remain ignorant of the truth whenever the answer might threaten liberal sensitivities. The modern "political correctness" movement is retarding scientific enquiry just as the medieval church forced Galileo to withdraw his thesis that the earth circled the sun rather than the sun circled the earth.

Genetics and Racism

As recently as August 1992, a new and equally shocking development has arisen. On May 1, 1992, the National Institutes of Health earmarked $78,000 to finance a conference on crime and heredity to be held at the University of Maryland. The conference had been approved by a peer-group review process, the approving body having included academic authorities drawn from diverse racial groups and even diverse disciplines. However, on July 15, NIH froze the funds, "until organizers can reshape the program," in the words of *Washington Post* reporter Lynne Duke, "to make it clear that NIH does not advocate a genetic explanation for crime." Apparently those who oppose the Conference are concerned that "such research could revive discredited theories that blacks are genetically inferior." Subsequently they cancelled the funding altogether.

What is meant by "inferior" was not explained. Blacks certainly are not "inferior" in many aspects involving physical sport; the World Olympics has shown their genetic "superiority" in many fields. And if the theories are "discredited," then surely further scientific research will either show them to be justifiably discredited, or else demonstrate that such theories were unjustifiably discredited. How can a nation that wants to stay in the scientific forefront of human progress ever say that any field of scientific research should be prohibited because it has already been "discredited"?

The real reason it was banned seems to have been objections by local black groups, because blacks have a disproportionately high crime rate in present-day America. Nationwide, 25% of young black males have spent a part of their lives in jail, and over 40% of young black males in Washington D.C. are either in jail or out on bail at any one time. The activists objecting to scientific enquiry into genetics and crime feared that any scientific evidence as to heredity influencing the criminal personality would be deemed to reflect badly on blacks and certain other minorities as a group. They alleged that this would lend support to "racist theories" and could lead to "a racist program of social control."

The Cancelled Conference

Presumably they preferred to ignore all efforts at scientific investigation of social problems, and to leave "social control" to the police and the present system of incarcerating offenders *after* the deed.

The full title of the conference was to be "Genetic Factors in Crime: Findings, Uses and Implications." Considering the high level of crime in America today, it would seem that for once the government was spending the taxpayers' money wisely. One would have thought that anything that might help our scientists find ways to understand the criminal personality, let alone reduce crime, would be welcome.

The seminar would have included scientists who had investigated the genetic contribution to human personality as well as scientists who were skeptical. Clearly, America's future is in danger if scientists are to be denied funds to allow them to investigate an issue whose outcome could be of the greatest importance in helping the nation to combat the ever-escalating crime rate.

Monkey Research and Neurochemistry

Work by Markku Linnoila and his colleagues at the National Institute on Alcohol and Alcohol Abuse has shown that persons who commit impulsive crimes—murder of total strangers, for example—have low serotonin [a neurotransmitter]. Men convicted of premeditated murder, on the other hand, have normal serotonin. Repeat arsonists—people who set fire to practically anything—have low serotonin. Men discharged from the military for repeated aggressiveness have low serotonin. Some psychiatrists say they can successfully treat humans with impulsive disorders with drugs that boost serotonin.

What makes an individual's serotonin high or low? The research shows that genes play a role, as does environment, including taking certain illicit drugs. The amphetaminelike street drug "ecstasy," for example, destroys brain cells that manufacture serotonin. After a single dose, experimental monkeys become more disposed to violence. Alcohol can play a role too. The occasional drink increases serotonin briefly—helping create a sense of relaxation—but chronic alcohol use has the opposite effect.

"What interests many of us is that the serotonin levels of monkeys—and their personality differences—can be traced back to the animal's early beginnings," [researcher Stephen J.] Suomi said. "It makes a big difference what kind of mothers they had and what their genetic heritage was. It's an interaction of the two—genes and environment—that shapes the animal's personality."

Boyce Rensberger, *The Washington Post*, March 1, 1992.

The part played by bad environment and "criminal subcultures" in promoting crime is widely recognized. The cultural and moral climate to which children are exposed is obviously important. Also pregnant mothers in inner cities, or elsewhere, who drink heavily or take drugs like crack can damage the central nervous system of any fetus they are carrying, and this may prevent their offspring from living a meaningful and productive life.

Current Research

Crime runs heavily in families. Dr. Allen Beck, a demographer at the Justice Department, found that more than half of imprisoned juveniles and a third of adult inmates have immediate family members who have been imprisoned. Thus much crime could be the result of bad family and peer group environments. Nevertheless, Dr. James Q. Wilson of the University of California in Los Angeles believes that the evidence for the heritability of personality does mean that research into the genetic basis of criminal-leaning personalities is "a very promising line of research."

Substantial research has been done on heritability and crime in Scandinavian countries, well known for their "liberal" preferences in social welfare. Meticulous records have been kept of the adoption of identical twins and their subsequent social histories, including criminal records. These records indicate that identical twins, reared under different social environments, tend to have closely similar criminal or non-criminal histories. If one identical twin turns to crime, the other twin, reared under quite different conditions, generally has a criminal record also. If one identical twin has been free from crime, the other, although reared in a different environment, is almost sure to have a crime-free record. This strongly indicates that criminal behavior is heavily influenced by personality.

Identifying Susceptible Individuals

This does not mean to say that there is any one gene which may be responsible for criminal behavior. What it does indicate is that the total personality may incline the individual to criminal behavior when placed in adverse environmental influences, while individuals who have inherited other personalities might well resist the temptation to crime.

If the progress of science eventually establishes the significance of genetics in determining criminal personalities, then it may confidently be expected that in the course of time it will be possible to identify potential criminals in advance of their committing crimes, and possibly some environmental conditions may be devised which will forestall their committing criminal deeds. Even before genetics advances to that level, the study of family histories in relation to criminal activities will produce fairly reliable indications as to which individuals *may* have a proclivity for crime. The emphasis here is on the word "may," but so it is with other kinds of "illness." Where families are known to have a high incidence of any particular disease, whether it be hemophilia, Down's Syndrome or simply heart disease, then medicine can and does prescribe suitable curative action which may be taken. Thus if we wish to reduce crime, and aspects of personality, including crime-susceptible personality, are genetically-influenced, it is imperative that science be permitted—or, more positively, actively encouraged—to enquire into this matter.

23

Let us simply say that sufficient research has already been done to indicate that personality *is* primarily heritable, and while not all potential psychopaths have to commit crime, those who have inherited tendencies to become criminals will be highly likely to commit crimes if the circumstances are right, whereas those whose personalities reject psychopathic solutions to their problems are much less likely to commit crimes in the same circumstances.

"The fault lies not in individual biochemistry and genes, but in the failure of America to deal with its most pressing problems."

Genetic Theories of Crime Are Racist

Peter R. Breggin and Ginger Ross Breggin

In 1992, the United States government announced a public health program aimed at fighting violent crime. The program's goal was to intervene in "at risk" families and neighborhoods, using psychiatric counseling and treatment in order to prevent violence. In the following viewpoint, Ginger Ross Breggin and Dr. Peter R. Breggin argue that federally funded research into a genetic predisposition to violence, proposed as part of this public health program, is baseless and potentially harmful to minorities. Ginger Ross Breggin is director of public education and Peter Breggin is director of the Center for the Study of Psychiatry in Bethesda, Maryland. The center is concerned with preventing abuse in psychiatric research.

As you read, consider the following questions:

1. According to the Breggins, what is the emphasis of "biological psychiatry"?
2. What are the inherent dangers of approaching "social problems" with medical or psychiatric intervention, in the authors' view?
3. What was the lesson of Nazi Germany, as described by the authors?

From "A Biomedical Programme for Urban Violence Control in the U.S." by Peter R. Breggin and Ginger Ross Breggin, *Changes*, March 1993. Reprinted with permission.

A storm of controversy has surrounded recent disclosures that the US government is planning a massive programme of psychiatric intervention into the inner cities aimed at identifying and treating young children with presumed genetic and biochemical predispositions for violence. The programme, called the violence initiative, was first described and promoted by psychiatrist Frederick Goodwin, director of the National Institute of Mental Health (NIMH). According to Goodwin, it is scheduled to become the number one funding priority for the federal mental health establishment in 1994. More recently, the overall biomedical thrust of the violence initiative received further support from a mammoth federally funded study by the National Academy of Sciences, entitled *Understanding and Preventing Violence*, edited by A. Reiss and J. Roth.

While confined to the United States, and not yet fully implemented, the violence initiative exemplifies the political use of biological psychiatry, and has historical roots in past abuses in both the United States and Europe. If it fails to fully materialize, the violence initiative will stand as a warning about the dangers inherent in approaching social problems from a biopsychiatric, medical or public health orientation. Meanwhile, despite widespread public controversy, federal officials have thus far refused to withdraw their plans.

Genetics and Racial Implications

Because most inner city children are African Americans, the violence initiative has been criticised as racist. While Goodwin himself never specifically referred to black people, his repeated references to "high-impact inner city" youth and urban poverty areas leave no doubt about the race of the proposed target population.

The National Academy of Sciences report specifically refers to "ethnicity" as one of the major predictors of violence. Under "Research Priorities" it lists "Key Questions." Question number one is, "Do male and *black persons* have a higher potential for violence than others and, if so, why?" While the study refers in passing to the possible social origins of black violence, its overwhelming emphasis is biological and genetic.

In addition to its racist implications, the violence initiative also reflects the current dominance of biological psychiatry with its emphasis on genetic and biochemical theories of human conduct, and physical interventions, such as drugs and electroshock.

The NIMH Violence Initiative

The violence initiative, as outlined in three speeches by Goodwin, plans to identify at least 100,000 inner city children whose alleged biochemical and genetic defects will make them violent-prone in later life. Treatment will consist of behaviour modification in selected families, special "day camps" for children with especially difficult backgrounds, and referrals to psychiatrists and neurologists. Children between the ages of two and eighteen will be targeted, with the main focus on younger ones.

The Offending Remarks

If you look, for example, at male monkeys, especially in the wild, roughly half of them survive to adulthood; the other half die by violence. That is the natural way of it for males, to knock each other off. And, in fact, there are some interesting evolutionary implications of that, because the same hyperaggressive monkeys who kill each other are also hypersexual, so they copulate more and therefore they reproduce more to offset the fact that half of them are dying.

Now, one could say that if some of the loss of social structure in this society, and particularly within the high-impact inner city areas, has removed some of the civilizing evolutionary things that we have built up, and that maybe it isn't just the careless use of the word when people call certain areas of certain cities jungles, that we may have gone back to what might be more natural, without all of the social controls that we have imposed upon ourselves as a civilization over thousands of years in our own evolution.

Frederick K. Goodwin, speech at February 11, 1992, meeting of the National Mental Health Advisory Council.

Since Goodwin emphasized presumed biochemical imbalances in potentially violent children, the major "treatment" inevitably will be drugs. This is consistent with the modern biological psychiatry establishment, as represented by the American Psychiatric Association, and its admitted "partnership" with the pharmaceutical industry. In a *Washington Post* article favourable to the violence initiative, government researchers openly discussed scientific findings that supposedly "show there are specific biochemical derangements in the brains of certain kinds of violent people—exactly the same chemical imbalances found in violent monkeys—and that these can be corrected with drugs. The same drugs work in both species."

The violence initiative ignores or minimizes environmental factors contributing to crime, as well as social, economic or political programmes to alleviate conditions within the inner city. Goodwin argues that there is no political "leverage" (political clout) in focusing on broader issues.

In presenting the violence initiative to the National Mental Health Advisory Council on 11 February 1992, Goodwin, as the government's highest-ranking psychiatrist, compared the inner city to a jungle that is going backward in evolution. He further compared inner city youth to rhesus monkeys who only want to kill each other, have sex and reproduce. These seemingly racist comments led to considerable controversy in the press. His observations, it turned out, were inspired by current federal research comparing violent rhesus monkeys to delinquent children with regard to presumed genetic factors, biochemical imbalances and responsiveness to drug treatment. This research is part of the already-evolving federal violence initiative research programme. . . .

A Government Study of Violence

Recently, fears concerning the violence initiative were confirmed by a much-anticipated report on violence in America by the National Research Council of the National Academy of Sciences. *Understanding and Preventing Violence* is funded by three federal agencies, the National Science Foundation, the Justice Department and the Centers for Disease Control (CDC). With a large board of research contributors, it purports to represent the latest in scientific research. It closely parallels Goodwin's proposals, focusing on the inner city and recommending that even younger children "as early as the age of four months" be studied for potential violence. The report points to "ethnicity" and "poverty" as the major variables predicting physical violence, and brings a heavy biological and genetic emphasis to bear.

The report discusses many supposed biological variables related to violence, including serotonin deficits and other "biomedical measures" or "neurological markers for violence potentials." Its final recommendations for "Research in Neglected Areas" use the same language as Goodwin's NIMH violence initiative, calling for "systematic searches for neurobiological markers for persons with elevated potentials for violent behavior." It also urges "systematic searches for medications that reduce violent behavior without the debilitating side effects of chemical restraint."

"Multi-community Longitudinal Studies" are proposed, including research on "neurobiologic measures . . . as is ethically and technically feasible" and "interventions" at the "biological" level. These are identical to Goodwin's proposed interventions in the inner city. Their most innovative aspect is described as the "unparalleled opportunity to examine the relationships between biomedical variables and violent behavior."

No conclusive evidence for the role of genetics in violence is found by the report, which nonetheless proposes further genetic research. Since the report identifies the inner city as the main arena of violence, the research will focus on minority populations, mostly African Americans. As noted earlier, the report openly declares that the number one research question for the future concerns whether or not black people are more violent than others.

The Conference on Genetic Factors in Crime

As the result of a national educational campaign initiated by the Center for the Study of Psychiatry and a coalition of members of the African American community, the government terminated funding for a conference entitled "Genetic Factors in Crime" at the University of Maryland, sponsored by the Genome Project of the National Institutes of Health (NIH) [NIH reauthorized funding in late 1993]. Since there are no known genetic factors in crime, critics of the conference felt it would give the misleading and potentially racist impression that genetic and other biological defects in black children and youth are responsible for crime in America's inner cities.

The brochure for the conference underscored advances in genetic research, noted the alleged failure of environmental approaches to violence, and suggested the possibility of drug interventions. As one of many ongoing projects anticipating the more massive proposed 1994 funding programme, the conference was but the tip of the violence initiative iceberg. . . .

The violence initiative ultimately puts children of all races in jeopardy. America's children are already subjected to massive psychiatric interventions, with more than a million children, mostly boys, taking methylphenidate (trade name, Ritalin), and tens of thousands being hospitalized. Despite widespread recognition that both the family and the schools are failing to meet the basic needs of children and youth, these societal problems are rejected in favour of subjecting young people to psychiatric diagnosis, drugs and hospitalization. If the violence initiative is fully implemented, America's children will come under increased psychiatric pressure.

While the initial focus of the violence initiative is on inner city children, 25% of American children, most of them white, live in poverty. If the violence initiative is allowed to proceed, it will eventually extend to other poverty-ridden populations, such as native American reservations and poor white communities. The National Academy of Sciences report advises extending its biomedical "intervention program to all children in a geographic area" in order to "broaden political support and to avoid stigmatizing high-risk children."

Research in the 1970s

In the wake of the black urban uprisings of the late 1960s, America became preoccupied with the threatening figure of the young black male as well as with the overall danger of rebellion and social chaos. Led by NIMH and the Justice Department, the federal government began to develop an overall programme for the biomedical control of violence that resembled the one proposed by Goodwin and the National Academy of Sciences. It included biological and genetic theories of violence, attempts at early identification and prediction, claims for research breakthroughs in diagnosis and treatment, and plans for behaviour modification programmes in controlled facilities. It too was inspired by fear of violence in the inner city and aimed at the control of young black males.

Three Harvard professors (neurosurgeons Vernon Mark and William Sweet, and psychiatrist Frank Ervin) were leaders in this 1970s violence initiative. They made the startling proposal that psychosurgery (brain mutilation by means of electrodes) could be used to control not only urban rioters but some black leaders who allegedly suffered from brain damage. Their psychosurgery research project, which only operated on white patients, was jointly funded by NIMH and the Law Enforcement Assistance Administration (LEAA) of the Justice Department. The grant also supported their genetic research in a prison containing a predominantly black population. In addition, acting alone, a neurosurgeon at the University of Mississippi, O.J. Andy, was performing neurosurgery on "hyperactive" and "aggressive" black children as young as five years in a segregated institution for people with learning disabilities. His method involved the implantation of electrodes, for multiple coagulations of brain tissue, on successive occasions.

During this time, proposals were made in Congress for funding a series of urban violence centres throughout the United States under the auspices of well-known medical schools. These centres would implement biomedical research and treatment programmes similar to those now being urged by Goodwin and the National Academy of Sciences. In addition, a new federal prison in Butner, North Carolina, was slated for development as a psychiatric-behaviour modification facility.

Due to efforts by the Center for the Study of Psychiatry and a coalition of concerned people and organizations, all federal funding was eventually cut off for the 1970s violence initiative, including psychosurgery for the control of violence, the genetic studies associated with that project, the violence medical centres and the psychiatric-behaviour modification programme at Butner. O.J. Andy was stopped from operating on children.

The Lessons of Nazi Germany

It has been amply described how Nazi Germany provided the largest experiment in the use of biomedical theory and practice for social control. Hitler's first legislation was aimed at the sterilization of a variety of individuals diagnosed as mentally ill. Eventually a scientifically and bureaucratically organised programme exterminated most of Germany's mental patients before the holocaust began.

The United States is not on the verge of becoming a totalitarian mental hygiene state similar to that of Nazi Germany. Nor is the violence initiative programme as extreme as proposals developed in Nazi Germany. But there are significant and threatening parallels in the proposed model for a state-controlled biomedical intervention into societal problems with focus on a feared and rejected racial minority. While the violence initiative would not, in the foreseeable future, lead to mass sterilizations or euthanasia, it would surely lead to vast encroachments on individual freedoms, to widespread psychiatric abuse, and to a great increase in racial prejudice disguised as medical science. If successful, it could open the way to further experiments in eugenics and social control.

University of California (at Berkeley) sociologist Troy Duster noted, "we will not see notions of Aryan purity and getting rid of whole populations of people. But we are in danger of returning to a kind of eugenics if we think of social issues like homelessness based upon their individual attributes. That's where the slippery slope begins down the easy reductionist path. I call this the back door to eugenics.". . .

The Dangers of Genetic Screening

The criminal justice system has already created a virtual institutional apartheid in which young black men are separated from their own communities and the remainder of America by the criminal justice system. This makes especially menacing the proposal to aim large-scale psychiatric interventions against the younger population of black children and youth, aged from two to eighteen years.

By itself, the proposed psychiatric screening of children is an unconstitutional federal encroachment upon schools, the privacy rights and well-being of children, and the integrity of the family. The current practice in which individual teachers voluntarily choose to refer large numbers of students and their families for psychiatric treatment has already led to widespread illegal and abusive practices, such as pressuring and forcing parents to drug their children as a pre-condition for going to school. It has encouraged the massive psychiatric drugging of children.

It is Orwellian, totalitarian and racist for the federal government to set up a massive screening programme of all city children with the aim of winnowing out potential criminals for preventive treatment. Neither the screening net, the theories behind it, nor

31

the proposed treatments have any scientific basis. The violence initiative is racially and politically motivated.

While Goodwin does not discuss drug interventions, he emphasizes . . . biochemical imbalances in the brain as "biochemical markers" and as causes for potential violence. These presumed biochemical imbalances can only be corrected by drug therapy. A considerable amount of federal research supports this approach, and some psychiatrists in the violence initiative network have advocated drugs for violence. The National Academy of Sciences report promotes the search for new drugs for the control of violence. Drugs are the only feasible mass intervention, corresponding with the needs of the pharmaceutical industry which is currently pushing these same drugs, including fluoxetine (Prozac), sertraline (Zoloft) and, forthcoming, paroxetine (Paxil) as their biggest potential money-makers. The schools, which already refer millions of children for psychiatric interventions, will become extensions of psychiatry and the pharmaceutical industry, creating a vast "third world" market for proprietary drugs within America's inner cities.

Politically, the violence initiative distracts society from the true causes of increasing violence. The fault lies not in individual biochemistry and genes, but in the failure of America to deal with its most pressing problems, such as white racism, poverty, unemployment, the degradation of the inner city, and the failure to provide in general for the needs of children.

The violence initiative gives an enormous political boost to biologically oriented psychiatry, which has already become the dominant wing of psychiatry throughout the United States and Europe. Western society does not need psychiatry to solve its social problems; it needs renewed dedication to fulfilling the basic needs of children through improving family life, the schools, and society. The violence initiative is embedded in the federal bureaucracy and the scientific community, and therefore will not disappear on its own. Under the guise of science, it is likely to survive the current political transition in America, unless sufficient public opposition can be mounted.

Authors' Note: These issues are documented and discussed in detail in the Breggins' book *The War Against Children: How the Drugs, Programs and Theories of the Psychiatric Establishment Are Threatening America's Children with a Medical "Cure" for Violence* (St. Martin's Press, 1994).

"Isn't a ghetto like a battlefield?"

Criminals Are Victims of a Violent Environment

Francis Flaherty

In the 1990s, battered spouses and abused children, defending themselves from criminal charges for killing or maiming their abusers, have claimed to suffer from a malady originally identified in war veterans, post traumatic stress disorder. In this viewpoint, Francis Flaherty argues that the ghetto environment can be as violently traumatic as a war zone; ghetto residents can suffer from PTSD as a result. He contends that if PTSD is a valid criminal defense for battered wives and Vietnam veterans, it should be a valid defense for some ghetto residents. Flaherty is a journalist and is on the editorial advisory board of the *Progressive*, a liberal monthly magazine.

As you read, consider the following questions:

1. According to the criticisms that Flaherty mentions, what is the difference between a battered spouse and a ghetto resident?
2. What are the conditions that make a ghetto a "war zone," in the author's view?
3. What does Flaherty mean by "social guilt"?

Francis Flaherty, "The Ghetto Made Me Do It," *In These Times*, April 5, 1993. Reprinted with permission.

When Felicia "Lisa" Morgan was growing up, her parents would sit down to meals with guns next to their plates. They were defending themselves—against each other.

"This was Lisa's dinner," explains attorney Robin Shellow. "She was seven at the time."

If nothing else, Lisa Morgan's childhood in a poor, inner-city Milwaukee neighborhood starkly illustrates the tragic effects of urban violence. "Mom shot Dad," Shellow says. "And Mom shot boyfriend. . . . [Lisa's] uncle, who was actually her age, was murdered. Two days later, her other uncle was murdered. Her sister's boyfriend was paralyzed from the neck down by gunfire. Her brother was shot at and injured. Her mother once had set her father on fire."

If this weren't enough tragedy in one young life, Lisa Morgan's mother was a drug addict and Lisa was raped at age 12.

The "Ghetto Defense"

So perhaps it's not too surprising that Morgan, as a teenager, committed six armed robberies and one intentional homicide in the space of 17 minutes in October 1991. The victims were girls; the stolen objects were jewelry, shoes and a coat. The dead girl was shot at point-blank range.

What *is* surprising—to the legal establishment, at least—is the approach Robin Shellow used in defending Morgan. In the girl's neighborhood and in her family, Shellow argued, violence is a *norm*, an occurrence so routine that Morgan's 17 years of exposure to it have rendered her not responsible for her actions.

This "ghetto defense" proved fruitless in Morgan's case. In court, the young woman was found both sane and guilty. Unless Shellow wins on appeal, Morgan will be behind bars well into the next century.

But despite its failure for Morgan, Shellow's "cultural psychosis" or "psychosocial history" strategy has taken hold. "I've gotten hundreds of calls from interested attorneys," Shellow says. Already, the defense is being floated in courtrooms around the nation. It's eliciting both enthusiasm and outrage.

The Defense Is a Medical One

Technically, Shellow's defense is a medical one. She believes that Morgan suffers from post traumatic stress disorder (PTSD) and other psychological ailments stemming from her lifelong exposure to violence.

Like other good lawyers, Shellow knows that the law abhors broadly applicable excuses, so she emphasizes the narrowness of her claim. Morgan belongs to a very small group of inner-city residents with "tremendous intra-familial violence," only some of whom might experience PTSD. She also stresses the unrevolutionary nature of the defense, medically and legally. PTSD has been recognized as a malady in standard diagnostic texts since 1980, she says, and it has been employed as a criminal defense for Vietnam veterans, battered wives and many other trauma victims.

They Have Begun Planning Their Funerals

In the past five years, 224 children younger than 18 have been killed in the District of Columbia either as targets of shootings or as bystanders. The carnage has been taken in by children who live close to the gunfire and by some children removed from it.

As they've mastered Nintendo, double Dutch and long division, some children have sized up their surroundings and concluded that death is close at hand. So they have begun planning their funerals.

According to interviews with about 35 youths and adults who work with them, children as young as 10 have told friends how they want to be buried, what they want to wear and what songs they want played at their funerals. Some young people dictate what they want their mourners to wear and say they want their funeral floral arrangements to spell out the names of their favorite brands of clothing. . . .

Douglas Marlowe, a psychologist at Hahnemann University Hospital in Philadelphia, says children often become fascinated with death during adolescence. Usually, he says, young people romanticize death or read literature about death in an effort to gain control over dying.

But Marlowe says planning a funeral is "extremely fatalistic" and is not a normal part of adolescent development. "Once they start planning their own funerals, they have given up. They are not trying to conquer death anymore," he says. "They are now turning themselves over."

DeNeen L. Brown, *The Washington Post National Weekly Edition*, November 8-14, 1993.

Despite Shellow's attempts to show that her defense is neither new nor broad, the case is ringing loud alarms. For, however viewed, her strategy sets up an inflammatory equation between inner-city conditions and criminal exculpation. The implication is that if you grew up in a poor, violent neighborhood and you commit a crime, you may go scot-free.

Yet why not a ghetto defense? After all, if a Vietnam veteran can claim PTSD from the shock of war, why shouldn't a similar defense be available for a young black reared in the embattled precincts of Bed-Stuy [Bedford-Stuyvesant neighborhood of New York City]? Sounds sensible, no? Isn't a ghetto like a battlefield?

Compare These Neighborhoods to War Zones

Alex Kotlowitz, who chronicled the lives of two Chicago black boys in *There Are No Children Here*, goes even further. He says the inner city can be worse than war. "You hear constant comparisons of these neighborhoods to war zones, but I think there are some pretty significant differences," he says. "In war, there's at least a sense that someday there will be a resolution, some vision that things could be different. That is not the case in the inner cities. There is no vision. And there's no sense of who's friend and who's foe."

There are other analogies that make the ghetto defense seem very legitimate. For instance, despite traditional self-defense principles, a battered wife in some jurisdictions can kill her sleeping husband and be legally excused for the homicide. The reason is the psychological harm she has sustained from her life of fear and violence.

Why not Lisa Morgan? Hasn't her life been debilitatingly violent and fearful?

These arguments make some lawyers hopeful about the future of Shellow's pioneering strategy. But most observers are pessimistic. "We'll get nowhere with it," says famous defense lawyer William Kunstler.

The Poor Instead of the Powerful

Why? One reason is that the American justice system often favors the powerful over the poor. For generations, for instance, the bloodiest crime in the nation—drunk driving—was punished with a relative wrist slap. By contrast, a recent federal law mandates that those convicted of the new crime of carjacking get socked with a minimum and mandatory 15-year sentence.

What explains these disparate approaches? Simple: protection of the affluent classes. Light penalties for drunk driving protect the affluent because they often drive drunk. Harsh carjacking penalties protect the affluent because they are the usual carjacking victims. "The middle class sees carjacking [laws] as protecting them from people coming out of some poor neighborhood and just showing up in *their* neighborhood and committing a crime in which they are at risk of dying," says Professor James Liebman of Columbia University School of Law.

Because the ghetto defense protects the poor instead of the powerful, Kunstler and others doubt it has a bright future. Other factors further dim the strategy's chances. Fear is a main one, says Professor Liebman. The ghetto defense brings a gulp from jurors because "their first thought is, 'If he's not responsible, then none of those people are,'" he reasons. And we all know what that means: riots, mayhem, Los Angeles.

Social guilt raises even higher the hurdles for the ghetto defense. To allow such a defense is a tacit admission that we—society—tolerate a situation so hobbling that its victims have become unaccountable for their actions. "If it ain't them who's guilty, it's us," says Michael Dowd, director of the Pace University Battered Women's Justice Center in New York. And "it's just too horrific for us to accept responsibility, too horrific to say, 'I'm responsible for what happened in L.A. [in April and May of 1992].' We will be able to accept the [ghetto] defense at the same moment that we are seriously moved to eradicate the realities behind that defense."

Television Violence and Crime

The entertainment industry can claim there are lots of other reasons young people act violently. They may have been exposed to crack while they were in the uterus, to malnutrition, to physical or sexual abuse, or both. They may have grown up in houses where there's lead in the paint, in neighborhoods where bullets fly, in schools where drug dealers roam school hallways.

But it's also true that television and movies saturate young people's lives with aggression and killings. The filmmakers are convinced violence is what sells; advertisers believe the same; and both purvey this material simply to make money.

The American Psychological Association reports that by seventh grade the average child has seen 7,000 murders and 100,000 acts of violence on television. When America's streets are then awash in rising tides of violent crime, most of it committed by teenagers, a trend unique among advanced nations, the entertainers' assertion of innocence rings hollow indeed.

Neal Peirce, *Liberal Opinion Week*, November 8, 1993.

What are the biggest criticisms of the ghetto defense? One focuses on the victim's identity. Battered spouses and battered children are accused of killing precisely those who hurt them. This endows the crime with a certain rough justice. But in a ghetto defense case, the victim is usually an innocent stranger.

Others, like Kotlowitz, worry that the ghetto defense might dislodge the cornerstone of our justice system: personal responsibility. "We have to be careful not to view people growing up in [inner-city] neighborhoods completely as victims; they are both victims and actors," he warns. "We can't absolve them from responsibility."

Lisa Morgan "went up to someone she didn't know, stole a jacket from her, and then just blew her away," he says. "There's no way as a society that we can excuse that. We can understand it, but we can't excuse it."

He raises a fundamental question. Everyone can point to scars from the past—alcoholic parents, tragic love, etc.—and claim exculpation. And if all are excused, who is responsible?

Another worry is diminished standards. "[The ghetto defense] lowers expectations," Kotlowitz continues. "It says, 'OK, I understand what you've been through, so it's OK to go out and hurt somebody.' And once you lower your expectations, particularly with kids, they will meet only those lower expectations."

A Disease Is a Disease

It's only fair to note that other criminal defenses also have these weaknesses. For instance, the victim of a PTSD-afflicted veteran is often an innocent passerby, and the battered-spouse doctrine certainly raises questions about personal responsibility and lowered expectations.

And if, as seems likely, some ghetto residents do have PTSD largely as a result of their living conditions, it's hard to see why this ailment should be exculpatory for veterans, say, but not for ghetto residents. After all, a disease is a disease, and how you got it is irrelevant.

How deep go the wounds from the ghetto? Here are two incidents in Morgan's life: "When Felicia was about 11, her mother put a knife to her throat and threatened to kill her," according to a psychologist's report in the case. "Felicia escaped by running into the basement, where she 'busted the lights out with my hand' so that her mother could not see her." Then, when she was 12, the landlord attacked her. "Felicia fought him off by throwing hot grease onto him, but he finally subdued her, tied her hands to the bed, stuffed her mouth with a sock and raped her."

How does one live like this? Morgan gives a hint. "My ears be open," she told the psychologist, "even when I'm asleep."

This was a *child*. Society did nothing to stop these daily depredations upon her. While the legal propriety of the ghetto defense is an important question, the biggest question of all in this story has nothing to do with personal responsibility. It has to do with society's responsibility to poor children like Morgan. What does it say about our society that such a defense was conceived? How can things have come to this pass?

"Blaming others for their predicament obscures from [criminals] the humiliating fact that they choose prison."

Criminals Are Not Victims

Theodore Dalrymple

In this viewpoint, Theodore Dalrymple expresses the opinion that criminals are not "victims" of their environments, but that they are sane human beings who choose to commit crimes. He argues that blaming society provides criminals with justification for further criminal activity. Dalrymple is a sometime prison doctor in England and a frequent contributor to the *Spectator*, a conservative British weekly magazine.

As you read, consider the following questions:

1. Why, according to Dalrymple, do prisoners "choose prison"?
2. What does Dalrymple mean when he says that criminals have an acute sense of justice?
3. What does the author mean by "medical absolution"?

Theodore Dalrymple, "Beyond Sympathy, Beneath Contempt," *The Spectator*, June 20, 1992. Reprinted with permission.

There is nothing quite like a little contact with hardened criminals for forcing one to revise (downwards) one's estimate of humanity. I have observed the liberal sentiments of several young doctors crumble to nothing, like a sandcastle before the tide, in the face of psychopathic murderers and rapists. They, the young doctors, enter prison convinced that incarceration is primitive, wasteful and serves no useful purpose whatever; a little later, they come out muttering that prisoners should never be released. Until then, their idea of evil incarnate had been the Tory [conservative party] Minister of Health of the day.

I admit that I love prison (at least, as an occasional visitor). It is the easiest and quickest way to travel to another continent, whose strange inhabitants have different rites and customs. I like the warders—their camaraderie, their gallows humour, even their rigidities and stubborn rituals. And I have seen many more acts of kindness done by them towards the prisoners than I have seen acts of brutality or cruelty.

As for the prisoners, they never cease to fascinate me. Much of the fascination is morbid, of course: to examine closely the hands of a strangler, the face of an arsonist, the mind of a poisoner, gives me the thrill which others derive from murder fiction. The extremes of behaviour invariably intrigue us even as they cause us unease.

But the prisoners also raise philosophical questions in acute and practical ways. In my youth, I studied philosophy with something approaching passion but, despairing of firm conclusions, gave it up as pointless and time-wasting. The prisoners, however, revive the old ultimate questions, of freewill and determinism, of good and evil, of the nature of explanation and the final unknowability of things.

Criminals Choose Prison Life

Often I meet prisoners who have committed the most terrible crimes, but repentance is rare, except in front of the parole board, where it is quite common. Of course, the majority of prisoners have committed only petty offences, small (but repeated) crimes against property, or rather against the people who own the property. They are often pathetic and inadequate individuals, thoroughly accustomed to prison life; the warmth and three square meals a day provided unconditionally in prison are for them an incitement to further crime. As for the loss of freedom, they welcome it: being told what to do all their waking hours obviates the need for thought and decision, processes which are infinitely painful for them.

This is not to say that they accept their lot, far from it. They may not be very intelligent or sensitive on the whole (I haven't met one who realises empathically how traumatic even petty crime is to many of its victims, or how it can change its victims' lives), but few are they who have not detected the liberal *Zeitgeist* of the last quarter of a century, who have not taken advantage of it to affix the blame for their behaviour elsewhere, and who do not descant at the first opportunity on the deformity of their own upbringing. This allows them to retain their sense of moral worth: it is they, not the people whom they have robbed or whom they have assaulted, who are the real victims. Furthermore, blaming others for their predicament obscures from them the humiliating fact that they choose prison, that it is the life they have come to prefer.

"THE DEFENSE CONTENDS THAT THE COURT IS AT FAULT BY PUTTING MY CLIENT ON PROBATION THUS PERMITTING HIM TO RUN FREE AND GET INTO MORE TROUBLE!"

But it is the notorious cases, the sadistic killers, the dismemberers and cannibals, the psychopaths and those who were once called the morally insane who present the greatest philosophical challenge (as well as providing the greatest *frisson*). To look into their cold, bright, dead eyes is to have all one's assumptions about life challenged.

Do such people really exist, or are they the product of our perfervid imaginations? Are there really people without morality, or do we invent them to distract ourselves from the intellectual difficulties in grounding our moral conceptions on any firm or indisputable basis? Are there beings so entirely different from us, morally speaking, that they form a separate and distinct class, or are they merely at the end of a behavioural continuum along which anyone may, in the right circumstances, slide? Victorian criminologists thought there was such a class, and that it was genetically determined. Thus Henry M. Boies, an American criminologist, writing in 1893:

> Everyone who has visited prisons and observed large numbers of prisoners together has undoubtedly been impressed, from the appearance of prisoners alone, that a large portion of them were born to be criminals. There would seem to be certain recognisable features which differentiate these from the rest of mankind, and set them apart as a criminal class, of which it might be assumed that, although any given individual might be reclaimed and saved, as a class the whole were destined to live and die criminals.

To the untutored eye, such a conclusion might still seem plausible enough and, in its way, reassuring. But one has only to consider the soul of Man under Nazism and communism, and reflect a little on the Khmer Rouge and their Peruvian imitators, Sendero Luminoso, to realise that the class of psychopaths can be indefinitely expanded.

A Criminal's Sense of Justice

Be that as it may, I have never actually met anyone who was morally insane, in the sense that he lacked the normal moral categories of thought. On the contrary, the worst of criminals often have the acutest sense of justice (or rather injustice): but they apply it only to themselves, and in obviously self-serving ways. It would be a mistake to conclude from this, however, that their sense of justice is insincere, for the human mind is a subtle instrument and quite capable of being morally earnest and viciously perverse at the same time.

I [once] encountered a remanded kidnapper of very high IQ who had kept a small child in a box for more than two weeks while demanding a ransom from her parents. When finally he was arrested, he was charged also with the sexual assault of another small girl, a crime which he steadfastly maintained he did not commit. He said that if he was found guilty—unjustly—of this second crime, he would kill himself in protest.

'Why?' I asked.

'I don't want people to think I'm a nonce,' he said.

'But you *are* a kidnapper,' I said. 'And kidnapping is a very serious crime. You are certain to get a long sentence.'

He fixed me with his expressionless, porcelain-blue eyes.

'I looked after her well,' he said. After a pause, he continued:

'She came out of it alive. But I'm not a nonce, and I won't allow the fuckers to pin it on me.'

At about the same time, I interviewed a convicted rapist who, with three accomplices, had broken into a house and raped an adolescent girl. He was sentenced to ten years (the judge believing him to be the ringleader of the gang), while his accomplices received seven years. His accomplices had now been released, and he was on hunger strike (which he later broke) because of what he saw as the terrible injustice done him. He was perfectly immovable on the subject; there was no Dostoyevskian realisation that any injustice done him—if such it were—was, compared with his terrible crime, trivial, a grain of sand set against the Himalayas. He was storing up his 'reasons' for his next monstrous act.

Community Consciousness and Criminals

The level of crime is deeply affected by the total community fabric. It is not enough for families to be strong, or schools to be fine educational institutions, and so on. To minimize crime, all of these elements must reinforce one another. Thus, in those parts of the country (and the world) where families are strong, schools teach moral values, communities are intact, and values command respect—as in Utah, for instance, with its Mormon-inspired community consciousness—crime is much lower than elsewhere. The national violent crime rate in 1990 was 730 per 100,000 people; in Utah, it was 284.

Even in the most intact communities, some individuals will—because of genetic, chemical, or physiological aberrations or deep-seated psychological distortions—act in an immoral manner. There is a hard core of psychopaths and criminals that the most dedicated parents, the most effective schools, and the most attentive and caring neighborhoods cannot reach. To cope with them, all communities require the hand of public authorities, lest people be subject to serial killers, wilding gangs, child abusers, and arsonists. To suggest that these people can be reached by involving them in positive community work, meaningful creative work, or national service is a fairy tale. They are the proper subjects for police and imprisonment. Their legal rights should be fully protected, but otherwise there is no denying that when it comes to hard-core criminals and dangerous mental patients, public authorities are a legitimate, morally appropriate way to protect the public.

Amitai Etzioni, *Utne Reader*, March/April 1993.

Many times have psychopaths burdened me with the responsibility for telling them why they do the things they do, and have mocked me because I have been unable to find the explanation. A murderer who drove a fence picket through his wife's chest blamed his doctor because he had gone to him the week before complaining of agitation and anxiety, and the doctor had done nothing. It was therefore, he told me, the doctor, not he, who was the *real* culprit. In the prison, an armed robber about to be released into the wider world came to tell me that in his fantasies he strangled, decapitated and disarticulated people he met in the street.

'Have you ever . . .' I began.

'Acted on my fantasies? Yes, I once strangled a lad I met down a dark alleyway at night.'

'But you let go before it was too late?'

'He was unconscious and I left him for dead. When they found him his jaw was smashed to pieces.'

'Were you ever charged?'

'They never knew it was me who did it.'

His sadistic leer was the most horrible expression I have ever seen. He thought that once he had informed me of his propensities, I had *ipso facto* released him from responsibility for them, and had granted him a kind of medical absolution for them in advance. But how he would have complained, if—on the basis of his confession—I had arranged a form of medical preventive detention for him!

The Locus of Moral Responsibility

I do not know any longer what it is to 'understand' another person, at least beyond banalities such as 'he ate because he was hungry.' There seems to me an irreducible gap between psychopathic behaviour and all hypothesised explanations of it. But I would make one general point, whose truth I cannot prove and which I admit is highly speculative: it is that the effort to explain psychopathic behaviour is itself likely to result in its spread.

In Brian Masters' book about Dennis Nilsen, *Killing for Company*, which is unlikely ever to be surpassed as an effort to comprehend the mind of such a man, we are told that on one occasion Nilsen said to the police that the real criminal, the person who should really be locked up, was in Number 10 [Downing Street—in other words, the prime minister of England], not in the police station confessing to 15 murders. And he later wrote a poem about one of his victims in which he accused society of hypocrisy, for it concerned itself with the murdered boy, who was something of a vagrant, only after his death: during his life it had cared nothing for him.

The locus of moral responsibility has departed the individual and settled on a distant abstraction. No doubt there will always be brain-damaged individuals who, for physiological reasons, cannot contain their rages and their impulses; but if, as is taught in the schools and the universities, in the churches and on the television, in the newspapers and in the secular sermons of the *bien pensants*, responsibility lies not with the individual but with society, it is scarcely surprising that crime and other forms of social deviance are inexorably on the increase. To deal justly oneself is a spiritual and intellectual discipline; to espy injustices elsewhere is often the merest self-indulgence.

"The drug economy, especially retail crack sales, is currently out-competing the legal, entry-level economy for the 'hearts and minds' of inner-city youth."

Poverty and Unemployment Cause Crime

Philippe Bourgois

In the late 1980s, economists suggested that crime is prevalent because the risks of punishment are low and the profits are higher than the wages of traditional careers. In the following viewpoint, Philippe Bourgois validates that theory as he describes a working-poor neighborhood where traditional job opportunities are limited. He argues that selling drugs is an attractive, economically viable career choice for young men in such neighborhoods. Bourgois is an assistant professor of anthropology at San Francisco State University and a visiting scholar at the Russell Sage Foundation in New York.

As you read, consider the following questions:

1. According to Bourgois, how are inner-city youths transformed into adult felons?
2. According to the author, drug "sellers frequently talk about 'going legit.'" Does he say what the attractions of "going legit" could be?
3. How does Bourgois relate the conspiracy theories of "The Plan" and "The System" to the failure of the public sector?

From Philippe Bourgois, "Growing Up: What Opportunities for the Young?" *The American Enterprise*, May/June 1991. Copyright ©1991 by the American Enterprise Institute. Distributed by the *New York Times* Special Features/Syndication Sales. Reprinted with permission.

I live with my family in a tenement in East Harlem opposite a large complex of public housing projects where I have been engaged since 1985 in ethnographic research. I am using the classical anthropological methodology of participant-observation fieldwork, focusing on a network of youths and adults who participate intensively in the underground economy—primarily street-level, retail crack distribution. This means I have spent hundreds of nights on the streets and in crack houses observing and tape recording dealers and addicts. I visit their families, attend their parties and intimate reunions—from Thanksgiving dinners to New Year's Eve celebrations—in order to collect life history interviews and to befriend their children, spouses, lovers, siblings, mothers, grandmothers, and—when possible—fathers and stepfathers. This allows me to situate the street dealing scene in its larger family and community context.

East Harlem, also referred to as *El Barrio*, or Spanish Harlem, is a 200-square-block neighborhood in New York City's upper East Side. Although the population is between 40 and 45 percent African-American, it is considered by both its residents and outsiders to be New York's quintessential Puerto Rican community. Most of the individuals I interact with are second- or third-generation New York-born Puerto Ricans.

An East Harlem Neighborhood

According to 1980 census data, 29 percent of the population in East Harlem was at 75 percent of the poverty level, 48 percent at 125 percent, and 68 percent at 200 percent. In other words, if one were to adjust for New York City's exorbitant cost of living, well over half of the population would fall into the ranks of the "working poor." One in three families in East Harlem is dependent on public assistance, and approximately half of all households are headed by women. The schools in the neighborhood have one of the highest drop-out rates in the country.

The neighborhood is visibly poor. Abandoned buildings, vacant lots, and streets strewn with rubbish are the rule here rather than the exception. My block is not atypical: I can get heroin, crack, powder cocaine, hypodermic needles, methadone, Valium, PCP, and mescaline within a two-block radius of my apartment.

Despite this active street scene and the visible social and economic crisis it reflects, the majority of the adult population of East Harlem abhors drugs. Most heads of households work nine-to-five-plus-overtime at entry-level jobs and shun illegal activity. Nonetheless, this majority, mainstream, working-class and working-poor sector is in retreat. Many residents, especially the elderly, live in terror, venturing outside only during daylight hours.

The street-level drug dealers I study are resented and shunned by the majority of the community. Unfortunately, however, they control the streets. Worse yet, they are offering on a daily basis an all-too-persuasive, violent, and self-destructive alternative to the youths growing up in the neighborhood.

Most of the hard-core inner-city "unemployables" have, in fact, worked at legitimate pursuits at some time or other in their lives. All of the crack dealers and addicts whom I have interviewed have worked at one or more legal jobs in their early youth. In fact, most entered the labor market at an earlier age than the typical teenager. Before their twelfth birthday, many were bagging groceries at the supermarket for tips, stocking beers (off the books) in local *bodegas*, or shining shoes. In fact, many dropped out of school in order to make money to obtain the childhood "necessities"—candy, sneakers, basketballs, baseball cards—that most preteens throughout the rest of America are able to buy with their allowances. What happens to these "eager-beaver" 12-year-olds that transforms them into the adult felons who terrorize their neighbors?

A Form of Moonlighting

Selling drugs has become a form of moonlighting, according to a study of drug dealers in the nation's capital. Seventy-five percent of the dealers interviewed reported holding legitimate jobs, averaging $7 an hour.

Dealing paid an average of $30 an hour with median earnings about $10,000 a year, working a mean average of four hours a day.

"It is indeed much more profitable on an hourly basis than are legitimate jobs available to the same persons," says the Greater Washington Research Center report, which interviewed dealers on probation. "On the other hand, few of the street-level dealers who made up most of this sample reported the kinds of incomes from which Mercedes and great fortunes spring.". . .

[Dealing is] not without risks. For each year of work, a dealer has a 1.4 percent chance of dying, a 7 percent chance of serious injury, and a 22 percent chance of going to jail for an average sentence of 18 months, the report estimates.

Vanessa Gallman, *New Dimensions*, January 1991.

The drug economy, especially retail crack sales, is currently out-competing the legal, entry-level economy for the "hearts and minds" of inner-city youth. Tragically, crack/cocaine is the only growing, dynamic, equal-opportunity-employer industry in East Harlem today. According to police records, millions of dollars' worth of drug sales are going on within a stone's throw of the youths living in my building. Why should we be surprised when they drop out of school to "get some of mine's"? And why should we wonder why they refuse low-prestige jobs in the service sector in favor of building up crack/cocaine enterprises where their identities, rooted in street culture, become an asset rather than a liability?

The youths on my block are not disorganized or apathetic. On the contrary, they are overly organized and energetic. Their mobilization, however, is destroying them and their community. The most determined, lucky, and ruthless of the children on my block are running thousand-dollar-a-day drug sales networks and are not yet 18. They keep regular hours and supervise half a dozen employees who work on consignment or on an hourly wage.

"Going Legit"

The most successful drive their Mercedes, Jaguars, and Porsches up to the fire hydrant on the block to be washed and waxed by local crack addicts while they stand triumphantly ten yards away and watch the neighborhood kids ogle their "ride" (car). To be this successful, they have to cultivate an aggressive and violent presentation of self or else they will lose credibility and be forced out of business, perhaps even killed. They believe with a vengeance in the traditional American dream: rags to riches through private entrepreneurship.

At the same time, contrary to what we hear in the media, the vast majority of the street sellers are not, in fact, making much money—on an average night, they might get $6 or $8 an hour. Of course, that is already twice minimum wage. But what is more important is that they are able to earn these "good wages" without having to demean themselves in jobs they believe compromise their sense of personal dignity. They do not want to adapt to the rules of a hostile outside world that is uncomfortable with their form of dress, their language, and their culture in general. In the crack economy, there is also a real possibility for dramatic advancement that is not easily replicated in the entry-level service sector, which is where the jobs available to them are located once they drop out of high school.

During the course of their lives, most of the street sellers cycle in and out of legal, just-above-minimum-wage jobs. Even the most hard-core sellers frequently talk about "going legit." In fact, one young man left the crack business when he was given a temporary job over the holidays with the Postal Service. Another street dealer recently took a union job as a porter for Woolworths; another now works as a bus driver for the New York City Transit Authority; yet another joined the Army. This shows that despite the strength of the underground economy, the

49

situation is not hopeless. There is still an arena within which the mainstream economy can compete for their allegiance. . . .

The Failure of the Public Sector

The miles and miles of abandoned buildings are powerful testimony to a profound infrastructure crisis. For the second summer in a row, the public swimming pool two blocks away that was the one healthy, popular, city-run activity center for youths in the neighborhood has been closed down while a corrupt construction company "renovates" it at a snail's pace. For the third year in a row, the basketball courts hedged in between the public housing towers are marred by deep potholes; only every other hoop on the courts is still in place, and the lighting systems for nighttime play never operate. Broken beer bottles, human feces, crack vials, and an occasional hypodermic needle litter the jungle gym where I take my two-year-old son to play on weekends.

Marginal Men—Going Nowhere

East Setauket [in suburban Long Island, New York] is not really all that far from East Harlem. If something is festering in the ghetto, something very similar is gnawing away in middle-income suburbs. A "way of life," as the cliché goes, is coming to an end, and in its place a mean streak is opening up and swallowing everything in its path. Economists talk about "deindustrialization" and "class polarization." I think of it as the problem of marginal men: They are black and white, Catholic and Pentecostal, rap fans and admirers of techno-pop. What they have in common is that they are going nowhere—nowhere legal, that is.

Barbara Ehrenreich, *Utne Reader*, May/June 1991.

It is unrealistic to expect most of the eight- and ten-year-olds playing tag in the ruins of the abandoned buildings or the pre-teenagers sifting through mounds of garbage piled on the sidewalks to develop healthy notions of public good and personal responsibility. The "common sense" emerging among this newest generation is that "The System" hates them. A disproportionate number of adults and teenagers believe virulent conspiracy theories about "The Plan"—that is, the evil intentions of the wealthy white-power-structure elite toward poor African-Americans and Puerto Ricans living in Manhattan. A fringe group has even postered the bricked-up abandoned buildings along several blocks with a picture of a black family struggling into the distance, carrying their possessions on their backs. The word "Genocide!" is written above the picture in red ink. This kind of rage and frustration will filter down in one form or another to the bulk of the children in the neighborhood, including those living in stable working households.

Perhaps the most ironic failing of the public sector is that the biggest crack-house landlord is the City of New York. Crack is most frequently sold out of abandoned building storefronts or in housing project stairways. Most people in the neighborhood assume that the police are paid off to ignore this activity, but in fact they do not need to be. The police are overwhelmed by the magnitude of crime; their morale is low; they cannot relate culturally to the community; and inadequate budgets are poorly managed.

Our tax dollars are not spent as effectively in the inner city as they are in the suburbs. How else can one explain the chipped paint and dirty floors of the local post offices, or the complaint scrawled on the blackboard in my neighborhood's police precinct in January 1990: "No more arrests until we get some heat in here!". . .

Scholars studying urban America are debating whether or not the structural transformations of the 1970s and 1980s have created a qualitatively as well as quantitatively new dynamic of poverty different from the one faced by new immigrants at the turn of the century or prior to World War II. As our cities have shifted from manufacturing to service economies, high school graduates can no longer find stable, unionized jobs that provide health and retirement benefits and pay a family wage. The debate over the social implications of these long-term structural transformations in our nation's economy is not academic; it has important policy ramifications. The inner-city crisis is "Made in the U.S.A."; it is not caused by new immigrants or by residual cultural influences. Right now, we are not even reaching out to the boys and girls who want to play by the rules.

Because I come from a discipline that systematically analyzes cultural processes, I have reached the conclusion that the experience of second-generation urban poverty in America today is qualitatively different from what it was in the recent past. Political and socioeconomic forces have coalesced, rendering street culture more persuasive and "economically logical" than it was in past generations. Concretely, this means that a much higher percentage than ever before of our best and brightest inner-city youths are pursuing careers with rugged determination that lead to violence and drug addiction. Worse yet, current public-sector policies and private-sector practices are merely compounding this crisis rather than addressing it.

6 VIEWPOINT

"Poverty doesn't cause crime; crime causes poverty."

Poverty and Unemployment Do Not Cause Crime

David Rubinstein and Carl F. Horowitz

Echoing the Kerner Commission's investigations into the causes of riots among blacks in the 1960s, a California Assembly Special Committee concluded that economic conditions in Los Angeles precipitated the riots there in April/May 1992. In Part I of the following viewpoint, David Rubinstein rejects that analysis. He presents what he maintains are fatally damaging discrepancies in the theory that crime is a "rational" choice for those who lack economic opportunity. Rubinstein is a professor of sociology at the University of Illinois at Chicago. Carl F. Horowitz, in Part II, shows that crime perpetuates conditions of neighborhood poverty in a number of ways. Horowitz is an urban planner and a housing and urban affairs analyst at the Heritage Foundation in Washington, D.C.

As you read, consider the following questions:

1. According to Rubinstein, why is crime of "doubtful economic benefit"?
2. What does Rubinstein mean when he says, "Ours is a materialistic culture"? What effect does this perception have on crime-fighting efforts, in his view?
3. According to Horowitz, what are the indirect costs of crime?

David Rubinstein, "Don't Blame Crime on Joblessness," *The Wall Street Journal*, November 4, 1992. Reprinted with permission of *The Wall Street Journal*, ©1992 Dow Jones & Company, Inc. All rights reserved. Carl F. Horowitz, "Getting It Straight: Crime Causes Poverty," *Human Events*, March 30, 1991. Reprinted by permission from Human Events Publishing, Inc., 422 First St. SE, Washington, DC 20003.

I

The California Assembly Special Committee on the Los Angeles crisis released its findings on the riots of [April 1992]. Unsurprisingly, the report echoes the Kerner Commission [National Advisory Commission on Civil Disorders, 1968] of a generation ago by emphasizing lack of economic opportunity as a major cause of the riots and the high crime rates in South Central Los Angeles.

The coincidence of crime and unemployment in places like South Central Los Angeles seems to confirm their connection. And it makes sense motivationally. Surely an absence of employment can make crime an attractive option, and so enhanced job opportunities ought to make it less so. University of Chicago economist Gary S. Becker won the Nobel Prize for this sort of reasoning.

Problems with Economic Models

But there are profound anomalies in this analysis. First, the place of crime in the life cycle is odd. One would think that limited job options would mean more to a man approaching 30 than to a teen-ager. But conviction rates for men between 25 and 30 are about one-third the rates for boys between 14 and 16. Similarly, a man with a family faces more urgent economic imperatives than a single man, and yet his inclination to crime is far less. It is noteworthy that women, despite various economic barriers, are invariably less prone to crime than men.

Also, it is hard to see crimes like rape, drug addiction, most homicides and assaults as substitutes for legitimate employment. Even profit-oriented crime is often of doubtful economic benefit. The take in most petty street crimes is so low that, even with a small chance of arrest for any single crime, a perpetrator will likely be jailed before he equals a year's income from a minimum wage job.

With a little ingenuity, the economic interpretation can be stretched to "explain" crimes that lack economic sense. While stabbing someone in a bar fight, using drugs or setting fire to a store are hardly substitutes for gainful employment, such crimes might be interpreted as "ultimately" reflecting the frustrations of blocked opportunities.

But all such theories founder on a striking fact: the nearly invisible relationship between unemployment and crime rates. Charting homicide since 1900 reveals two peaks. The first is in 1933. This represents the crest of a wave that began in 1905, continued through the prosperous '20s and then began to *decline* in 1934 as the Great Depression was deepening. Between 1933 and 1940, the murder rate dropped nearly 40%. Property crimes reveal a similar pattern.

53

Between 1940 and 1960 the homicide rate remained relatively stable. In the early '60s, a sharp increase began that peaked in 1974, when the murder rate was more than double that of the late 1950s, and far higher than it had been in the depths of the Depression. Between 1963 and 1973 homicides in New York City tripled. Again, property and most other forms of crime followed a similar pattern.

"At least I know where I'll be for the next 5 to 10 years. . . . Have you given any thought to your own future?"

The cause of this remarkable increase in crime, certainly was not unemployment—which was, by contemporary standards, enviably low. In 1961, the unemployment rate was 6.6% and the crime rate was 1.9 per 1,000. By 1969, unemployment had dropped to 3.4% while the crime rate nearly doubled to 3.7 per 1,000. The incidence of robbery nearly tripled. Interestingly, the recession of 1980 to 1982 was accompanied by a small but clearly discernible drop in crime. As the economy revived, so did the crime rate.

These patterns are well known to criminologists. A review of several studies by Thomas Orsagh concluded that "unemployment may affect the crime rate, but even if it does, its general effect is too slight to be measured." Another survey by Richard Freeman concluded that the relationship is so weak that, if unemployment were cut by 50%, the crime rate would drop by only 5%. Some criminologists seriously entertain the thesis that crime, like any other form of "business" activity, turns up in good times.

Despite this evidence, the idea that crime can be substantially cut by enhanced employment opportunities remains deeply entrenched, even in the social sciences. Ours is a materialistic culture. We believe that people are driven by calculations of economic gain and that money can solve a host of social problems. But human motivation is far more diverse, and often darker, than this. Just as money spent on health care can do little to counter the effects of destructive life styles, and money spent on schools cannot overcome a lack of motivation to learn, pouring money into America's inner cities to enhance employment opportunities will do little to make them safer.

Crime in One Poor Neighborhood

When considering what to do about crime in places like South Central Los Angeles, it is worth recalling the relationship between crime and economic deprivation in a different part of California at a different time: "During the 1960s, one neighborhood in San Francisco had the lowest income, the highest unemployment rate, the highest proportion of families with incomes under $4,000 a year, the least educational attainment, the highest tuberculosis rate, and the highest proportion of substandard housing. . . . That neighborhood was called Chinatown. Yet in 1965, there were only five persons of Chinese ancestry committed to prison in the entire state of California."

This quote, taken from *Crime and Human Nature* by James Q. Wilson and Richard Herrnstein, suggests that economic theories tell us more about our misunderstandings of human motivation than about the causes of crime. It also suggests that policy planners would rather speak of factors that are within the reach of government programs than those, like weak families and a culture that fails to restrain, that are truly related to crime.

II

One of the most enduring misconceptions about urban life in America is that conditions in poor neighborhoods "force" residents into a life of crime. This view initially gained popularity after the urban rioting of the 1960s and was enshrined in the report of the National Advisory Commission on Civil Disorders, better known as the Kerner Commission Report.

Poverty and crime are related. But the cause and effect are generally the opposite of what the "experts" say. Poverty doesn't cause crime; crime causes poverty. . . .

How Crime Causes Poverty

Most obvious, of course, are the immediate costs of crime: the victim's injuries and the loss of property. The poor usually suffer most not just because they have little wealth to lose, but also because they live in neighborhoods where crimes are common.

Less obvious are the indirect costs of crime, affecting not only the person robbed but anybody living in the same neighborhood.

Gary S. Becker's Economic Analysis

No serious student of crime claims that the solution to the crime puzzle is simple. There are many interrelated and complicated causes. However, one cause is clearcut: the economics of crime. Indeed, Gary Becker of the University of Chicago was awarded the Nobel prize in 1992 for his work on that topic. Professor Becker's work shows that crimes are not irrational acts. Instead, they are voluntarily committed by people who compare the expected benefits with the expected costs. Hence, one reason crime rates are surging is that, for many people, the benefits of criminal activity outweigh the costs.

Crime pays, in part, because the cost of committing a crime is so low. That cost can be measured by determining the "expected punishment" associated with various criminal acts. Expected punishment is calculated by first multiplying four probabilities times each other: that of being arrested for a crime after it is committed, that of being prosecuted if arrested, that of being convicted if prosecuted and that of receiving punishment if convicted. The product of that arithmetic is the probability of being punished. To complete the calculation of expected punishment, we must next multiply the probability of being punished times the penalty for an offense.

Steve Hanke, *The Washington Times*, January 1, 1993.

First, there is fear. Fear of criminals discourages families from moving into and staying in neighborhoods. This depresses property values. If potential buyers of property, whether occupied or vacant, believe it is in a high-crime neighborhood, they offer a lower price for the property than they would in the absence of crime.

This chain of events, though obviously not new, continues to have a devastating effect on the poor. Thirty-eight per cent of Americans in below-poverty-line households own their own homes. As a result of crime, their principal asset is devalued. It is the equivalent of criminals' robbing a family's savings account.

If residents are apartment owners, they may be unable to find any buyers when they wish to sell; they also may have difficulty finding responsible renters. This also discourages the landlord from spending money on maintenance, which increases the likelihood of more crime, and further impoverishes the neighborhood.

The resulting property deterioration and abandonment is documented in every urban neighborhood in America where criminals reign. It is especially true in public housing. In Chicago, for example, more than 5,000 publicly owned dwellings stand vacant, most as a result of vandalism and youth gang violence.

Thus, reducing crime is a key to neighborhood revitalization and economic improvement.

"The policies of the right are moving us toward a way of life—a civilization—that is destructive of the institutions that sustain personal character and social order."

The Culture of Social Irresponsibility Causes Crime

Elliott Currie

"Greed is good" was a popular attitude in the 1980s. In this viewpoint, Elliott Currie argues that the conservative policies of the 1980s promoted a market society that emphasized personal gain over social responsibility. Market society values erode traditional American values, Currie asserts; with social responsibility gone, crime becomes a legitimate way to satisfy needs. Currie is a criminologist with the Institute for the Study of Social Change at the University of California, Berkeley. He is the author of *Confronting Crime: An American Challenge*.

As you read, consider the following questions:

1. How does the author distinguish between a market economy and a market society?
2. According to Currie, what is the relationship between poverty (economic deprivation) and crime? Why does he believe America is a special case in this regard?
3. How does a market society undermine families, according to Currie?

Elliott Currie, "Crime in the Market Society: From Bad to Worse in the Nineties," *Dissent*, Spring 1991. Copyright 1991 Foundation for the Study of Independent Social Ideas, Inc. Reprinted with permission.

To say that we are losing the war on crime is a cruel understatement. Today we are a nation reeling from rates of violent crime that in many places outstrip anything we have seen before in our history. The basic outline of this American tragedy is easy to sketch.

According to data from the U.S. Public Health Service, a young American male, aged fifteen to twenty-four, is seventy-three times more likely to die of deliberate homicide than his counterpart in Austria, forty-four times more likely than a Japanese youth, and about twenty times more likely than a young Englishman or Dane.

Worse, the risks of violence in America have *risen* in the past few years: and they have risen in the face of what by conventional measures was (until recently) touted as one of our longest sustained periods of "prosperity."

The year 1990 [was one of] the most violent *ever* in many of our cities: the rate at which Americans killed one another in the first half of 1990 was a stunning 20 percent higher than in the same period in 1989 in cities of over a million population—and rates for 1989 were already an all-time record in many of those cities. Still more ominous, that rising violence exists together with the institutionalization of a larger and larger proportion of our population.

A City of One Million

Our incarceration rate—more than triple that of our closest Western European competitor, the United Kingdom—has been rising even faster than the criminal violence it was supposed to stop. Our prison and jail population, having passed the one million mark in 1989, now constitutes a city about the size of Detroit. If we add those on probation or parole, we have a city of four million, making it the second largest in the United States.

It is predominantly a city of the young and the poor and especially, but not exclusively, the young *minority* poor. According to an analysis by Marc Mauer of the Sentencing Project, nearly one-fourth of young black men in the nation aged 20 to 29 [as of June 1990 were] either behind bars, on probation, or on parole. In New York State, as a study by the Correctional Association of New York and the New York State Coalition for Criminal Justice points out, twice as many young black men are under "correctional supervision" as are attending college. And it is a city whose staggering costs have helped to bankrupt our other cities; in New York State the size of the prison budget is increasing by a stunning $50 million a month.

Beyond the bare numbers, the violence in our cities reflects a deepening social and spiritual disaster. Some examples, drawn almost at random from a pile of newspaper clippings:

59

- the annual burning of parts of Detroit on Halloween, which [in 1990] destroyed nearly two hundred buildings and left over a dozen families homeless;
- the beating, slashing, and, in one case, hacking to death of homeless men in New York that same Halloween by a gang of masked young men shouting "trick or treat";
- the rape, beating, and stabbing one hundred thirty-two times of a young black crack addict in Boston by a gang of kids looking for "a female to rob";
- seven killings in seven hours in New York City, including the shooting to death of a sixteen-year-old as he tried to defend a friend from robbers who wanted his Chicago Bulls jacket.

The Roots of Black Crime

The old liberal wisdom held society to blame for all criminal problems. The new conservative wisdom exonerates society and puts the blame on personal responsibility.

Actually, both theories are at least partly right. Every individual bears personal responsibility for his or her actions. You commit the crime, you do the time. But a society bears responsibility for its condition, too, and our society is in a breathtakingly violent condition.

Although the roots of black crime can be found in poverty and prejudice, a new, angry nihilism seems to have gripped a growing number of the ghetto poor. It grows out of violent childhoods and truncated opportunities, and it seems to be feeding on itself, reducing the sense that one's own life or anyone else's has value.

Clarence Page, *Liberal Opinion Week*, October 18, 1993.

It is sometimes argued that the rising tide of urban violence in the United States only reflects the deadly imperatives of the drug trade—especially the crack "epidemic." The implication is that when the epidemic subsides, so will the plague of violent crime. Crack thus becomes an oddly comforting scapegoat for a crisis whose roots are deeper and more tangled. Crack—and other hard drugs—are certainly a big part of the reason for the violence in the cities; but they are only a part and not necessarily the most important part. In Washington, D.C., for example, while homicides [rose] to new highs in 1990, the drug-related proportion has *fallen* substantially (to about a third) in the past few years.

The fear and outrage generated by endemic violence is compounded by a sense of helplessness. It is dramatically apparent that the conservative "solution" to crime has failed, but the vision of feasible alternatives has also receded. For many Americans, the roots of the disintegration of social life in the cities remain mysterious, the remedies elusive.

That is partly because of the quite successful effort by those running the country [in the 1980s] to minimize the connections between the mounting urban violence and a decade of their own social and economic policies. Partly, too, it is because those of us who see those connections have failed to bring them sufficiently to light.

Let me suggest several ways in which conservative policies have aggravated the criminal violence that has made most of our cities nearly uninhabitable. These connections are deep and complex: it isn't just, for example, that a decade [1980s] of conservative policy has increased urban unemployment. It's that the policies of the right are moving us toward a way of life—a civilization—that is destructive of the institutions that sustain personal character and social order.

Looking at several of those effects at once is crucial to understanding crime in the United States. It helps explain why some factors taken individually—say, the unemployment rate, or levels of poverty—may not always fit well as explanations of crime, a point much seized upon by some conservative observers. Looking at the role of these factors through a more holistic perspective helps us understand why poverty, for example, predictably breeds crime in some societies, at some point in their development, and not in others.

The Concept of Market Society

First let me make a distinction between "market economy" and "market society." All societies make some use of market mechanisms to allocate goods and services. Assessing what the market does well and what is best accomplished by other means is often an empirical question.

But "market *society*" is a different animal altogether. By market society I mean one in which the pursuit of private gain becomes the organizing principle for all areas of social life—not simply a mechanism that we may use to accomplish certain circumscribed economic ends.

In market society all other principles of social organization become subordinated to the overarching one of private gain. Alternative sources of livelihood, social support, and cultural value—even personal identity—become increasingly weakened, so that individuals, families, and communities are more and more dependent on what we somewhat misleadingly call the "free market" to provide for their needs—not only material needs but cultural, symbolic, and psychic ones as well. (I say

61

somewhat misleadingly because in existing market societies some groups are increasingly able to protect themselves against the market's uncertainties.) The United States has long been the most market-dominated of Western industrial countries, the one with the least developed alternatives to the values and institutions of the market. And under the [Ronald] Reagan and [George] Bush administrations, that domination has significantly increased. As a result, we are something of an experiment in the consequences of market-driven social policy. Rising crime is only one of those consequences—but one of the most visible. Here are five links between the advance of market society and the rise in crime.

Economic Inequality and Crime

1. *Market society promotes crime by increasing inequality and concentrated economic deprivation.*

In the United States the rise in violent crime has gone hand in hand with the sharpest rise of economic inequality in postwar history. The rise in economic inequality can be traced to several trends. One is the deterioration of the private and public labor markets, in which a great many former 'middle-level' jobs—especially but not exclusively in blue-collar industry—have disappeared, replaced by a significant rise in extremely well-rewarded jobs at the top—and a much larger increase in poor jobs, including unstable and part-time ones, at the bottom.

That shift in the labor market is not a matter of "fate" or even of politically neutral changes in technology or demographics. It has been driven by conservative social policy in several ways:

• through the flight of capital and jobs to low-wage havens in the United States and overseas;

• through the lowering of the real value of the minimum wage, which ensures that new job creation has been overwhelmingly concentrated in poverty-level employment;

• through the weakening of the labor movement's capacity to organize in areas of new job creation and to hold the line against wage cuts.

The resulting tendency toward an "hourglass" income distribution is compounded by two other effects of conservative market policy: the erosion of income-support benefits for low-income people and the unemployed and a pattern of systematically regressive taxation. In the late 1970s our income-support benefits— already among the most meager in the developed world— brought about one in five poor families above the poverty line. In 1991, according to the Center on Budget and Policy Priorities, the figure was closer to one in nine. Meanwhile, since 1977 the top 1 percent of income earners have seen their pretax income rise by 85 percent and their tax burden drop by 23 percent, while the bottom 20 percent of the population suffered a real income decline of about 12 percent and saw their tax burden *rise* by 3 percent.

Today we not only have about seven million more poor Americans than at the end of the 1970s: they are typically much poorer. And as the job structure has narrowed and income support shriveled, it is now far more difficult for them to get out—at least through legitimate means, a fact that is not lost on the urban poor, especially the young.

The "Greed Is Good" Culture

In 1835, Alexis de Tocqueville wrote that in America "no natural boundary seems to be set to the efforts of man." In his 1989 book *The Hunger for More*, business writer Lawrence Shames notes that there has always been a tenuous connection between the American dream and civilized behavior. The peculiar feature of the dream that emerged in the '80s was its insatiability, each success creating a more acute sense of hunger. This chronic drive for *more* is a fertile breeding ground for a culture of wilding. Me, Me, Me, hollered the relentless voices from inside; look after number one, echoed the reassuring voices from high places. The new operational credo: Anything goes. As French sociologist Emile Durkheim observed long ago, if the ceiling on ordinary expectations is removed, the conventional restraints on pursuing them will also rapidly disappear. . . .

Sociologist Robert Merton wrote that crime is a product of a disparity between goals and means. To weave grandiose materialist dreams in an era of restricted opportunities is the ultimate inducement for social wilding. Wilding is American individualism run amok. And just as insider trading and leveraged buy-outs symbolized the Reagan-era "greed is good" credo in the corporate suites, dealing crack and grabbing handbags were signs of the times on ghetto streets.

Charles Derber, *Utne Reader*, March/April 1993.

---

2. Market society promotes crime by eroding the capacity of local communities for support, mutual provision, and effective socialization of the young.

Under the sustained impact of market forces, communities suffer both from the loss of stable livelihoods and from the excessive geographic displacement that results from that loss. These losses are compounded in the United States by the crisis in housing for low-income people, as market forces drive up the cost of shelter at the same time that they drive down wages. The loss of stability of shelter, in turn, helps destroy local social cohesion.

Local communities suffering these stresses begin to exhibit a phenomenon some researchers call "drain." As the ability of families to support themselves and their children drops below a certain critical point, they can no longer sustain those informal networks of social support that might be a buffer against the economic grinding of the market. A family having tough times can't lean on neighbors or cousins—even if they still live in the same community—because *they* are having tough times too. This, in turn, helps us understand the third link:

3. *Market society promotes crime by isolating the family and subjecting it to stress.*

Economic deprivation and community fragmentation have put enormous pressures on family life. Conservatives talk endlessly about the importance of family values, but the reality is that market policies have brought disaster to low- and even middle-income families across the country, and that disaster is deeply implicated in the crime problem.

The long-term economic marginalization of entire communities inhibits the formation of stable families in the first place—as the sociologist William Julius Wilson has argued—by diminishing the "pool" of marriageable men—men seen as capable of supporting a family.

At the same time, the deterioration of the labor market and the spread of poverty-level wages have meant that many families—especially young families—can only stay afloat by working at two or even three jobs. The real incomes of families headed by someone under twenty-five dropped by over 23 percent between the early 1970s and the late 1980s, and that level has been maintained only because family members are working harder and longer. That has given us a generation of parents, especially young parents and single parents, who have virtually no leisure time and who are under constant stress.

To recognize the troubling results of these strains isn't to blame the parents. But it is true that the nurturing capacities of many families have been weakened and their children too often thrown back on their own resources and their own peer groups. Conservatives, of course, make much of this result in their own explanations of rising crime but conveniently ignore its *causes*.

The resulting "social impoverishment" fuses with economic deprivation to produce overwhelming stresses—stresses long associated with domestic violence and child abuse. (I do not think it's an accident that the foster-care caseload in New York City tripled during the reigns of the Reagan and Bush administrations—or that child-abuse reports in California rose by over 300 percent.)

Crime and American Society

4. *Market society promotes crime by withdrawing public services from those already stripped of economic security and communal support.*

Before the eighties, the United States was already notable for the absence of health care and family supports for all its citizens. The conservative ascendancy of the 1980s undercut already meager public services, which could have stalled some of the damage inflicted by economic deprivation, family stress, and community disintegration.

For an understanding of urban crime, we can single out the effects of declining preventive health care and mental health services that might help some of the children most "at risk" of delinquency and drug abuse, the absence of intervention for families at high risk of severe child abuse, and the lack of adequate child care for low-income families whipsawed by low wages and overwork.

Competition for Status

5. *Market society promotes crime by magnifying a culture of Darwinian competition for status and resources and by urging a level of consumption that it cannot provide for everyone.*

This cultural context helps explain why economic deprivation is so significant a source of crime in a market society and not necessarily in others.

The corrosive effects of market culture on social stability have been a theme in the study of crime for close to a century. Almost sixty years ago the great Dutch criminologist Willem Bonger argued that "[t]o make prosperity and culture as general as possible" was the "best preventive against crime." But he stressed that he meant "prosperity, not *luxury*": for "[t]here is not a weaker spot to be found in the social development of our times than the ever-growing and ever-intensifying covetousness, which, in its turn, is the result of powerful social forces." Bonger would surely be amazed by the degree to which "covetousness" has suffused American social life in the 1990s.

A market culture promotes crime by holding out standards of economic status and consumption that many cannot legitimately meet, thereby creating pressure for meeting them in illegitimate ways: and, more subtly, by weakening values supportive of the intrinsic worth of human life and well-being. Much violent street crime in America today directly expresses the consumerist values of immediate gratification; some of our delinquents will cheerfully acknowledge that they blew someone away for a pair of running shoes (or a suede jacket). The point is not simply to bemoan the ascendancy of such values among the urban young but to recognize that they are, as Bonger said, the "result of powerful social forces."

We also need to consider the impact on crime of the specifically psychological distortions of market society—its tendency to produce personalities less and less capable of relating to others

65

except as consumer items or as a means to the consumption of goods or the attainment of social status. And we need to consider the long-term political impact of market society—in particular, its tendency to eclipse alternative political means by which the dispossessed might express their frustration and desperation.

It's not simply by increasing one or another discrete social ill that conservative market policies stimulate crime: it's through the growth and spread of a way of life that at its core is inimical to social order and personal security. In the words of another keen critic of market culture, R.H. Tawney, it is a "false magnetic pole that sets all the compasses wrong."

These trends have had their strongest impact on the young. As we move closer to a full-fledged market society in America, young people are increasingly left to grow up on their own, without consistent support or guidance, sometimes with untended physical or psychological damage; always with the lure of the consumer marketplace before them and with little opportunity to participate fully in that marketplace. This neglect is a recipe for disaster, and it helps explain why our American cities are the most dangerous in the developed world.

"The new culture holds that . . . crime isn't pathological. . . . It is rebellion—the manly response that Americans have shown to oppression since the Boston Tea Party."

The Culture of Personal Irresponsibility Causes Crime

Myron Magnet

Following the April/May 1992 riots in Los Angeles, then-President George Bush reiterated conservative criticism of Lyndon Johnson's Great Society as "failed social programs." In the following viewpoint, Myron Magnet amplifies that criticism. He argues that the counterculture of the 1960s, which he says romanticized freedom from personal and societal restraint, undermined the traditional value of personal responsibility. It thus lowered the barriers to crime and created a culture of poverty. Magnet is an editor of *Fortune* magazine and the author of *The Dream and the Nightmare: The Sixties' Legacy to the Underclass*, from which this viewpoint is taken.

As you read, consider the following questions:

1. Why does Magnet trace the current crime wave to the 1960s?
2. What, according to Magnet, is the relationship between Norman Mailer's "The White Negro" and Eldridge Cleaver's *Soul On Ice*?
3. According to the author, what is the effect of crime on the lives of the Haves? on the lives of the Have-Nots?

It had all the makings of one of those heartwarming Hollywood movies where the tough but loving schoolteacher, sporting a red-and-black-checked lumberman's shirt, charms and bullies his delinquent pupils into changing their ways and becoming model citizens, teenage-style. Here, in real life, was George Cadwalader, a central casting dream: an ex-Marine captain wounded in Vietnam, he was big, rugged, and handsome, with smiling crinkly eyes, bushy brows, limitless courage and self-confidence—and a plan irresistible in its mixture of idealism, toughness, and adventure. He would gather up a crew of hardened delinquent boys from the toughest urban neighborhoods of Massachusetts and transport them to a wild, deserted island, with all its associations of sagas from *Robinson Crusoe* to *Treasure Island*. There they would build their own house, grow and cook their own food, cut the firewood that would both warm them and heat their dinner. By coming to grips with the basic realities of life, they would learn self-reliance, responsibility, and teamwork, discover their own inner strength and confidence, and be converted.

But it was Cadwalader who got converted.

The "Castaways" Experiment

He woke up one morning to discover all the chickens his little community was raising for food fluttering helplessly on the ground, dazed with pain. In a paroxysm of sadism, each chicken's two legs had been savagely twisted and smashed, wrenched out of their joints and hanging useless. All that could be done for the broken creatures was to put them out of their misery. Which boy had done such a deed in the dead of night Cadwalader never knew for certain, nor did he ever know the motive.

But he knew beyond a doubt that the certainties with which he'd started his experiment in rehabilitation had crumbled within him. He and his associates had begun by holding "without question the assumption that bad kids were simply the products of bad environments," he recalls in *Castaways*, his striking account of the experiment. "We believed changing the environment could change the kid. . . ." Yet the vast majority of his charges didn't change, despite transplantation to the radically different, militantly salubrious environment Cadwalader had designed for them.

Far from it. When he followed up the first 106 boys who had gone through his program, he discovered that in seven years they'd been charged with 3,391 crimes, 309 of them violent. . . .

The theory that Cadwalader felt he had disproved, much as he would rather have confirmed it, is central to the new worldview of the Haves. And because it tends to excuse criminals from personal responsibility for crime, pinning it on social circumstances instead, the theory has given potential wrongdoers exactly the wrong message. Moreover, it has produced a criminal justice system, administered by a generation of judges steeped in the new culture of the Haves, that confronts actual criminals with a leniency offering little deterrence to crime.

Theories of crime have to make an assumption about whether men are predisposed by nature to force and violence or whether violence gets into their hearts from some outside source. Cadwalader's original assumption about man's inborn character—a key assumption of the new culture of the Haves—is that men are intrinsically peaceful creatures, inclined not to disturb their fellows and, when necessary, to cooperate harmoniously with them. As nature formed them, they don't attack and invade each other. Crime is an artificial growth, grafted onto human life by the development of societies and governments. . . .

America's Liberal Philosophy of Crime

Americans don't have to go back to Revolutionary times for firsthand knowledge of government-sanctioned oppression. They can think of Southern slavery; they can recall, firsthand, the outrages of institutionalized racial discrimination. With respect to their black fellow citizens in particular, many Americans are readily inclined to believe that crime is the fault of society, not of the criminal. Crime may be either the product of unwholesome social conditions or a rebellion—perhaps even a justified rebellion—against injustice and oppression.

These ideas were always alive in American culture, but they became dominant only at the start of the sixties. Michael Harrington gave voice to this interpretation of crime just as it was becoming widespread. Speaking of black delinquents and then of all delinquents, he concluded in *The Other America*: "[T]heir sickness is often a means of relating to a diseased environment." Ramsey Clark, Lyndon Johnson's attorney general and assistant attorney general in the [John F.] Kennedy administration, is a luminous example of how quick were the Haves at their most established to embrace such an understanding of crime as part of the new era's revolutionized worldview. Clark takes an utterly uncompromising tack. "[C]rime among poor blacks . . . flows clearly and directly from the brutalization and dehumanization of racism, poverty, and injustice," he wrote in 1970, summing up his experience as the nation's top law enforcement officer. "[T]he slow destruction of human dignity caused by white racism is responsible."

Just look at the unwholesome environment racism has produced, Clark demands. "The utter wretchedness of central city slums . . . slowly drains compassion from the human spirit and breeds crime." For this the Haves are most emphatically to blame. "To permit conditions that breed antisocial conduct to continue is our greatest crime," Clark concludes. . . .

Inevitably, ghettos will breed violent crime and even rioting. "You cannot cram so much misery together," says Clark, "and not expect violence."

Asay, by permission of the *Colorado Springs Gazette Telegraph*.

This whole structure of thought, most of it still completely orthodox today, rests on theoretical foundations that George Cadwalader found false. But it is a further sign of the times that once Cadwalader had grappled with the discovery that aggression and violence come from some source deep within individuals, not from the social environment, he was stumped. With his old theory in pieces, he had no new one to put in its place. . . .

The Other Tradition

[Another] tradition, for most of history the dominant stream in Western political philosophy, best explains the origin of crime. This tradition takes as its starting point the irreducible reality of human aggression. It holds that as men come from the hand of nature . . . they are instinctively aggressive, with an inbuilt inclination to violence. . . .

The fundamental purpose of the social order, of the civilized condition itself, is to restrain man's instinctual aggressiveness, so that human life can be something higher than a war of all against all. The great seventeenth- and eighteenth-century political theorists, most notably Thomas Hobbes, imagined that that restraint was accomplished by a social contract: driven to desperation by the universal warfare that made their lives "solitary, poore, nasty, brutish, and short," in Hobbes's famous phrase, men in the early ages of the world entered into an agreement, by which each man renounced his unlimited freedom of aggression in order to promote the security of all. . . .

Sigmund Freud offers a still more up-to-date version of this line of thought. The taming of aggression and the replacement of the rule of force by the rule of law isn't something that happened only in the history of the race, Freud argues. It takes place in each individual's history, too.

In early childhood, under the continual pressure of parental demands, each person is made to renounce the unlimited aggressiveness with which he was born. During this protracted process, central to early childhood, one's innermost being is transformed. As one internalizes the civilizing demands of one's parents and the community that speaks through them, one acquires an entirely new mental faculty, a part of one's inner self given one not by nature but by society. This, in Freud's rather unlovely term, is the superego, analogous to the conscience; and like conscience, it punishes one with feelings of shame and guilt, while speaking with the voice not of divinity but of society. . . .

Crime and Socialization

Seen in this light, crime takes on the closest links to culture. For though the whole governmental structure of force and threat—police, judges, and prisons—is a key means by which society restrains aggression and crime, it isn't the principal means, according to this tradition. The most powerful curb isn't force at all: it is the *internal* inhibition that society builds into each person's character, the inner voice (call it reason, conscience, superego, what you will) that makes the social contract an integral part of our deepest selves. . . .

Crime and the Community

When crime flourishes as it now does in our cities, especially crime of mindless malice, it isn't because society has so oppressed people as to bend them out of their true nature and twist them into moral deformity. It is because the criminals haven't been adequately socialized. Examine the contents of their minds and hearts and too much of what you find bears out this hypothesis: free-floating aggression, weak consciences, anarchic beliefs, detachment from the community and its highest

71

values. They haven't attained the self-respect or the coherent sense of self that underlies one's ability to respect others.

This is a predictable result of unimaginably weak families, headed by immature, irresponsible girls who are at the margin of the community, pathological in their own behavior, and too often lacking the knowledge, interest, and inner resources to be successful molders of strong characters in children. Too many underclass mothers can't enforce the necessary prohibitions for children—or for themselves. And most underclass families lack a father, the parent that Freud, wearing his psychoanalyst's hat rather than his political philosopher's, sees as the absolutely vital agent in the socialization of little boys and in the formation of their superegos.

When the community tells people from such families that they are victims of social injustice, that they perhaps are not personally to blame if they commit crimes, and that it is entirely appropriate for them to nurse feelings of rage and resentment, it is asking for trouble. Worse, the new culture holds that, in a sense, such crime isn't pathological; it is something higher and healthier. It is rebellion—the manly response that Americans have shown to oppression since the Boston Tea Party, the response that Robin Hood and his outlaw band gave to injustice before America was even thought of. . . .

Crime as Rebellion

But one could hardly articulate the idea of the criminal as rebel more explicitly or forcefully than Norman Mailer did in his incendiary manifesto, "The White Negro." Today, the essay reads like a firework sparkler fiercely sizzling until it sputters out in a wisp of smoke. But it was as hugely influential as it was startling when it appeared in 1957, just as Mailer was becoming a national celebrity and assuming his role as an avant-garde figure at the very forefront of the cultural revolution of the Haves.

Mailer threw down the gauntlet in "The White Negro," indicting modern society as nothing but an engine of oppression, repression, and destruction. What has it produced but the Nazi concentration camps and the atom bomb? And the modern social order holds in reserve yet another form of extinction—"a slow death by conformity with every creative and rebellious instinct stifled."

In this manmade wasteland, blacks inhabit the deepest circle of oppression and victimization. They have "been living on the margin between totalitarianism and democracy for two centuries," says Mailer. In the injustice of our capitalist order, they are Marx's impoverished industrial reserve army, "a cultureless and alienated bottom of exploitable human material." Given not just the economic violence but also the visceral hatred that as-

72

saults blacks, says Mailer, "no Negro can saunter down a street with any real certainty that violence will not visit him on his walk. . . . The Negro has the simplest of alternatives: live a life of constant humility or ever-threatening danger." He "know[s] in the cells of his existence that life [is] war. . . ."

"[W]hether the life is criminal or not, the decision is to encourage the psychopath in oneself." Rebel, rebel—even if lawless rebellion leads to such psychopathic extremes as murder. Even in such rebellion, according to Mailer's Americanized version of European existentialism, you will at least assert your freedom and selfhood.

To be sure, Mailer admits, all this may not look so heroically manly at first blush. Arguably "it takes little courage for two strong eighteen-year-old hoodlums . . . to beat in the brains of a candy-store keeper. . . . Still, courage of a sort is necessary, for one murders not only a weak fifty-year-old man but an institution as well, one violates private property, one enters into a new relation with the police and introduces a dangerous element into one's life. The hoodlum is therefore daring the unknown, and so no matter how brutal the act, it is not altogether cowardly."

Monstrous, but influential. After the publication of Mailer's work, after other writers had expressed similar views, the idea that violent black crime was a kind of regenerative rebellion gained a certain currency. Not that the majority of mainstream Haves embraced Mailer's version of it wholeheartedly or uncritically: rather, they flirted with it; they were prepared to believe that in some, even many, cases it might be true. Crime *might* be rebellion—and so crime became problematical, no longer simply crime, no longer compelling unqualified condemnation. . . .

From Norman Mailer to Eldridge Cleaver

Shortly after Norman Mailer had helped propagate the idea of the criminal as rebel throughout the general culture, well-known black writers embraced it with an extremism all the more disturbing for being presented so matter-of-factly. Black Panther party member Eldridge Cleaver, for example, declared that the most heinous crime could be an expression of political activism. This declaration went only one step beyond the ideology of Cleaver's Black Power group, which had already wedded politics and violence by espousing the idea of armed black rebellion against oppressive American society. In *Soul On Ice*, a best-seller in the sixties and still taught in some college courses, Cleaver argued that for a black man to rape a white woman was a political act, protesting against his oppression and striking out against his oppressor.

Insidiously, such a politicized view of criminals saturated the inner cities during the sixties. In his memoir *Brothers and*

Keepers, for instance, author John Edgar Wideman paraphrases his brother Robby's ruminations on what led him to the criminal career that ended with a prison sentence for murder. In the ghetto, says Robby, "all the glamor, all the praise and attention is given to the slick guy, the gangster especially. . . . And it's because we can't help but feel some satisfaction seeing a brother, a black man, get over on these people, on their system without playing by their rules." After all, those rules "were forced on us by people who did not have our best interests at heart." So it's not surprising that black people look upon black gangsters "with some sense of pride and admiration. . . . We know they represent rebellion—what little is left in us."

The rebelliousness that breeds crime, Robby says, is ingrained deep in ghetto life. In his own adolescence, "it was unacceptable to be 'good,' it was square to be smart in school, it was jive to show respect to people outside the street world, it was cool to be cold to your woman and the people that loved you. The things we liked we called 'bad.'. . . The thing was to make your own rules, do your own thing, but make sure it's contrary to what society says or is." You keep your dignity and integrity by your rejection of right and wrong as defined by the society that oppresses you. With all values turned upside down, it doesn't take much to turn crime into heroic, or at least honest, defiance. "Robbing white people didn't cause me to lose no sleep back then," Wideman quotes Robby as saying. "How you gon feel sorry when society's so corrupt?". . .

Such a view of the admirably defiant criminal still holds the underclass in thrall. "They want us to settle for a little piece of nothing, like the Indians on the reservation," as one inner-city resident who grew up in a Harlem housing project said recently, summing up his vision of the larger society. "They got us fighting and killing each other for crumbs. In a way, the ones in jail are like political prisoners, because they refused to settle for less.". . .

Overturning the Barriers to Crime

The cultural revolution left none of the barriers to crime undisturbed. Not only did it undermine the inner inhibitions, but it also weakened the external deterrent, the threat of official punishment. Guided by the idea that society systematically oppresses the poor and the black, the Haves increasingly hampered the governmental apparatus that upholds the law by force.

Government, according to this view, tends almost reflexively to be an instrument of injustice against the Have-Nots, above all in its law enforcement capacity. As William Ryan put it in *Blaming the Victim*, all experts know that "the administration of justice is grossly biased against the Negro and the lower class defendant; that arrest and imprisonment is a process reserved almost exclusively for the black and the poor; and that the major function of the police is the preservation not only of the public order, but of the social order—that is, of inequality between man and man." However overwrought, Ryan's statement contains this element of somber truth: racial discrimination did taint police treatment of blacks when Ryan was writing, and in the South police did act as oppressors of blacks, as the nation learned indelibly when Freedom Riders were arrested in Jackson and elsewhere in Mississippi in 1961 or when Chief Bull Connor viciously attacked civil rights demonstrators with police dogs, clubs, cattle prods, and fire hoses in Birmingham, Alabama, in 1963.

Properly indignant at such viciousness, the majority culture responded by throwing a cordon around the government's police functions, aiming to confine the police within the narrowest channel so they couldn't surge out of control. . . .

The inevitable result was that criminals became harder to convict, and punishment for crime became rarer. As the judges issued their rulings on suppressing evidence in the sixties, the prison population declined. By the mid-seventies, the average Chicago youthful offender got arrested over thirteen times before being sent to reform school. In big cities, more than nine felony convictions in ten result not from trials but from plea bargains, in which penalties are lighter and criminals are left with at least some sense of having beaten the system. Today, thanks partly to plea bargaining, your chance of *not* going to jail if you're *convicted* of a serious crime is two to one. . . .

Decline of the Community

For all Americans, the wholesale overturning of the bars to crime and disorder has scrambled the moral order. What becomes of the sense of justice when, almost daily, people violate the fundamental principle of the social contract? What becomes of the sense of personal responsibility for actions when people are not held accountable even for the most evil deeds? With the ground on which the sense of values rests giving way beneath their feet, no wonder many reel with moral vertigo.

For all Americans, Haves and Have-Nots alike, the weakening of the protections against crime and disorder has debased urban life, overlaying it with fear and suspicion as well as real injury. The disproportionate number of crimes committed by underclass lawbreakers has heightened racial hostility, straining the social fabric. Straining it too are the menacing rowdiness and graffiti, the dope selling, and the occupation by the homeless of public spaces everywhere. . . .

However much the erosion of the barriers to crime and disorder disrupted the lives of the Haves, that disruption pales compared to the disruption it inflicted on the lives of the Have-Nots.

More than any economic change of the [sort] William Julius Wilson [describes in *The Truly Disadvantaged*], it is the explosion of violent crime that has turned inner cities into blighted wastelands, virtual free-fire zones. Repeated holdups and street robberies of employees drove out small tradesmen and larger businesses alike. Crime made fear ever-present for hardworking, law-abiding ghetto citizens—who, though you might not think so from reading William Julius Wilson on the flight of upwardly mobile blacks from the ghetto, certainly do exist.

The almost daily reports of gunfire crackling outside the projects, of people cowering on the floor of their apartments, of innocent passersby getting caught in the crossfire, become numbing by their very familiarity. But it is true that a young black man has a greater chance of being murdered in the inner city than a soldier had of being killed in the jungles of Vietnam. It is true that you can send your kid to the grocery store and never see him again alive. . . .

After a nine-year-old girl in a crime-ravaged Brooklyn ghetto had just been shot in the head by a thug's stray bullet, a neighbor—a law-abiding family man living across the street from a crack house—lamented: "Our lives have been reduced to the lowest levels of human existence." In such an anarchy, it's a wonder not when people fail to achieve the civilized excellences but when, like the family man quoted above, they succeed.

The primary function of any society is to guarantee the social contract. What but anarchy can you expect if the legitimate force of society has eroded? What can you expect when the guardians of that force cannot bring themselves to exercise it, like a New York judge who vibrated with protective sympathy for the defendant before him, a callously brutal eighteen-year-old murderer? The judge, trying to quell the prosecutor's outraged complaints about the defense lawyer's procedural pettifoggery, cried out feelingly: "This is only a murder! Only a murder!"

Periodical Bibliography

The following articles have been selected to supplement the diverse views presented in this chapter.

Natalie Angier — "Elementary, Dr. Watson. The Neurotransmitters Did It," *The New York Times*, January 23, 1994.

Gary S. Becker — "How to Tackle Crime? Take a Tough, Head-On Stance," *Business Week*, November 29, 1993.

Richard Blow — "A Social Disease," *Mother Jones*, May/June 1993.

Fox Butterfield — "Studies Find a Family Link to Criminality," *The New York Times*, January 31, 1992.

Brandon S. Centerwall — "Television and Violent Crime," *The Public Interest*, Spring 1993.

Charles Derber — "A Nation Gone Wild," *In These Times*, May 20, 1992.

Ted Gest and Gordon Witkin — "Rooting Out the Violent," *U.S. News & World Report*, November 23, 1992.

Nathaniel Hupert — "Reducing Urban Violence: A Critique of the New Public Health Approach," *The Pharos*, Winter 1994.

John Kurzweil — "Crime Story," *National Review*, June 8, 1992.

John Leo — "The Psychologizing of Crime," *U.S. News & World Report*, December 7, 1992.

Charles Murray — "The Legacy of the 60's," *Commentary*, July 1992.

Charles Murray et al. — "After LA: Causes, Root Causes, and Cures," *National Review*, June 8, 1992.

Hal Pepinsky — "Violence as Unresponsiveness," *Peace Review*, Winter 1992.

Morgan O. Reynolds — "Crime Pays; but So Does Imprisonment," *Journal of Social, Political, and Economic Studies*, Fall 1990.

Thomas Sowell — "Scoring Points," *Forbes*, February 28, 1994.

Louis W. Sullivan — "U.S. Violence Studies Are Free of Racial Bias," *The New York Times*, October 2, 1992.

Anastasia Toufexis — "Seeking the Roots of Violence," *Time*, April 19, 1993.

James Q. Wilson — "What Is Moral, and How Do We Know It?" *Commentary*, June 1993.

2 CHAPTER

What Will Prevent Crime?

CRIME AND CRIMINALS

Chapter Preface

In his 1994 State of the Union address, President Bill Clinton proposed a "three strikes, you're out" law, saying, "Those who commit repeated violent crimes should be told, when you commit a third violent crime, you will be put away and put away for good." The proposed law is intended to keep repeat felons from committing more crimes by mandating life terms on their third conviction, or "strike." Supporters say the law will cut crime by imprisoning the worst criminals.

A study by economist Marvin Wolfgang that has been widely quoted asserts that the majority (70 percent) of crimes are committed by a small minority (7 percent) of criminals. Citing these statistics, a *Wall Street Journal* editorial supporting three strikes laws concludes that locking up this small minority of repeat offenders for life will reduce the crime rate. In the *Journal*'s view, the biggest cause of crime "is the early release of violent criminals who commit more violence," and "three strikes" laws will keep these criminals from being released.

On the other hand, Federal Bureau of Investigation statistics indicate that most crime is committed by young people between the ages of fifteen and thirty. For Philip Heymann, former U.S. deputy attorney general and a vocal critic of the three strikes idea, this means that "the vast majority of street violence is committed by robbers who grow out of the occupation at a relatively early age." Because most criminals are growing out of this age group by the time they receive their third conviction, "three strikes" laws, in Heymann's opinion, will not target the group that is committing the majority of crimes and therefore will not reduce crime.

"Three strikes, you're out" laws—debated in the following chapter—are "tough" measures that are intended to prevent crime by taking criminals off the street. An enduring issue in the debate is whether such tough laws effectively target the most active criminals.

"Only when residents feel they can work closely with police will fear of crime subside."

Community-Based Policing Will Prevent Crime

Carl F. Horowitz

The following viewpoint outlines some common proposals for increasingly popular community-based policing plans: cooperation between police foot patrols and neighborhood crime watch groups; problem-solving in high crime areas, such as public housing projects; and anti-crime education for young people. Carl F. Horowitz argues that promoting cooperation between police and neighborhood residents is a deterrent to crime; citizens should help police prevent crimes from happening rather than have police respond only after a crime has been committed. Horowitz is a policy analyst in Washington, D.C., and has written several books on housing and urban planning.

As you read, consider the following questions:

1. How does Horowitz view the relationship between crime and poverty?
2. According to the plan the author presents, what role should governments play to establish foot patrol programs?
3. What role should citizens (or citizens' groups) play in conjunction with police foot patrols, according to Horowitz?

There is a growing realization that the best strategies for fighting crime in residential neighborhoods are those where the police work closely with resident organizations. Such community-based strategies require residents to believe that others in their neighborhood are committed to a crime-free environment. Then they will be more willing to take part in public or private anti-crime programs, and be mobilized by police forces. "Community-oriented policing," as this is known, attempts to prevent crimes rather than investigate them after the fact. As crime experts James Q. Wilson, Collins Professor of Management at UCLA, and George Kelling, Fellow at Harvard's John F. Kennedy School of Government, write:

> Community-oriented policing means changing the daily work of the police to include investigating problems as well as incidents. It means defining as a problem whatever a significant body of public opinion regards as a threat to community order. It means working with the good guys, and not just against the bad guys.

Community groups and police forces now have a considerable body of experience drawn from successful experiments in community-oriented policing. This evidence suggests that several tactics are key to a successful approach, and that government policies can help in a number of ways.

Create More Police Foot Patrols

The evidence indicates that deploying more foot patrol police officers in a high-crime neighborhood can make substantial headway against crime. Charleston, South Carolina, is a case in point. When Reuben Greenberg in 1982 took over as Police Chief of that city of 80,000, he inherited one of the nation's most crime-ridden cities for its size. One of his first steps to tackle the problem was to create an elite unit of foot patrolmen. Friendly and cooperative with neighbors, yet tough and agile enough to chase and catch a fleeing suspect, these patrolmen have deterred criminals, especially drug dealers, from preying on poor neighborhoods.

Under Greenberg, crime in Charleston has fallen 42 percent. So successful is his strategy viewed that he was invited by Mobile, Alabama, with a population of 200,000, to design a similar program for that city. Five months after Mobile adopted the Greenberg plan, Mobile's serious crime fell by 18 percent.

Results from other cities are also encouraging. In Flint, Michigan, a city of nearly 150,000, foot patrol officers since 1979 have been trained to refer citizens to social service agencies when the police detect domestic problems or alcohol and drug abuse. The idea is to prevent residents with such problems from falling into a pattern of crime. In the fourteen experimental areas established by the Flint police as high-crime districts, crime rates declined an average of 8 percent in the first three years of the program; by contrast, rates rose 10 percent in areas without the program. In Los Angeles, a foot patrol program, Secured Areas Footbeat Enforcement (SAFE), begun [in 1990] but now discontinued due to budget cuts, was popular in several of that city's poorer neighborhoods.

Foot patrol programs have proven to be a successful method of deterring street crime. The U.S. Justice Department and state justice departments should consider making law enforcement assistance to localities contingent upon local government at least exploring the merits of a police or private guard foot patrol program.

Create Citizens' Patrols

Unarmed community volunteers, working together and with the local police force, also seem able to deter street crime. Like police foot patrols, their presence itself warns drug dealers and other criminals that the neighborhood has been put "off-limits."

A good example is in Washington, D.C., where more than 130 neighborhood crime watch groups involve about 6,000 residents. In several neighborhoods, residents armed with video cameras and walkie-talkies film drug transactions and write down license plate numbers, later relaying the information to the police. The aim is to target drug customers rather than dealers, and thus to reduce the demand for drugs. Their effort has closed dozens of crack houses and reduced open-air drug dealing. Other Washington neighborhoods have expressed enthusiasm for similar groups.

Establishing community patrols makes residents appreciate their own power to change the neighborhood. Explains Jim Foreman, coordinator of the Metro Orange Coalition, the umbrella organization for local crime watch groups in Washington, "Usually when you go out to see a group, they are afraid about what is on the street. Once you get them there, they see the power of togetherness, what they can do."

The Guardian Angels pioneered such neighborhood patrols. The organization first gained national attention a decade ago for their efforts in fighting crime in New York City's subways. No volunteer organization has done more to make America's streets less dangerous. With dozens of active chapters, the Guardian Angels are scrupulous about maintaining good relations with local police. They enter a community only at the invitation of residents. They have substantially reduced crime in a number of Washington, D.C.-area apartment complexes. The Angels have worked hard at building a reservoir of good will among public officials. Francis Keating, General Counsel for the U.S. Department of Housing and Urban Development (HUD), acknowledges that they are a key element in HUD's Drug Elimination Program, which makes available grants to housing authorities to assist in the elimination of drug-related crime in public housing projects.

Community Policing to Empower Citizens

A goal of community policing is to empower citizens to act on their own initiative in close coordination with the police to solve and resolve problems. Not only do citizens require empowerment, but police employees need to feel as though they can make a difference in the quality of life in neighborhoods. Do the citizens and the police feel confident that no problem is beyond resolution if they join in partnership?

Everyone must take ownership of neighborhood problems. No one has a right to say that crime, gangs and drugs are someone else's problem. A cooperative and productive partnership is a far superior alternative to holding the police solely accountable for crime.

Wayne R. Inman, *Corrections Today*, August 1992.

Governments should seek ways to establish citizen crime patrol programs in low-income neighborhoods. The bureaucratic obstacles to such arrangements have been overcome where neighborhood groups and police work closely. HUD, for example, works with housing authorities around the country in providing technical assistance to tenant anti-crime patrols. In Baltimore, for instance, elderly residents in the city's public housing projects, with walkie-talkies, report to local police suspicious and illegal behavior they see.

Localities should encourage low-income resident associations to take the lead in establishing patrols. Besides patrolling, these patrols could provide literature to neighborhood residents to encourage them to leave on their lights at night, trim their shrubs and bushes for greater visibility, and arrange for the Post Office not to deliver mail when they are out of town. These groups also could give city building inspection and police departments information on vacant dwellings, especially those that may function as drug houses.

Make Public Housing Safe

Crime rates in public housing projects tend to exceed the city average. Thus, while Chicago's serious crime rate already is almost quadruple the national average, the rate in three of its most notorious projects—Cabrini-Green, Stateway Gardens, and Rockwell Gardens—ranges from double to quadruple even that of the whole city.

In the late 1980s, federal and local agencies began taking decisive action to tackle public housing project crime. HUD Secretary Jack Kemp was prompted to do so after the March 1989 murder of an Alexandria, Virginia, police officer who tackled a crack dealer holding a tenant hostage in a public housing project. It subsequently was learned that other project residents knew that the apartment long had been used for drug dealing and had complained to housing officials. Complex eviction procedures, however, had made it impossible to remove the drug-dealing tenants. Under this procedure, it normally took one to two years to evict someone from public housing. Since the Alexandria murder, HUD has waived these eviction requirements for close to 40 states and the District of Columbia.

A police response to public housing tenant requests for better protection can reduce crime. When the Chicago Housing Authority (CHA) in late 1988 asked police to raid suspected gang hideouts and crack dens in one of the Rockwell Gardens buildings, violence dropped dramatically, and residents no longer felt they had to sleep in closets and bathtubs for safety from flying bullets. . . .

Public housing authorities should establish comprehensive programs to combat crime and drug abuse in public housing. These programs should include better screening of prospective tenants; neighborhood foot patrols; information-sharing with police and housing authorities on criminals, suspected drug activity, and vacant apartments; and tenant drug education and referral outreach services.

In each program, tenant involvement is critical. Without it, the fear established by drug dealers and other criminals will not be removed. The housing authorities of Orlando, Florida, and Savannah, Georgia, have taken major steps in this direction. In both cities, police act as community organizers working closely with tenants. Officers take children on field trips and to ball games, introducing them to a world of non-criminal activities. As a result of this, drug activity in projects of both cities, especially Savannah, has been greatly reduced. . . .

Create Physical Barriers to Crime

An increasingly common technique of community policing is limiting access to a neighborhood. In many cases, the police, with the cooperation of resident leaders, erect barricades and guard posts at street intersections. Well-known is the Los Angeles Police Department's "Operation Cul-de-Sac." When a crack cocaine epidemic hit the south Los Angeles neighborhood of Newton in the late 1980s, gang members terrorized the neighborhood. Of the 873 murders in Los Angeles in 1989, 100 were in Newton.

Working with residents, police created a "Narcotics Enforcement Area" in February 1990. Police limited access to the community by constructing entry gates at street entrances and exits. They also interrogated suspicious persons where there was a legal basis to do so. As a psychological barrier, the police put up the sign OPEN TO RESIDENTS ONLY at each gate. The program enjoyed the strong support of the residents, many of whom had been too terrified to leave their homes after dusk. Within six weeks, violent crime in Newton had fallen by 90 percent; attendance at the nearby 2,600-student Jefferson High School had risen by 150 to 200 students a day; and residents rededicated a park that previously had been controlled by gangs. Then the barricades were removed—and crime, including several drive-by shootings—returned. The police brought back the barricades. Los Angeles police also instituted street barricade programs in the Sepulveda area of the San Fernando Valley. Within months, crime had been cut by about one-third.

Through close links with community leaders, local governments can adopt the tactics of Operation Cul-de-Sac to limit access to some neighborhoods. This of course needs broad neighborhood support, lest the operation harass and thus anger law-abiding persons living in, visiting, or passing through these neighborhoods. Police departments, with the help of neighborhood groups, should identify where the crime problems are, and then cordon off the key intersections and provide residents with opportunities to report suspicious-looking behavior. . . .

Steer Children Away from Crime

The evidence shows that reaching troubled children during their pre-adolescent years has the greatest effect on deterring them from becoming adult criminals. Instilling values of respect for property, hard work, and the nuclear family reduces criminal behavior. By contrast, children who become criminals often have suffered parental abuse or neglect.

Several police forces well understand the importance of preventing crime by exposing children to its futility. "We absolutely have to target the real young kids," states [former] Philadelphia Police Commissioner Willie Williams, adding that police and community leaders must "completely educate them about drugs, sex and how to protect themselves from family members leading them to drugs." The Los Angeles Police Department sponsors several youth intervention programs, such as the Jeopardy Program, in which officers visit the parents of youth involved with gangs, and DARE (Drug Abuse Resistance Education), in which officers come into school classes, and lecture students about the dangers of drug abuse. Similarly, New York City has launched a program, "Cops and Kids," aimed at keeping children in school, improving reading skills, preventing drug addiction, and creating after-school jobs and sports programs, among other activities. These police-sponsored programs are models for other cities.

Community Policing and Fear of Crime

Low level street crime and nuisances combine to make life in many urban neighborhoods *feel* as dangerous as actual life-threatening situations. Collectively, street disturbances, vandalism, prostitution and the like create a hostile environment that invites more serious crime, and at the very least, intimidates law-abiding citizens. Ultimately, a safe environment and the *perception* of a safe environment are important to the long-term health of the city.

I believe that community policing is essential to insure both the perception and reality of the public safety and quality of life in the city.

Lee P. Brown, *Vital Speeches of the Day*, July 1, 1992.

Community groups and private institutions have established similar programs. In Washington, D.C.'s Kenilworth-Parkside Gardens, a former public housing project now owned by its tenants, the managers sponsor a program that teaches youths how to develop business skills that will keep them out of trouble. Children also are employed in project-sponsored businesses to bake, package, and sell cookies. Working on commission, many youngsters earn up to $45 a day. Also, D.C. police are sponsoring nighttime basketball games to get teenagers off the streets during hours in which they might be tempted by crime, and involve them in recreation that tests their strength and athletic skills. Working with the D.C. local government, the National Basketball Players' Association, Anheuser-Busch Companies, and the Coca-Cola Company are acting as co-sponsors of this "Late Night Hoops" program.

The federal and state government should promote youth intervention programs. One possibility would be to use Project Head Start more frequently as a crime prevention program. Local police can work with parents of assisted children to educate them on the dangers of drugs.

Public school drug education programs should shift some of their emphasis away from students in high school and junior high school and toward those in elementary school, since most—though not all—children that age have not yet begun to use drugs and deal in them. States and localities should establish educational tax credit voucher programs that enable low-income parents to choose private schools that provide a drug-free environment.

Principles for Public Officials

Reducing crime is a key to neighborhood revitalization and economic improvement. The evidence is clear that one of the best ways of accomplishing this is by forging resident-police programs to discourage crimes rather than simply using the police to investigate crimes after they have happened. Only when residents feel they can work closely with police will fear of crime subside.

The argument that crime is of secondary concern, and is a byproduct of poverty, misunderstands the causal relationship between poverty and crime. Tackling crime is the precondition to a successful war on poverty—tackling poverty is not the key to reducing crime.

In tackling crime, public officials at all levels must adhere to the following principles:

• A police anti-crime program in low-income neighborhoods requires maximum face-to-face communication with resident leaders.

• Crime prevention is less expensive and more effective than crime investigation.

• No neighborhood or housing project, no matter how seemingly hopeless, can be written off. Success stories can and have happened even in the most crime-ridden neighborhoods.

• Economic development strategies to help the poor will work best when linked to areas with local crime prevention programs.

• Neighborhood space should be perceived by resident and non-resident alike as being under control of the law-abiding, not the lawless. Removal of graffiti, abandoned housing, litter, and other evidence of decay must have a high priority in municipal budgets.

• The drug culture must be eliminated. This means above all educating children and adolescents about the destructive and self-defeating nature of the drug world, and giving landlords and housing authorities the right to evict drug dealers with a minimum of impedance from misguided "civil rights" groups.

To rid poor urban neighborhoods of their criminal element, public officials at all levels must encourage the creation of new relationships between low-income resident organizations and local police forces. Central to this strategy is to give residents the confidence that they can take steps themselves to reduce crime. In this way, America may one day have a real chance of declaring victory in a war on urban poverty.

87

2 VIEWPOINT

"The move towards community-based policing can serve to divert attention away from grassroots efforts to establish real police reform."

Community-Based Policing Does Not Prevent Crime

Nicolas Alexander

In the wake of the March 1991 videotaped beating of Rodney King by officers of the Los Angeles Police Department, many people called for community-based policing as the best proposal for police reform. In the following viewpoint, Nicolas Alexander argues that community-based policing is often only a cosmetic reform; police do not want citizen involvement or oversight, he charges, and they often co-opt or resist neighborhood groups. Only activist citizen oversight groups can promote adequate reform, according to Alexander. The author is a contributing editor to *Third Force*, a journal published by the Center for Third World Organizing to examine issues and actions in communities of color.

As you read, consider the following questions:

1. According to Alexander, what was the original goal of the Neighborhood Watch program? Why does he feel that it has failed?
2. According to the author, why do two neighborhood councils operate in some communities?
3. Alexander quotes Earl Ofari Hutchinson as saying that some people, particularly African Americans, have a "'schizoid mind' about police reform." What causes this ambivalence, in Hutchinson's view?

Nicolas Alexander, "Taming the Paramilitary Monster," *Third Force*, September/October 1993. Reprinted with permission of the Center for Third World Organizing, Oakland, California.

Haunted by the national outcry against police brutality in the wake of Rodney King, law enforcement agencies throughout the country have latched onto a catchall buzzword for police reform: "community-based policing." It's hard to find a precise definition of the term, but it is clear that the on-the-ground reality in communities where the program is being implemented will depend on whether it's the community or the cops who get to define the specifics.

On one level, some of the proposed reforms that fall under the rubric of community-based policing are changes that community groups have demanded for decades: More accountability to the community, a return to beat cops who take the time to get to know the neighborhood, less emphasis on heavy-handed law enforcement and more on crime prevention and so on. On another level, however, community-based policing in some areas might be a "reform" along the lines of "low-intensity warfare," the Reagan administration's smoke screen for its war on Nicaragua, which was anything but low-intensity for the unfortunate people on the receiving end.

"Community-oriented policing usually involves some sort of decentralization of command, a return to the beat cop," says noted police reform advocate Jerome Skolnick, author of a book on police abuse entitled *Above the Law*. "The idea is for officers to feel responsible for a neighborhood; this will lead to more positive interactions between the cops and public." Such interactions may have a humanizing effect on police departments as cops get past stereotypes about entire communities that can lead to the use of excessive force. "Police begin to focus on 'bad acts' [instead of] 'bad people.'"

Community-Based Policing and Abuse

But, as Wilson Riles, Jr., chair of the Mayor's Task Force on Community Policing in Oakland, California, points out, the key deterrent to police misconduct in communities of color is "significant grassroots political organizing to monitor police behavior in the neighborhoods." He says that a minimum reform package should include elected review boards with independent investigative authority and the rights of districts to establish localized community-initiated policing methods.

For community organizations working to change abusive police behavior in communities of color, community-based policing is a mixed bag. As Skolnick admits, community-oriented policing as an antidote to police violence has not been implemented on any significant scale in low-income communities of color. In some areas, the move towards a "softer" style of policing has actually undermined community efforts for more substantive, comprehensive reforms.

Although it has gotten a lot of attention [recently], the concept of community-based policing actually emerged in the aftermath of the 1965-71 period of unrest in Los Angeles and other cities. As a way to deal with some of the complaints raised, LAPD [Los Angeles Police Department] Chief Ed Davis created the now widespread Neighborhood Watch as the basis of a larger strategy to rebuild community support in Black and Latino communities for the police by establishing a territorial identity between cops and neighborhoods.

One Police Officer's View of Community Policing

This is the usual horseshit. The chief tells everybody that we're community-oriented, but we still don't know what that means. The chief goes out and makes speeches about it, but when we ask the sergeant what we should say to people if they ask us about this, he tells us to keep in mind the department's rule that we're not allowed to criticize any department policy or official. I guess it would be critical to tell people we have no idea what the difference between community-oriented policing and what we used to do is, so we just smile and nod.

Anonymous police officer, quoted in Jerome H. Skolnick and James J. Fyfe, *Above the Law*, 1993.

The goal of Neighborhood Watch, which was developed through experimentation and collaboration between police department reformers and academics, was to replace aggressive paramilitary crime-fighting tactics and eliminate the officer's view of the entire community as the "enemy." However, Neighborhood Watches are police-organized and very pro-police, and so while the organizations may improve police relations with some sectors of the community, they never confront the police department over abuse, brutality or mistreatment of residents. In some cities where the Neighborhood Watch organizations have tried to assert a more independent role, the police have simply disbanded them.

One police officer captures the essence of the program: "Neighborhood Watch is supposed to work like a wagon train in an old-fashioned cowboy movie. The neighbors are the settlers and the goal is to get them to circle their wagons and fight off the Indians until the cavalry can ride to the rescue." The obvious danger of a program that conscripts citizens to become police informers is that it inevitably stigmatizes certain groups, such as inner-city teenagers, who may be subject to flagrant stereotyping.

In Portland, Oregon, for example, where people of color say

African American teenagers are routinely stopped by police and accused of being in gangs, local activist Aaron Ross attended a police advisory council meeting in a white neighborhood. A resident asked an officer about the problem of teenagers from the city's African American community entering their area and "enticing their children" to commit crime. The officer's answer: "Take down the license plates of cars not usually in the neighborhood and our department will take it from there."

In Seattle, a community policing plan is a recent innovation by a police department that has often been criticized for its attitudes towards people of color. Harriet Waldon, a member of Seattle's Mothers Against Police Harassment (MAPH), says the police advisory boards in the city's low-income neighborhoods are dominated by white homeowners and business people who often demand a more aggressive policing style. She says African Americans, especially youth, the main victims of unchecked police abuse, have stopped attending the meetings out of frustration that their concerns about police abuse are ignored. In some Seattle African American communities, two neighborhood councils operate: One that monitors police harassment, verbal abuse and discourtesy, and the other sponsored by the Seattle Police Department.

Barricading Communities of Color

In some cases, the slogan "community policing" has simply been pasted over the same old "us against them" mentality. For example, the Christopher Commission, which uncovered widespread cases of improper police conduct and racist practices inside the LAPD and L.A. County Sheriffs Department, cited as an example of current community-based programs the experiment begun in 1989 known as "Operation Cul de Sac." In the program, the police erected barricades and street barriers and posted signs proclaiming NARCOTICS ENFORCEMENT AREA—OPEN TO RESIDENTS ONLY. Officers on foot, horseback and bicycle saturated the area and required identification of people entering. Even the commission report criticized the program for operating only in communities of color and for the harsh treatment meted out to some residents.

Initiated by an inner circle of police officials and academics, community-oriented policing has for the most part been implemented from the top down (despite the populist cachet), and the slogan has often been little more than good public relations for police departments whose paramilitary approach remains essentially unchanged. In some cases, funding for "community policing" programs is being used as bait for cities to accept the Weed and Seed Program, which allows federal involvement in harsh crackdowns on suspected gang members and drug dealers in low-income neighborhoods, in exchange for funds for social services. In Seattle, community policing in the form of expanded foot and bike patrols is intended for the "transition period" after "violent criminals" are pushed out of the community. Where the police department is unaccountable to the community—or where community organizations do not have enough power to hold the police accountable—the move towards community-based policing can serve to divert attention away from grassroots efforts to establish real police reform. In Los Angeles, where activists believed that the police were politically vulnerable following the Rodney King incident, there were expectations that an elected civilian review commission with some real power could be established. But much of the African American establishment and many progressives fell in behind the blueprint for police reform issued by the Christopher Commission, which called for limiting the police chief to a five-year term, strengthening the LAPD's internal affairs office, and more aggressive prosecution by the district attorney of officers accused of brutality. The commission stopped short of recommending even limited civilian control over the department.

Police Reform in Los Angeles

Many were hopeful that the selection of Willie Williams as L.A.'s first African American police chief would lead to significant internal reforms. Williams said he was amenable to a "community policing" model developed by some local activists providing for locally elected police advisory councils to address both crime prevention and police abuse. However, Michael Zinzun, founder of the Coalition Against Police Abuse, faults the civil rights establishment and some elements of the left for getting too excited about Williams's ideas, diverting energy from a campaign to pass a sweeping proposal for police reform that called for an elected civilian review board with its own independent staff of investigators, subpoena power, and special prosecutor. He says it was the strongest plan against police abuse and for police accountability in the country, but that the push for community policing was presented as an alternative more palatable to the city's powerful corporate and municipal interests.

Despite the euphoria over Williams, the structural problems "of police violence, misconduct and racism" have not been solved, says Zinzun.

The elected "community policing boards" established under Williams are now largely defunct, with only about half of the original people still active. People who had an independent attitude about the council structures have dropped out as reports of police abuse continue unabated. [Referring to the chief of police in Los Angeles during the Rodney King beating and subsequent riots], "It's basically back to the 'Daryl Gates model' of community policing," says Joe Hicks, executive director of the Los Angeles chapter of the Southern Christian Leadership Conference. "You can't have authentic community policing," adds Zinzun, "without community control."

Most Community Policing Is Cosmetic Reform

In Oakland, where grassroots organizing around police brutality has tended to be sporadic and reactive, a new liberal city council is pushing for a comprehensive reform package that would include community-oriented policing. On the other hand, as in L.A., the plan may end up being a glorified Neighborhood Watch without community pressure to counter the political power of the Oakland Police Officers Association, which argues that the existing Block Watch program is "community policing."

In Oakland, as in other cities, the police can undermine support for substantive reforms by playing on people's fear of crime—both in communities of color and in white neighborhoods. This can have a strong whiff of racism, as when the police campaign against reform by arguing that only they stand between "nice" (i.e. white) areas of the city and the crime-ridden urban core. The police argue that community policing will "turn cops into social workers" when their real job is to fight crime. Politicians who push for reform risk getting labeled as "soft on crime."

"Community-oriented programs" can also exhibit the same disregard for people of color reflected in the distribution of other public services. In Portland, officers on foot and bicycles are concentrated in white suburbs and the central business district, where they develop friendly relationships with local residents, says Aaron Ross. But despite community demands, foot patrols and beat cops are almost completely absent in low-income African American neighborhoods, where police continue random patrols and enforce "drug free zones" with street barriers and barricades.

The bottom line is that community-oriented programs as conceived by the police give the community little real power. Bureaucratic and political resistance to the changes makes it virtually impossible for small pilot programs to succeed in the long run. Initiated with little input from the community, they tend to be easily co-opted by vested interests within the department. Absent a strong grassroots movement, the programs have seldom served as a handle for real reform of brutal police departments and are in most cases cosmetic at best.

Ambivalence in Communities of Color

Though the demands of community advocates for real power over the police are almost invariably absent from so-called "community-oriented programs," in a few cities community groups have appropriated the rhetoric to push their law enforcement agencies in a reform direction.

In Chicago, a multiracial, politically inclusive coalition was able to pressure the city to start a limited pilot program that will go city-wide [in 1994], but so far the plan is severely circumscribed. John McDermott, of the Chicago Alliance for Neighborhood Safety, says the coalition is pushing for elected members of police advisory councils, now appointed by the precinct commander, for a mechanism for community input into hiring and firing beat cops, and for officer training with less "abstract seminars on developing communications skills" and more interaction with community groups.

Mary Powers of the Citizens Alert, a local coalition against police torture and brutality, says the plan is a step in the right direction. "If beat officers are known to the community, it's more difficult for them to hide behind a veil of secrecy, more difficult for fellow officers in the same beat to fall behind a code of silence." But, she points out, faced with pressure to reduce crime, too many members of the coalition are willing to accept limited reforms that do nothing to reduce police abuse.

Even the most ardent advocates of police reform admit that communities of color are divided about what should be done. As Earl Ofari Hutchinson, author of *The Mugging of Black America*, points out, "there is a deep ambivalence in the community (regarding police reform). On the one hand, there is not a Black person walking around who has not had a negative experience (with cops) . . . certainly not a young Black male. They understand how the police have been used as a repressive vehicle, not to 'protect.' On the other hand, there is a deep fear of crime and the perception that we need the police to protect us . . . so what you have is a 'schizoid mind'" about police reform.

Joe Hicks agrees, and admits to being pessimistic about the chances that this latest reform fad to come down the line will change much in communities of color. "Community-based policing," he says, "is a hollow phrase. It has not been articulated in a way that would threaten the police. If community-based policing can't [give the community control over the police] then it's a sham and a hoax. The police reform movement is basically back to square one in trying to control this huge paramilitary monster in our midst."

:

"One thing is beyond debate: Prison incapacitates chronic, repeat offenders."

Harsher Sentences Will Prevent Crime

Mary Kate Cary

A popular theory among conservative criminologists is that most of the criminal violence in American society is perpetrated by a very small group of violent offenders, who commit crimes whenever they are out on the streets. Mary Kate Cary argues that keeping these criminals locked up will incapacitate them and thereby reduce crime. In the following viewpoint she calls for "swifter and surer" sentencing of criminals, harsher sentencing, and more jail time as a deterrent to crime. Cary, former deputy director of the Office of Policy and Communications within the Justice Department, is now director of First Freedom Coalition, a group that advocates strengthening the U.S. criminal justice system.

As you read, consider the following questions:

1. According to Cary, why is the Bail Reform Act of 1984 significant?
2. What is this author's view of the purpose of sentencing? Of parole?
3. What relationship between incarceration and the crime rate does Cary describe? Why is this so, in her view?

Violent crime remains at intolerably high levels. Gang violence is spreading across the country. And juveniles are committing more and more serious crimes. At the same time, crime is becoming more ruthless and wanton. Too many Americans—especially residents of the inner cities—have become prisoners in their homes, behind bars and chains. It is not surprising, therefore, that the strongest support for tougher law enforcement is found among inner-city, largely minority residents.

Despite this plague, a powerful bloc of liberal lawmakers in Congress prevented the passage of tough anti-crime measures proposed by the [George] Bush Administration. If President Clinton is to launch a war on crime, he will have to overcome this resistance on Capitol Hill.

As Bill Clinton prepares his own initiatives on crime, he would be wise to examine the recommendations of the report released in 1992 by former Attorney General William P. Barr. The report, entitled "Combatting Violent Crime," focuses on actions which can be taken at the state and local levels. President Clinton should call on governors and state legislators to act on the recommendations, and he should frame federal legislation and policies to complement the proposals.

Federal and State Partnership

When the federal government works with state authorities, the combined assault on crime can yield real results. Working with local police under "Operation Triggerlock," for example, federal prosecutors were able to charge over 10,000 dangerous criminals who used firearms in the operation's first eighteen months alone (Summer 1991–Winter 1992). The average sentence for three-time felons was eighteen years without parole. In another operation, 300 FBI agents were transferred from counterespionage to anti-gang squads in 39 cities across the country, and the federal RICO (Racketeer Influenced Corrupt Organizations) statutes were used in many cases to dismember violent gangs. Under the innovative "Operation Weed and Seed," law enforcement resources were combined with social programs at the local level to reduce crime in 20 targeted cities. And U.S. Marshals, in one ten-week period, rounded up thousands of dangerous fugitives in a massive manhunt named "Operation Gunsmoke."

The Clinton Administration should continue to assist state and local law enforcement officials in these ways. At the same time President Clinton should build upon the progress made by Presidents Ronald Reagan and George Bush in strengthening the federal criminal justice system. During the 1980s, federal legislation reformed bail laws to establish pretrial detention for dangerous offenders; sentencing guidelines were initiated to ensure firm

96

and consistent punishment; mandatory minimum sentences were created and federal parole was abolished to bring the amount of time served closer to the amount of time imposed in criminal cases. In addition, substantial resources were invested in federal law enforcement. The number of prosecutors and federal law enforcement officials increased significantly, and President Bush doubled federal prison capacity in just three years.

"LAST SPRING YOU ROBBED ME AND GOT 3 YEARS. LAST MONTH YOU NAILED ME AGAIN AND GOT 5 TO 10... HAVEN'T YOU LEARNED YOUR LESSON YET?"

Stayskal. Reprinted by permission: Tribune Media Services.

Nevertheless, the impact of federal policy necessarily is limited, since 95 percent of crimes fall within the jurisdiction of state and local governments. But state and local law enforcement agencies, with limited resources, are under great strain to deal effectively with the increase of violence in this country. To fight violent crime on the state and local levels, Attorney General Barr made 24 recommendations in his report. Developed in partnership with a broad array of non-partisan law enforcement officials, these recommendations are a sound framework for state and local policy makers seeking tough action on crime. And if the Clinton Administration should fail to follow through on candidate Clinton's anti-crime rhetoric, or weaken existing law enforcement programs through the appointment of liberal jurists to the federal bench, it will be all the more important for state and local officials to strengthen law enforcement in their jurisdictions. . . .

State officials must address a simple fact: The United States is in the grip of a violent crime wave. The number of violent crimes has jumped dramatically in the last thirty years, over three times the rate in the 1990s as in 1960. Measuring the increase in terms of population over the same time period, the U.S. population has increased by 41 percent, while the violent crime rate has increased by more than 500 percent. As Heritage Foundation Distinguished Fellow William J. Bennett, former National Drug Control Policy Director, observes, "The rate of violent crime in the U.S. is worse than in any other industrialized country."

The victims of violent crime tend to be disproportionately poor and members of racial and ethnic minorities, particularly blacks. "Given current crime rates," observes Bennett, "eight out of every ten Americans can expect to be a victim of violent crime at least once in their lives."

Most of the criminal violence in American society is committed by a very small group of chronic, violent offenders—hardened criminals who commit many violent crimes whenever they are out on the streets. They begin committing crimes as juveniles, and they go right on committing crimes as adults, even when on bail, probation, or parole.

The first duty of government is to protect its citizens. If law enforcement officials are to make any progress in reducing violent crime, their top priority must be to identify, target, and incarcerate these hard-core, chronic offenders.

The Barr report indicates ways in which state legislatures can take decisive action to protect citizens.

Pretrial Detention of Dangerous Defendants

Every state should grant statutory and, if necessary, state constitutional authority to its trial judges to hold, without bail, those defendants who are a danger to witnesses, victims, or the community at large—both before trial and pending appeal.

A study by the Department of Justice's Bureau of Justice Statistics (BJS) of individuals on pretrial release in 75 of the nation's most populous counties found that 18 percent of released defendants were known to have been rearrested for the commission of a felony while on pretrial release. Two-thirds of those rearrested while on release were again released.

This revolving door justice adds significantly to crime and destroys public confidence in the criminal justice system. Law-abiding citizens understandably are reluctant to inform police of criminal activities when they know that those arrested will be back on the street in a few days, or even in a few hours. Citizens fear retaliation, intimidation, and harassment by returning criminals if they help police.

At the federal level, the Bail Reform Act of 1984 grants federal judges the authority to deny bail or pretrial release to defendants who pose a danger to specific individuals or to the community in general. Under the Act, criminal defendants with serious records, including the commission of crimes while on release and those charged with serious drug felonies, are presumed to be a danger to the community and therefore unsuitable for release. The Act also creates a strong presumption that a convicted offender will remain imprisoned during any post-conviction appeal.

Pretrial detention has helped federal prosecutors cripple organized crime and drug rings. When pretrial detention is foregone, defendants have the opportunity to intimidate or harm witnesses before their trials. But when pretrial detention is enforced, dangerous defendants are put behind bars until trial, where they are unable to obstruct justice or pose a threat. Pretrial detention also increases the protection afforded to witnesses and victims of crimes.

The Statute's Proven Effectiveness

Despite the proven effectiveness of the federal statute, and its soundness as federal constitutional law (the Supreme Court rejected a constitutional challenge to the pretrial detention provisions of the Bail Reform Act in *United States v. Salerno*, 481 U.S. 739 [1987]), only a few states have effective pretrial detention provisions. In many states, pretrial detention is not currently possible because of an absolute right to bail in the state constitution. Thus where state constitutional reform is necessary to remedy this, it should be enacted.

States also should consider other key provisions of the Bail Reform Act of 1984, such as the serious penalties for jumping bail and enhanced penalties for crimes committed while on release.

In Philadelphia in 1986, for example, a judge placed a limit on the number of criminals that could be housed in the Philadelphia jail, in order to prevent overcrowding. Released because of this order were dangerous arrestees who otherwise would be held without bail or on very high bond. The result was an increase in violent crimes committed by the releasees. In the face of this crisis, the federal government stepped in to use federal pretrial detention in cooperation with state authorities. Over 600 gang members, who would have been turned loose by state judges because there was no room to hold them, were placed in federal facilities under federal law while awaiting trial. The homicide rate in Philadelphia declined as a result.

Imprisoning the hard-core population of chronic, violent offenders will reduce the level of violent crime in America. The reason: When these criminals are on the streets, they are victimizing citizens; when they are in prison, they are not committing crimes against the public. While liberals may question the deterrent and rehabilitative aspects of imprisonment, one thing is beyond debate: Prison incapacitates chronic, repeat offenders.

Consider the American experience of the last three decades. In the 1960s and early 1970s, incarceration rates dropped and violent crime rates skyrocketed. Conversely, when incarceration rates jumped in the 1980s, the rate of increase of crime was substantially reduced. This is all the more impressive, considering the mid-1980s "crack" drug epidemic and its associated violence.

Truth in Sentencing

The average time served in confinement fell by several months in the 1980s. Most convicted criminals spend only about one-third of their sentences in prison. On average, convicted rapists spend barely 5 years in prison; robbers spend 3.9 years; assaulters and burglars spend barely 2 years; and drug traffickers spend less than 2 years. Only 42% of reported murders result in a prison sentence; most convicted murderers spend well under 10 years behind bars.

The Swiss cheese of mandatory sentencing laws has left little room behind bars for petty, first-time or nonviolent criminals. More than 93% of state prisoners are violent criminals, repeat criminals (with two or more felony convictions) or violent repeat criminals. Most of the "property offenders" behind bars have long criminal histories and a propensity for violence. Within 3 years about two-thirds of all probationers get into serious trouble with the law again, and 20% of released property offenders are rearrested for a *violent* crime.

John J. DiIulio Jr., *The Wall Street Journal*, January 26, 1994.

The best way to reduce crime is to identify, prosecute, and incarcerate hard-core criminals. Study after study shows that a relatively small portion of the population is responsible for the lion's share of criminal violence in this country. For example, one California study found that 3.8 percent of a group of more than 236,000 men born in 1956 were responsible for 55.5 percent of all serious felonies committed by the study group.

Putting chronic offenders in prison for long periods, especially upon second and third convictions, is the most effective way to reduce violent crime.

An axiom of effective law enforcement is that punishment should be swift, certain, and severe. Yet in too many jurisdictions, it is none of these. In fact, most violent offenders who are sent to state prison serve only a small fraction of their sentences. According to the Bureau of Justice Statistics, analysis of release practices in 36 states and the District of Columbia in 1988 shows that although violent offenders received an average sentence of seven years and eleven months imprisonment, they served an average of only two years and eleven months in prison—or 37 percent of their imposed sentence. Overall, 51 percent of the violent offenders in the survey were discharged from prison in two years or less, and 76 percent were out in four years or less.

The Failure of Parole

This huge gap between the nominal sentence given and the real time served is dishonest, and it is bad policy. It is dishonest because the public—especially victims of crime—is often under the impression that the sentence will be served in full, when in fact no such thing happens. It is bad policy because it puts the public at risk.

There are several reasons why states should restrict parole practices. First, parole is based on the mistaken idea that the primary reason for incarceration is rehabilitation (prisoners can be released as soon as they are rehabilitated, so the argument goes), and ignores the deterrent, incapacitative, and retributive reasons for imprisonment. A clear and truthful sentence increases the certainty of punishment, and both its deterrent and incapacitative effects.

Second, in too many cases parole simply does not work. Studies of the continuing failure of parole obscure the terrible human cost to law-abiding citizens. For example, Suzanne Harrison, an eighteen-year-old honor student, three weeks from graduation, left her home in Texas with two friends, nineteen and twenty years old, on May 4, 1986. Her body was found the next day. She had been raped, beaten, and strangled. Her two companions were shot to death, and their bodies were found ten days later in a ditch.

Their killer, Jerry Walter McFadden (who calls himself "Animal"), had been convicted previously of two 1973 rapes, and sentenced to two fifteen-year sentences in the Texas Penitentiary. Paroled in 1978, he was again sentenced to fifteen years in 1981 for a crime spree in which he kidnapped, raped, and sodomized a Texas woman. Despite the fact that his record now contained three sex-related convictions and two prison terms, he was released again on parole in July 1985. McFadden's crime spree finally came to an end when he was convicted of the capital murder of Suzanne Harrison and sentenced to death in 1987. McFadden raped and killed Harrison and killed her two friends less than a year after being released on parole. This tragic example is all too common, and the cost of failed parole practices to the public safety is all too high.

Enact Mandatory Minimum Sentences

Parole sometimes is used as an answer to prison overcrowding. This is hardly a reasonable justification for the premature release of violent criminals into the community. The answer to a lack of prison space is to build more prisons, not to release dangerous criminals.

Until recently, the Texas prison system was not expanding rapidly enough to house that state's criminals. Under federal court order to remain at a maximum of 95 percent of capacity, the Texas prison system responded by increasing the number of inmates released on parole. The number of felons on parole increased by 430 percent during the 1980s, and inmates served an average of only sixty-two days for each year of their sentence. As a result, reported crime rates in Texas increased 29 percent in the 1980s, according to the FBI, while they fell for the nation as a whole.

States should enact "truth in sentencing." Parole should be restricted so that the sentence served more closely matches the sentence imposed. While "good behavior" incentives may be used to control prisoners, the mechanism should not exceed federal standards requiring 85 percent of sentence to be served.

In many states, sentences for violent crimes are too short. To many criminals, jail time is little more than a brief cost of doing business. For example, in 1988, of an estimated 100,000 persons convicted in state courts of murder, rape, robbery, and aggravated assault, some 17 percent—or about 17,000 violent criminals—received sentences that included no prison time at all.

State legislators should enact mandatory minimum sentences for aggravated crimes of violence, and for such crimes committed by repeat offenders. Every state should follow the example of federal law, which mandates imprisonment where a firearm is used or possessed in the commission of certain serious felonies.

Every state should also enact laws similar to the federal armed career criminal statute, which targets repeat violent criminals who possess a gun. Under federal law, any person who has been convicted of three violent felonies or serious drug offenses, and who illegally possesses a firearm, is sentenced to at least fifteen years imprisonment without possibility of parole. There are graduated, lesser penalties for those who have been convicted of one or more prior felonies and illegally possess a gun. . . .

On the federal level, President Clinton should use the power of his office to continue the federal effort against crime. In so doing, he should build upon the progress of his predecessors, Presidents Reagan and Bush, in strengthening the criminal justice system.

At the same time, state legislators and judicial officials can and should take concrete steps to make America safer. Concerned citizens, victims of crime, and law enforcement leaders are working to strengthen the criminal justice system. Law-abiding citizens, however, are asking if their state and local public safety laws are as effective as those of the federal government and the more rigorous states. They want police and prosecutors to have the tools they need to combat gangs, drug dealers, and chronic violent offenders. They want states to ensure that dangerous criminals are in prison, not in their neighborhood. And they want victims of crime to have the same say as the criminals do in the system.

"Mandatory minimums are increasingly being attacked from the left and the right as frustrating, draconian, unjust, racist and completely ineffective."

Harsher Sentences Will Not Prevent Crime

Chi Chi Sileo

The following viewpoint was written in response to the adoption of mandatory minimum sentences as part of the 1993 crime bill passed by the Senate. Chi Chi Sileo cites opinion leaders who argue that mandatory minimums are ineffective in preventing the types of crime and locking up the criminals that most people are concerned about, namely violent crime and criminals. Sileo is a contributing editor to *Insight on the News*, a weekly newsmagazine published by the *Washington Times*.

As you read, consider the following questions:

1. What was the original purpose of mandatory minimum sentences under the Boggs Act, according to Sileo?
2. Why, according to the author, do drug "kingpins" serve less of their sentences than low-level offenders?
3. According to the sources cited by Sileo, what is the effect of mandatory minimums on rehabilitation?

Laura Graser, a Portland, Ore., defense lawyer, is under no illusions about her clients. Known as a tough, law-and-order type, Graser believes in harsh punishment and describes the average drug dealer as a "selfish, whiny jerk." But ask her about Michael Irish and she says, without hesitation, "He's the finest human being it's ever been my privilege to represent."

If ever the quality of mercy were absent in a courtroom, Graser says, it was in Irish's case. Irish, a carpenter with no criminal background who was known as hardworking, honest and devoted to his family, was offered a deal one day—several hours of work in exchange for more money than he had ever made in a year. It was an offer someone in comfortable circumstances might have considered, and Irish was in desperate straits. His wife's cancer had wiped out the family's savings, and he had recently been laid off from his job. The three hours' work was unloading boxes of hashish from a boat. Caught and tried in federal court, Irish was convicted and sentenced to twelve years in prison with no possibility of parole.

If he had been tried in state court, he might have gotten two years' probation. But drug cases are now routinely tried at the federal level, and the punishments are meted out according to mandatory minimum sentencing rules.

If Irish had been convicted of murder, he would be serving only half as long.

The Original Intent of Mandatory Sentencing

According to Stuart Taylor Jr., a writer with the *American Lawyer*, mandatory minimums "may well represent the most complete triumph of political cowardice and public ignorance over common sense and fundamental fairness in the history of our nation's criminal justice system."

Strong words, but Taylor is not alone. Mandatory minimums are increasingly being attacked from the left and the right as frustrating, draconian, unjust, racist and completely ineffective. Opponents maintain that there are detailed federal sentencing guidelines already on the books that should be used instead.

Proponents of mandatory minimums say they relay a message of swift and certain justice and let criminals know they will be dealt with harshly. These supporters decry the effectiveness of the current sentencing guidelines (which have never been fully implemented) and insist on even more minimums.

The two sides have polarized along increasingly inflexible lines, with accusations of unfairness, ignorance, softness on crime and bleeding-heart liberalism emerging as favorite fighting words.

It wasn't supposed to be this way. When mandatory minimum sentencing was first introduced in the Boggs Act of the 1950s, it was intended to end sentencing disparity so that everyone committing the same crime did the same time, regardless of family connections, race or other factors. In the 1970s, mandatory minimums were abolished because of concerns that they were overly harsh and inflexible; then-Rep. George Bush of Texas was among those who praised this return to "more equitable actions by the court" and "fewer disproportionate sentences."

Existing Mandatory Sentencing Laws

But Congress quickly forgot history, and was doomed to repeat it. In 1984, with the advent of the war on drugs, Congress took two mutually contradictory actions. First, it passed the Sentencing Reform Act, the main feature of which was the presidentially appointed U.S. Sentencing Commission, which was supposed to draw up detailed sentencing guidelines for more than 2,000 crimes. Curiously, however, Congress immediately negated the intent of the new law when it passed a large number of mandatory minimum sentences two years later, thus ignoring both the failures of the Boggs Act and the work of the Sentencing Commission, which released the results of its painstaking efforts in 1986.

Those mandatory minimums were followed swiftly by others, buried in the 1986 and 1988 Anti-Drug Abuse Acts. The same era saw passage of the Armed Career Criminal Act; not to be outdone, the Justice Department joined the parade in 1990 with Operation Triggerlock, which encouraged resentencing for earlier crimes.

The dizzying result of all this legislation is a still-dismayed Sentencing Commission and a collection of about sixty statutes for mandatory minimums, only four of which are used with any regularity. These four, dealing with drug and gun-related offenses, account for more than 90 percent of the mandatory minimum sentences handed out.

Resurrecting Sentence Disparity

Laying aside arguments for and against mandatory minimums, two things are undeniable: mandatory minimum sentencing has led to a huge increase in the federal and state prison populations—the "land of the free" now has an incarceration rate three times higher than those of South Africa or the former Soviet Union—and no one feels any safer.

Critics charge that mandatory minimums have resurrected the very monster they were supposed to slay; sentencing, they say, is now even more confused, and confusing, than it was under previous systems. That's largely because under mandatory minimums, sentences can be modified only by prosecutors—who can do so only in cases in which the defendant can trade valuable information—rather than by judges as in traditional sentencing. In 1991, the Sentencing Commission presented a report to Congress stating that prosecutorial discretion and uneven application of the minimums had led to a marked and clear reintroduction of sentencing disparity.

"Mandatory minimums are to sentencing uniformity what a meat ax is to brain surgery" is the blunt summation offered by Henry Scott Wallace of the National Legal Aid and Defender Association. "Sentencing," Wallace says, "is the art of rationally individualizing a punishment to fit a crime. You have to consider things such as levels of violence or threat of violence, criminal background, mitigating circumstances, quantities (say, of drugs sold or items stolen)—all the things that are routinely weighed for other offenses. Mandatory minimums don't permit any of these individual factors."

Unintended Consequences

Chief Justice of the United States William H. Rehnquist, in a speech June 18, 1993, said that mandatory minimum sentences are a "good example of the 'law of unintended consequences.' There is a respectable body of opinion which believes that these mandatory minimums impose unduly harsh punishment for first-time offenders—particularly for 'mules' [runners] who played only a minor role in drug distribution schemes. . . . [They] have also led to an inordinate increase in the federal prison population and will require huge expenditures to build new prison space."

Charles S. Clark, *CQ Researcher*, February 4, 1994.

This is particularly evident in trials for drug offenses. Since only prosecutors can reduce a mandatory minimum sentence, they often use that reduction as a way of bargaining for important information on other criminals.

The only problem is that low-level offenders, particularly in drug cases, rarely have access to high-level information. In fact, studies show that low-level offenders serve, on the average, 70 percent to 80 percent of their given sentence; mid-level dealers, 62 percent; and high-level kingpins, 60 percent.

There also are anecdotal accounts of defendants bargaining their way into reduced sentences by turning in innocent people.

Nicole Richardson of Mobile, Ala., has firsthand experience of this skewed justice. Her mistake was dating the wrong guy, not unusual for a twenty-year-old. One day an undercover agent asked her where he could buy LSD; she told him that her boyfriend was a dealer. For that level of involvement, she was sentenced to ten years in prison with no possibility of parole. Her boyfriend had some tips on other dealers. He got five years.

"All right, let's accept the premise that we have to give stiff punishments to drug traffickers," Wallace says. "Do we want to then send the message that if you're going to get involved in drugs, you better become a big-time kingpin so you can get a smaller punishment? Is that a useful message to send to society?"

Fifty percent of the cases now in federal courts are for drug offenses. The trend is part of a greater one of federalizing crimes, which is clogging federal courtrooms with cases that used to be handled by the far larger state courts system and is commandeering time and resources from state law enforcement efforts.

Federal vs. State Jurisdiction

Supreme. Court Chief Justice William Rehnquist noted that mandatory minimums were fueling the overfederalizing of crimes. At the National Symposium on Drugs and Violence in America, Rehnquist warned that huge amounts of resources will be necessary to run the federal courts "unless we reach a different allocation of jurisdiction that both supports state efforts and preserves federalism. And the federal courts will be changed, perhaps irrevocably, unless the current federalization trends are halted." He also tentatively opposed mandatory minimums, saying they "frustrate the careful calibration of sentences, from one end of the spectrum to the other, which the sentencing guidelines were intended to accomplish."

That's precisely the point, say mandatory-minimum advocates such as Sen. Phil Gramm, a Texas Republican who calls the rules "a massive no-confidence vote by the American people in the discretionary powers of our judges."

That's only partially true. Americans are extremely concerned about violent crime and many agree that justice needs to be swifter and harsher, but most people don't believe in the indiscriminate locking-up of small-time offenders. Regarding the drug war, Bureau of Justice Statistics figures note that 40 percent of Americans would direct the majority of resources to educating the young, 28 percent to working with foreign governments to control the influx of drugs, only 19 percent to arresting drug pushers and 4 percent each to treatment programs and to arresting users. A 1993 poll commissioned by the National Rifle Association found similar results: When people were asked what they thought was the "single most important thing that can be done to help reduce violent crime," the top answer was preventive programs, followed in descending order by stricter prosecution and penalties, the teaching of values, more law enforcement efforts and gun control.

A common thread in arguments made by supporters of mandatory minimums is that people want to see "violent criminals" locked up. The word violent is repeated like a mantra; even when talking about nonviolent offenders, these supporters are fond of using terms such as "deadly," "brutal" and "dangerous" to describe federal inmates.

That confusion between violent and nonviolent offenders is the most frustrating one for those who want to repeal mandatory minimums. These critics repeatedly draw the distinction between violent and nonviolent offenders, but often find their careful delineations overwhelmed by voices warning of city streets filled with marauding murderers if mandatory minimums are abolished.

Not so, respond these critics, who maintain that allowing the sentencing guidelines to work would keep tough sentences in place for tough offenders and still allow for some flexibility. The guidelines, they say, are complete and carefully drawn, and if implemented would result in fairer overall sentencing at both ends of the criminal spectrum. "If we could go back and start over," says Kent Larsen, a spokesman for the Sentencing Commission, "people would see that these guidelines would really work."

Mandatory minimums, in fact, are often used against nonviolent offenders. A 1992 Sentencing Commission report found that 50 percent of those incarcerated for drug offenses were nonviolent offenders who had no criminal record for 15 years prior to their convictions. These offenders, who have a high rate of rehabilitation when given a chance through alternative sentencing, are serving tougher sentences than the violent criminals that mandatory-minimum advocates rail against. (The average federal sentence for a drug conviction is 6.5 years, nearly twice that for manslaughter or assault.)

In fact, one of the great ironies of mandatory minimum sentencing is that burglars, rapists and murderers are being released early to make room for people such as Michael Irish and Nicole Richardson. In North Carolina, violent offenders are serving one month for every year of their sentences. The state of Florida repealed its mandatory minimum policy after finding that violent criminals were serving less than half their sentences so that prisons could accommodate drug offenders. According to Wallace, "Florida is the federal system a few years down the road.". . .

The Price Tag for Mandatory Minimums

Stories about jails and prisons being finishing schools for crime are not new. With mandatory minimums, however, the new twist is a growing problem with prison discipline. Michael Quinlan, director of the Bureau of Prisons under Presidents Reagan and Bush, says of prisoners coming in under mandatory minimums, "The things that matter to other inmates just don't matter to them. You can't get them to behave or cooperate because they know they're not going to get any time off for good behavior, or have to worry about qualifying for parole."

A stint in stir costs around $30,000 a year per inmate. Even opponents of mandatory minimums agree that's not too high a price to keep a truly dangerous person out of society, but they also point out that alternative sentencing, by comparison, costs very little. It almost pays for itself, they note, because nonviolent offenders have a low rate of recidivism and often make a speedy return to respectability, getting jobs, paying taxes and raising families.

Quinlan says: "We also need to think about the costs we're paying for loss of tax revenues from these incarcerated people, and also for increased social services that their families are using. If the offender is a male supporting a family, that family might have to go on welfare, or they might need the help of social workers. They become huge burdens on the state." Adds Bill Maynard, a defense lawyer in El Paso, Texas: "What happens when these people come out of jail? How can they compete in the job market? It's easy to say, 'Well, they should have thought of that before they committed the crime,' but we're the ones who end up paying."

Mandatory Minimums Convey a Message

In practice if not in theory, mandatory minimums convey the message that there is no such thing as rehabilitation. Despite the fact that the majority of Americans believe in the concept of rehabilitation and that rehabilitation for nonviolent offenders is an attainable and inexpensive goal, current drug war policies deny ex-offenders any certainty that their efforts at reentering society will be acknowledged.

A case in point is that of Bill Keagle, one of Maynard's clients. Keagle, who Maynard admits is "no one's idea of an angel," had a criminal record for nonviolent burglaries he committed as a young man. He served six years in prison for those crimes, but came out and "turned his life around," Maynard says. "He got a job and stayed out of trouble. He got married and adopted his wife's two boys, to whom he became extremely attached. It was a complete turnaround—this was a shining example of rehabilitation."

Keagle had a couple of guns that he used for target shooting. When he was laid off from his job, he sold the guns to a pawn shop to pay some bills. What he didn't reckon on was a recently passed federal statute, the Armed Career Criminal Act, which mandates prison time for any ex-felon in possession of firearms who has three prior convictions that involved either violence or drugs. The catch in the law is that violence is defined amorphously, so that even though Keagle never assaulted anyone, never used a gun or any other weapon, his crimes were considered "potentially violent" and therefore qualified for the same punishment. Keagle was turned in to the local agent of the Bureau of Alcohol, Tobacco and Firearms and, like Irish, ended up in a federal court.

If Keagle had been tried in Texas courts, his offense might have netted him two years' probation at most; in some states, where the right to own firearms is eventually reinstated to ex-convicts, not even that. What he got was the federal mandatory minimum: 15 years.

"This law," Maynard says, "was intended for a person who can't obey the law, who's a danger to society. Not for someone like Bill Keagle. The logic here is that you can't ever be rehabilitated, that you're a career criminal for life." He notes that the act makes no allowance for recidivism or recency of crime and that the average murderer serves five or six years. "Where is the justice here? Look, I believe that long prison terms should be used to protect society from a dangerous person, or to punish someone for a particularly evil crime. But Bill Keagle did nothing against the laws of God, nothing that was inherently evil. Let's put it this way: No one in El Paso was locking their doors at night because they were afraid of Bill Keagle.". . .

Who Will Pay?

No one doubts that something needs to be done, both about violent crime and about prison overpopulation. Quinlan predicts that by 1999, the state and federal prison populations will have swelled from the current 740,000. No one, he adds, talks about who will pay. (In a *New York Times* op-ed piece, Gramm said the cost of incarceration was cheap compared with the "$430,000 a year" cost imposed by "an active street criminal," but that description does not fit most of these federal inmates.)

"We'll be spending more on prisons than on schools," says Wallace. "More than on hospitals, on keeping libraries open. The choice will come down to these versus prisons."

Predicts Maynard, "We're going to have an unbelievably huge, clumsy bureaucracy regulating us. This is the same government that wants to end poverty, create a government in Somalia and reduce pollution. How well do we think they've done at those? And where is the money supposed to come from? All we can see as an outcome of this 'war on crime' is the tremendous suffering and sorrow that it's wrought."

Critics of mandatory minimums echo the same refrains: Let's reserve those costly prison slots for violent, dangerous offenders. Let the sentencing guidelines work.

Supporters of the minimums have their own chorus: Let's show criminals we mean business. Let the mandatory minimums do the dirty work of levying harsh punishment.

111

Both sides make appeals to emotion—critics to compassion and humanity, supporters to public safety and frustration with the justice system. Neither side predicts any drastic changes anytime soon. Supporters of the minimums have vowed to fight for them at every opportunity, in every crime bill. Even the fiercest opponents of the sentences admit that they have an up-hill battle, and that any changes will be in baby steps.

Much of the work for change seems to rest with individual defendants and their attorneys, trying to interject a human element into a harsh policy debate. Nicole Richardson spoke at congressional hearings and has appeared on television to discuss her case. Maynard has asked Clinton and Attorney General Janet Reno to commute Bill Keagle's sentence. And in Portland, Laura Graser steels her voice and vows, "I don't care what it takes. On this one, I'm just not quitting."

"Our new law locks the revolving door on [criminal] careers."

"Three Strikes" Laws Prevent Crime

John Carlson

In November 1993, voters in Washington state approved the nation's first "three strikes" law. The law mandates life sentences for violent criminals convicted of three serious felonies. In the following viewpoint, John Carlson presents evidence that the criminals who are "striking out" are the violent, repeat offenders the law is intended to target. He argues that the new law will reduce crime by taking these felons off the street and deterring others. Carlson, who is president of the Washington Institute for Policy Studies in Seattle, led the campaign for the Three Strikes, You're Out initiative in Washington.

As you read, consider the following questions:

1. What two kinds of criminals are targeted by the "three strikes" law, in Carlson's view?
2. What are the "three other benefits" of the "three strikes" law that Carlson mentions?

John Carlson, "'Three Strikes' Works for Us," *The Washington Post National Weekly Edition*, March 14-20, 1994. Reprinted with permission.

President Clinton received roars of approval when he rousingly endorsed the "Three Strikes, You're Out" anti-crime proposal during his [1994] State of the Union Address. But now the idea of locking criminals up for life after their third serious felony is being attacked by critics as good politics but bad policy—as a catchy slogan with an expensive price tag that does little to protect people's security and covers too many crimes that aren't serious.

We heard those same concerns voiced in Washington state. But on Election Day [1993], nearly 77 percent of the voters launched the national movement for "three strikes" by approving Initiative 593 to put felons permanently behind bars after their third serious conviction. And ironically, while "three strikes" is under fire in the nation's capital, some opponents of the 1993 initiative now support the new law.

"Sentencing Law Isn't Striking Out" reads the lead editorial in the February 10, [1994], *Spokesman-Review* from [House Speaker] Tom Foley's hometown of Spokane. "We grudgingly admit the new law appears to be working," said the paper, which encouraged a "no" vote on 593. "We felt, and still do," the paper wrote, "that it will add greatly to the increasing cost of incarceration. We also worried that too many small-fry would be caught in the three-strikes net. We didn't want to see relatively harmless felons taking up prison space at age 60, 70 or 80."

"Maybe we've done too much hand wringing," the *Spokesman-Review* conceded, and pointed out that the new law was catching the two kinds of criminals it targeted: "high-profile predators who rape or kill repeatedly; and offenders who terrorize the community with chronic strings of lesser but still serious crimes, such as robbery."

Targeting Career Criminals

Precisely. At present eight criminals are facing the prospect of "striking out" here in Washington state. Three are sex criminals, all of whom have attempted murder (one successfully). Another is a four-time armed robber. The other four are career criminals. One, Larry Fisher, was described in the *New York Times* as a two-time felon. In fact, he has sixteen prior criminal convictions—six felonies, ten misdemeanors and numerous probation violations. Another has five felonies and nine misdemeanors. A third has four previous felonies and fifteen misdemeanors, and the fourth has had fifteen convictions in eight years, five of them felonies. That's sixty-four convictions among four street criminals. Essentially, whenever these fellows weren't in the joint they were out ripping off people's homes and businesses. Our new law locks the revolving door on their careers.

But in the nation's capital, a rehashed version of Washington state's election debate has resulted in a weak White House version of "three strikes" that would not cover six of our eight criminals, including two of the three violent rapists. Philip Heymann, the former number-two official with the Department of Justice, contends that some of the crimes weren't serious enough to be covered by "three strikes," such as second degree robbery, which he characterized as knocking someone down to steal a purse.

"Three Strikes" Is Worth It

Despite the strength of the "three strikes" idea, [some people] have raised legitimate questions about its consequences. One objection is that the law would not affect enough criminals to do any good. In 1992, of 25,000 offenders imprisoned in New York State, only 286 were sentenced as three-time violent offenders. Thus a "three strikes" law would have kept "only" 286 murderers, rapists, armed robbers and other violent felons off our streets.

If that number seems small, imagine the public outcry if we announced that instead of locking these felons up for life, we intended to release that many. If a "three strikes" law prevented only one rape, one murder, one assault, it would have been worth the trouble to pass the legislation.

Mario M. Cuomo, *The New York Times*, January 29, 1994.

That's theory. Here's reality. The first criminal to face the "Three Strikes, You're Out" charge in our state is Cecil Emile Davis. His first strike was second degree robbery back in 1986. But Mr. Davis didn't knock down a lady while snatching her purse. He robbed a convenience store and beat both the clerk and a customer so severely that the judge noted at sentencing his "deliberate cruelty to the victims." So how long did Davis spend behind bars for that attack? Two years. Often, criminals are not charged with a crime or given a sentence that matches the severity of their actual offense, a reality not addressed by the Clinton version of "three strikes."

Davis is charged with abducting a young woman, repeatedly raping her, stabbing her in the throat and throwing her down the recessed stairwell of a church. She managed to survive and has identified Davis as her assailant. If convicted, Davis will "strike out" and be gone for life. Had he committed that crime on government soil, the Clinton bill would not have applied to him.

Other Benefits

As for the costs of incarceration, only 3 percent to 4 percent of most state budgets is spent on corrections, and several studies show that it's much cheaper to lock up a common criminal than allow him to roam free. However, if the governor is convinced that an aging third striker is too old to do harm any longer, our "three strikes" law reaffirms his power to grant pardons or clemency.

Three other benefits to our law should give pause to even its most liberal critics. First, although statistics haven't yet been tabulated, police officers report that the new law is already deterring criminal activity. Second, the tough new penalties are forcing some criminals to seek treatment and counseling they previously refused. Third, the new law is unquestionably driving criminals out of Washington state. In Seattle alone, since "three strikes" passed, seventeen registered sex offenders have moved out of state because their next offense would be their last. That may be good news for people here, but it will only be good for America if lawmakers across the country, including Congress, make the climate for crime as chilly in their states as it now is in Washington state.

"Any effort to really enforce such a ["three strikes"] law will require a massive increase in prison spending."

"Three Strikes" Laws Will Not Prevent Crime

Jonathan Simon

"Three strikes, you're out" is the popular catchphrase used to describe a proposal to impose life sentences on career criminals convicted of three serious felonies. In the following viewpoint, Jonathan Simon argues that "three strikes" and other tough sentencing policies will require huge expenditures on prison building at a time when state budgets are already being cut. Further, he contends that tough sentencing policies have failed to deter criminals as advertised. Simon is an associate law professor at the University of Miami and author of *Poor Discipline: Parole and the Social Control of the Underclass, 1890-1990.*

As you read, consider the following questions:

1. Why are violent offenders now being released, in Simon's view?
2. What two things were tough sentences supposed to accomplish, according to Simon?

Jonathan Simon, "How Many Prisons Must We Build to Feel Secure?" *Los Angeles Times,* January 17, 1994. Reprinted with permission.

"Three strikes and you're out," the proposal to imprison three-time felons for life, is drawing considerable attention from politicians. Governors as different as [New York's] Mario Cuomo and [California's] Pete Wilson, who share little more than bad polling numbers and impending elections [in 1994], have rushed to embrace the proposal. This is not surprising. The idea, like the slogan, is simple, satisfying to express and capable of channeling the overwhelming tide of popular anger about violent crime rising in America. Any politician who does not ride on this wave has good reason to fear being dragged under it.

The arguments against the proposal are solid, persuasive and boring. Any effort to really enforce such a law will require a massive increase in prison spending when states like California and New York have been slashing budgets for years. Wilson promises to build six more prisons on top of the five he has already built on top of those built by his predecessor. Cuomo, too, promises to wring New York's budget dry to pay for more cells.

The Costs Will Go Up

Life sentences involve a lot more whimper than bang. The twentysomethings with a seemingly insatiable appetite for violence become forty-, fifty- or sixtysomethings. Their propensity for violence goes down but the cost of maintaining them (in human as well as fiscal terms) goes up. In the meantime, correctional officers will have to deal with a burgeoning population of inmates with little left to lose.

So many violent offenders are now being released without serving their full terms because mandatory sentencing laws for drug offenders have already filled our prisons, forcing early release of felons without mandatory minimums. "Three strikes" would add yet another monolithic mandatory sentencing policy that robs our courts of the ability to make commonsense distinctions of degree between crimes and criminals.

But, look, don't bother the public with the fiscal details, or the fact that plenty of horrible crimes . . . get committed by people with no record of felonies. Like the ball game from which the slogan derives, the "three strikes" proposal has an almost mythic quality that sustains its capacity to endure in our hearts over many seasons of disappointment. This is the stuff that dreams (and governors) are made of. Indeed, variations on this theme, life terms for "habitual" offenders, have been around since the 19th Century and in some form or another sit in the laws of virtually every state in the union, the relics of earlier crime panics and campaigns.

Before this wave crests, leaving behind yet more evidence for the proposition that Lincoln should have been more worried about fooling most of the people most of the time, two aspects

118

are worth considering.

While "three strikes" may seem to fit in with the "get tough" policies toward crime legislated over the last decade or two, it really reflects an admission of bankruptcy on the part of that philosophy. They used to tell us that tough sentences would cut through the confusing messages of the "rehabilitative" penal philosophy, and that the promise of stiff punishment would deter crime. Now, billions and billions of dollars later, "three strikes" implicitly acknowledges a fact too painfully obvious to conceal any more: Deterrence did not work to prevent crime. And, guess what? The new solution to the old solution looks like the same solution: more prisons.

Steve Kelley. Reprinted by permission.

Californians, like people all over America who are toasting the "three strikes" proposition, are expressing genuine frustration over the loss of personal security in this country. Contrary to the received wisdom that Americans want their government to go away and leave them alone, millions of Americans are saying that they expect government to take an active role in improving the conditions that make life so fearful, and they are willing to be taxed if they believe it will go to a serious effort.

What form should that effort take? Criminal-justice experts, liberal and conservative, share a surprising degree of consensus on programs that will have both short- and long-term impacts on public safety, such as: targeting early intervention at juvenile offenders; improving drug treatment and education programs in prison so that first-time felons do not graduate to careers in crime; and boosting police presence in the schools, parks and shopping districts where law-abiding citizens must be made to feel secure if our cities are to remain economically viable.

None of these proposals has anything like the magic ring of "three strikes and you're out." Creating a thoughtful strategy to reduce crime and increase public confidence in the safety of their communities will be as boring as a pitchers' duel. The question is whether the political leadership and the taxpayers will give the serious, low-key approach a try before or after the next multibillion-dollar monument to political mendacity is constructed.

7 VIEWPOINT

"One of America's best-kept secrets is that our huge investment in building prisons . . . has produced a tremendous payoff: Americans are safer and . . . crime has fallen steadily."

Imprisoning More Criminals Will Prevent Crime

Eugene H. Methvin

In the following viewpoint, Eugene H. Methvin interprets crime statistics released in the FBI's Uniform Crime Report, the Bureau of Justice Statistics' National Crime Survey, and various studies. Methvin concludes from the statistics that an increase in incarceration rates during the 1980s has resulted in a decrease in crime. He argues that increased incarceration of serious habitual offenders will result in a further sharp drop in crime rates. Methvin is a senior editor with *Reader's Digest* and served on the President's Commission on Organized Crime from 1983 to 1986.

As you read, consider the following questions:

1. Why does Methvin rely more heavily on measures of robbery and burglary than murder and aggravated assault?
2. According to studies cited by Methvin, how much did Michigan spend on new prisons in the late 1980s? How much did people in Detroit save, by his calculations? What was the basis for these calculations?
3. How many hard-core, violent, repeat offenders does the author estimate there are in America?

Eugene H. Methvin, "The Dirty Little Secret About Our Crime Problem," *The Washington Post National Weekly Edition*, January 13-19, 1992. Reprinted with permission.

One of America's best-kept secrets is that our huge investment in building prisons—an estimated $30 billion in the [1980s] to double capacity—has produced a tremendous payoff: Americans are safer and, as the Justice Department reported in 1991, crime has fallen steadily

Moreover, some pioneering research and police field testing suggest that if we again double the present federal and state prison population—to somewhere between 1 million and 1.5 million—and leave our city and county jail population at the present 400,000, we will break the back of America's 30-year crime wave.

Liberal opponents will howl, of course. They have convinced many Americans that imprisonment is a failed policy and don't want to hear otherwise. The Edna McConnell Clark Foundation bombards influential media, declaring: "Our prison population has gone up by more than 200 percent in the last 15 years with no resulting decrease in crime." The director of the American Civil Liberties Union's National Prison Project, Alvin Bronstein, writes that "no jurisdiction has ever . . . had an impact on crime rates by an expanded incarceration policy." *Washington Post* columnist Colman McCarthy insists that prisons don't succeed but "work-release or community-service programs, structured therapy, in-prison job training, restitution, house arrests with electric monitoring and halfway houses do."

Other pundits and experts will point out that a numerical correlation—between increased incarceration and decreased crime rates—does not prove a causation and that other demographic variables may be at least partly responsible for the trend. They are usually the same people who nonetheless find correlations between crime and joblessness, poverty and illiteracy and who argue that public money is better spent addressing these "root causes."

The Economics of Crime and Punishment

Despite our high prison population, punishment for crime is near an all-time low, Texas A&M University economist Morgan O. Reynolds observes. He did a 38-year comparison of serious crime and probable punishment—that is, the expected days in prison as determined by the median prison sentence for all serious crimes and weighted by probabilities of arrest, prosecution, conviction and imprisonment. He charted the two lines from 1950 to 1988. His chart shows a big horizontal "X."

Probable punishment turned sharply down in 1954, and crime soared. Thus, in 1950 we had 1.8 million serious crimes, and the average criminal risked 24 days in prison. By 1964 imprisonment risk dropped in half, to 12.1 days, and crimes had increased to 4.6 million. By 1974, the criminals risked a mere 5.5 days in prison and America had 10.3 million crimes. Finally, in

1975, punishment turned slightly up, and the crime increase slowed. In 1988, the prison risk was 8.5 days and the number of crimes was 13.9 million.

"Why is there so much crime?" asks Reynolds. "The main reason is that crime pays for millions of criminals and potential criminals. Only 17 in 100 murders result in a prison sentence. The imprisonment rate for rape is 5.1 percent, for assault 1.5 percent and for auto theft only 0.3 percent. . . . Even though police make 13 million arrests each year, less than 2 percent of them result in a prison sentence."

The Case for More Incarceration

In 1992, a short publication titled "The Case for More Incarceration" published by the Justice Department . . . showed:

- That incarceration is cheaper than letting a criminal out on the streets.

- That although the crime rate is horrifically high, the actual rate of increase of violent crime has been going down since we started putting more people in prison.

- That much violent crime is committed by people who have already been in the criminal justice system (that is, people who have been arrested, convicted, or imprisoned, or who are on probation or parole).

- That prison time served, despite some mandatory minimum sentencing laws, has gotten somewhat shorter.

- That prisons do not create criminals.

- That blacks and whites are treated equally and that the vast majority of law-abiding African-Americans would gain most from more incarceration of criminals because African-Americans are more likely to be the victims of violent crime.

Ben Wattenberg, *The Wall Street Journal*, December 17, 1993.

A related analysis produces similar conclusions. During the 1960s, total prison population fell from a then-historical peak of about 219,000 in 1961 to about 195,000 in 1968. During the same decade, crimes soared from 3.4 million in 1960 to 8 million in 1970, according to the FBI's Uniform Crime Reports (UCR) based on incidents reported to police.

Only after 1972 did the prison population start upward, surpassing the 1961 peak in 1975, then soaring to 771,243 by Jan. 1 [1991]. And, wonder of wonders, crime declined significantly—whether measured by the FBI's long-standing UCR or by the

Justice Department's National Crime Survey of households conducted by its Bureau of Justice Statistics (BJS). The distinction between the two surveys is important. The FBI's UCR, begun in 1929, includes only crimes reported to police; in 1973 Justice began its scientific BJS surveys to estimate actual victimization totals, including crimes not reported to police—which the department estimated at 62 percent in 1990 (and more than half of all violent crimes). The two sets of figures frequently produce seeming contradictions and must be interpreted carefully. For example, the latest BJS report shows that the percentage of assaults reported to police increased from 43 to 47 in 1989-90—which alone would produce an increase of almost 10 percent in the FBI's reported assaults even if there were no actual increase.

Differences In Crimes

Moreover, there are differences in crimes. Half or more murders and aggravated assaults are once-in-a-lifetime crimes of passion that involve acquaintances; robbery and burglary are almost always crimes of deliberation by predators who repeat and repeat and repeat. I rely more heavily on the latter two categories than on others when measuring the effectiveness of imprisonment rates. There are other variables as well. The crack cocaine epidemic, which began in 1985, clearly has produced an increase in criminality since then—including murderous battles over turf. Rape and theft remain the most underreported crimes of all, though efforts by police and victims groups to encourage rape reporting are having some success. And much depends on what year is used as a baseline.

Given these caveats, it is not surprising that the FBI could report that the number of reported crimes in the nation in the first half of 1991 increased 2 percent over the first half of 1990, continuing an upward trend evident since the mid-1980s—while the BJS could report at the same time that actual criminal victimization (reported and unreported) *decreased* 3.9 percent, continuing a "*downward* trend . . . that began a decade ago. [emphasis added]" Contradictory? Not really. They are describing different groups of crimes over different periods of time.

Both surveys, in fact, show a long-term downward trend. Even without adjusting for increased population, increased reporting to police or the crack phenomenon of the late 1980s, the FBI's reported murder rate for the 1981-90 decade declined 8 percent and the burglary rate 26 percent—though the robbery rate increased 5 percent. The broader BJS survey documents an overall 9.2 percent decline in violent crimes since its first survey in 1973; robbery is down 16 percent, burglary 41 percent and rape 33 percent. In sum, the BJS found, the rate of crimes against people was 25 percent lower in 1990 than in 1973 and the rate of household crimes 26 percent lower. The number of personal or household crimes, it added, fell from 41 million in 1981 to 34 million in 1990—a decline of 7 million in a decade.

The Lessons Learned from Texas

Michigan, California and Texas in the 1980s have conducted revealing demonstrations of contrasting "deprisonization" and "lock 'em up" policies.

• Case 1. Michigan tried it both ways. In the late 1970s, legislators and voters refused to build new prisons, and the state soon was forced to deal with severe overcrowding. The governor granted emergency releases to 20,000 inmates in four years, some more than two years early. Michigan became the only state to record a prison population decrease in 1981-85, dropping from 15,157 in 1981 to 14,604 in 1984 but then jumping sharply to 17,755 in late 1985 after a *Detroit Free Press* series on early release of prisoners.

The violent-crime rate for Michigan reported by the FBI soared 25 percent, and public outrage mounted. Starting in 1986, a crash prison-building program doubled inmate population in five years. And, wonder of wonders, Michigan's crime rate dropped. Robbery and burglary rates fell more than 25 percent; in Detroit the decline was even more impressive—burglaries down 32 percent, robberies 37 percent. (Murders decreased at lesser rates— 12 percent in the state and 4 percent in the city, an apparent anomaly probably explained by new and deadly warfare among crack cocaine gangs in Detroit, as in Washington.)

Success in Michigan wasn't cheap. The state voted $888 million to build and expand prisons by 1992, and operating them costs additional millions each year. But there were savings too. In 1988, U.S. Sentencing Commission criminologist Mark A. Cohen calculated the cost of 10 crimes to their victims by combining direct costs such as lost property and wages with estimates of pain, suffering and fear based on known jury awards. Cohen calculated the cost of a rape at $51,050, a robbery at $12,594, an assault at $12,028, a burglary at $1,372. By this measure, the decrease in just two prominent "fear" crimes—robberies and burglaries—saved Detroiters $113,546,000 in a single year.

• Case 2. [From 1982 to 1991] Californians have approved $3.7 billion in bonds to build prisons. From 1980 to January 1991, inmate population quadrupled from 22,600 to 98,000. By the 1990s, murder, rape and burglary rates fell a whopping 24 percent to 37 percent from their 1980-82 peaks—which translates as an annual reduction of nearly a thousand murders, 16,000 robberies and a quarter of a million burglaries.

• Case 3. Conversely, Texas learned that skimping on prisons inflates crime disastrously. Prison costs had soared because of a burgeoning inmate population, a doubling of the guard/prisoner ratio and a federal judge's order to make costly changes—some indisputably necessary, such as better medical care but others of dubious value, such as free college courses. The yearly cost per prisoner would eventually rise from $2,920 to $14,000 in the 1980s, but in an early effort to slow it, the legislature in 1983 adopted a turn-'em-loose-faster approach. Thus, while the imprisoned convict population grew by 2½ times, the average term served dropped from 55 percent of sentence to less than 15 percent and the number of convicts on parole increased by 21 times.

Crime Pays

The reason we are deluged by a tidal wave of fear and violence in America, with nearly 6 million incidents of violent crime yearly, is that crime pays. Crime, in fact, is attractive because, simply put, the criminal's cost of doing business—his risk of being arrested, tried and convicted and doing a substantial amount of jail time—is low relative to the potential economic gains, whether he is a common thief or a Mafia don.

Phil Gramm, *The Washington Times*, June 28, 1991.

Texas A&M professor Reynolds calculated the consequences. The expected punishment for a serious crime dropped 43 percent (from 13 days to 7.4) from 1980 to 1989, though for the nation as a whole it rose by about 35 percent (from 5.5 days to 8.8) in roughly the same period. Factoring the probability of arrest, conviction and imprisonment, a potential criminal in Texas today risks little. Fewer than one out of every 100 serious crimes results in a prison term, and those who land in prison serve an average of only 10 months. For murder an offender risks 24 months, for rape 5.3 months, for robbery 2 months and for burglary 7 days.

Result: The crime rate soared 29 percent in the 1980-89 decade, though nationally it dropped 4 percent, making Texas the second most crime-prone state. In 1980 no Texas city had ranked in the 20 worst American cities in property crimes; in 1988, 13 of the nation's worst 20 cities were in Texas.

If increased incarceration cuts crime, how many convicts should we keep locked away in this "land of the free"? When can we stop? And how much can we afford? We've spent an estimated $30 billion to double our prison population in the past decade, and yet today our prisons crowd in perhaps 140,000 more than they should.

University of Pennsylvania criminologist Marvin Wolfgang compiled arrest records up to the 30th birthday for every male born and raised in Philadelphia in 1945 and 1958 and published a 1990 study comparing the two cohorts. In both, about 35 percent of the young men collected one arrest and most never tangled with the law again. The real hard-core predators were an astonishingly small group of repeaters who were rarely punished; just 7 percent of each age group committed two-thirds of all violent crime, including three-fourths of the rapes and robberies and virtually all the murders. Moreover, this 7 percent not only had five or more arrests by age 18 but went on committing felonies and, for every arrest made, got away with about a dozen crimes.

Locking Up "Serious Habitual Offenders"

Incredibly, only 14 percent of the first five arrests resulted in punishment; in the other 86 percent, no charges were brought. Even the 14 killers among the 1945 cohort averaged an appallingly lenient four years behind bars. Yet when punishment was tried, it worked. The few who were imprisoned committed fewer and less serious crimes afterward.

What can be done? Wolfgang's studies suggest that about 75,000 new young, persistent criminal predators are added to our population every year. They hit their peak rate of offenses at about age 16. Locking up all of them from the time of a third felony conviction until, say, age 30 would almost double our present prison population to about 1,230,000. But such long-term imprisonments may not prove necessary if punishment is applied early and consistently.

Another measure of the size of our hard-core criminal population comes from a Justice Department program begun in 1983 and based on the Philadelphia findings. Justice persuaded 20 cities to have their police, prosecutors, schools and welfare and probation workers pool information and focus on the worst offenders, generally youngsters with three or more arrests by age 18. A "serious habitual offender" (SHO) gets priority attention from probation authorities, and if he is arrested anew, investigators and prosecutors throw the book at him with escalating penalties (coupled with rehabilitation efforts) in an effort to stop the revolving door.

In all 20 cities, SHOs consistently accounted for less than 2 percent of all juveniles arrested, or about 18 to 25 youngsters per 100,000 population. Thus, out of 250 million Americans, we would have a maximum of maybe 62,500 SHOs between their 14th and 18th birthdays at any one time. Putting them all behind bars until 30 after the third offense—or even permanently, as is the law in many states, though rarely enforced—would be a relatively inexpensive way to cut a huge chunk out of our still atrocious crime rates.

California's only participating city, Oxnard, began a concerted effort to get the city's active SHOs behind bars, and in 1987 violent crimes dropped 38 percent, more than double the drop in any other California city. By 1989 all 30 of Oxnard's identified active SHOs were behind bars—almost exactly the predictable total for a city of 130,000—and its citizens experienced the lowest crime of a decade. Murders declined 60 percent, robberies 41 percent and burglaries 29 percent.

Based on these social yardsticks, I'd hazard a guess that America's hard-core violent repeaters number upwards of a million. That in turn suggests that if we increase federal and state prison populations to between 1 million and 1.5 million and keep our jails (usually operated by cities and counties for misdemeanor sentences of a year or less) at the present level of about 400,000, we may see a sharp drop in our horrendous crime rates.

And what about those alternatives to imprisonment Colman McCarthy touts?

The American Institutes for Research in the Behavorial Sciences, a non-profit Washington think tank, studied 350 high-repeat Illinois delinquents and found imprisonment was significantly more effective in reducing subsequent arrests from their previous levels. Judges committed the 159 worst prospects to incarceration and sent another 191 to foster or group homes for community "treatment" programs; the latter recorded subsequent arrest reductions of 56 percent to 68 percent while those imprisoned registered 71 percent fewer. Moreover, those not imprisoned were free to continue committing untold crimes while in "treatment."

In short, lock 'em up and you slow 'em down. Turn 'em loose and you pay an awful price.

"The seeming logic of the lock-'em-up campaign is defeated by a combination of demography and justice-system inefficiency."

Imprisoning More Criminals Does Not Prevent Crime

Ted Gest

In the following viewpoint, Ted Gest uses FBI and Justice Department statistics on crime to argue that increased spending on prisons and increased numbers of prisoners have done little to prevent crime. Incarceration does not affect the crime rate, he maintains, because there is a new crop of juvenile criminals every year. In addition, Gest charges, inefficiency in the justice system leads to a revolving door on prisons. He believes that rehabilitative programs are a better alternative. Gest is a senior editor with *U.S. News & World Report*.

As you read, consider the following questions:

1. According to Gest, what group of people constitutes the majority of those arrested for serious crimes?
2. What is creating the greatest need for prison space in California, in Gest's view?

For a generation, crime and politics have been inseparable. In April 1991, the nation's attention was riveted on the last-minute maneuvering that surrounded California's first execution in 25 years [April 21, 1992]. In May 1991, there was more alarming news: the relentless rise in violent crime. FBI data show that reports of violence increased 5 percent in 1991. But the true extent of the problem could be much worse. One crime-victim group estimates the actual rape total at 683,000, nearly seven times the FBI count. Most disturbing, crime rates are growing despite the mammoth expansion of prisons in the past 10 years. And that is prompting a fresh debate about the incarceration strategy that has been the core of the war on crime.

"The choice is clear: more prison space or more crime," argues [Bush Administration] Attorney General William Barr, who summoned crime fighters from across the country to the nation's capital for a "summit" on punishment policy. He and George Bush hoped to score political points and further a new building boom that would expand the already unprecedented rise in imprisonment. The number of inmates in U.S. prisons has doubled over the past decade; on any given day, 1.2 million Americans are behind bars—leading to the highest incarceration rate in the world.

The Shortcomings of the Lock-'em-up Strategy

But do more prisons—and more prisoners—really mean less crime? If so, it is not obvious from the statistics. California criminologists James Austin and John Irwin compared crime and imprisonment rates in each state during the 1980s and found no firm correlation. South Dakota's incarceration rate was twice that of neighboring North Dakota, for example, but crime in both states rose and fell at roughly the same rates. And while, nationally, property crime seems to have stabilized over the past decade, violent crime began rising again in 1990 after reaching a plateau for several years.

The shortcomings of the lock-'em-up strategy in crime busting are particularly evident in California, one of the most aggressive states pursuing this policy. A buildup that began when Ronald Reagan was governor [1966-74] put 111,000 criminals behind bars in 1993. When rising crime rates fueled public dissatisfaction, legislators stripped from prison officials the power to release inmates. The word *rehabilitation* was removed from the penal code and a scheme of fixed sentences began, quadrupling the number of prisoners and requiring $4.5 billion for new lockups.

Yet as new convicts kept pouring in, crime totals fluctuated wildly. The most visible violent acts—homicides—fell from 3,405 in 1980 to 2,640 in 1983, then jumped to 3,562 in 1990. Burglaries declined by 26 percent over the same period, paralleling a national trend, but the drop was completely offset by a 74 percent rise in vehicle thefts. Robberies, the bellwether street crime, fell 7 percent in the early 1980s and then shot up to a 1990 level about 25 percent higher than that of a decade earlier. "There is no evidence of imprisonment's deterrent effect," declares Malcolm Feeley, a criminal-justice expert at the University of California at Berkeley.

The Benefit-to-Cost Ratio

The seeming logic of the lock-'em-up campaign is defeated by a combination of demography and justice-system inefficiency. Each year, a new crop of youths in their upper teens constitutes the majority of those arrested for serious crimes. "When major-league criminals are removed from the field, a new group of minor leaguers is elevated to the top," says criminologist Irwin, who teaches at San Francisco State University. And even California's aggressive law enforcement—40,000 felons enter state prisons each year—deals with only a small fraction of those who commit 1 million serious crimes annually in the state.

©1993 Joel Pett/*Lexington Herald-Leader.* Reprinted with permission.

Large-scale imprisonment obviously works at a certain level. It keeps truly violent felons behind bars longer and prevents them from committing more crimes. One estimate suggests that the most predatory street criminals commit an average of 15 or more crimes each per year. But the benefit-to-cost ratio declines when it comes to short-term lockups, which cost taxpayers large sums without preventing much serious crime. California slaps long terms on heinous criminals—the proportion behind bars five years or more doubled to 10 percent in the 1980s—but it also sweeps up throngs of lesser lawbreakers.

It is the imprisonment of this vast new class of criminals that is creating the greatest need for more prison space. The percentage of incoming prisoners convicted of violent crimes dropped from 56 to 41 between 1985 and 1991. A policy of tightening the screws on inmates after release, mainly by stepping up drug testing, makes parole violators by far the largest category of entries each year, almost half the total. "The justice system is eating its young," charges Dale Sechrest of California State University, a former corrections official. "It imprisons them, paroles them and rearrests them with no rehabilitation in between."

This change in the composition of the inmate population is evident at San Quentin, the most infamous of the state's 23 prisons and the place where Robert Alton Harris was executed. As recently as the mid-1980s, it housed many of the state's most violent men; now, with the exception of about 300 on death row, the iron gates serve mostly as rapidly revolving doors. Half of the 5,575 inmates serve less than two years; others wait up to 10 weeks for assignment elsewhere.

Rehabilitation Efforts Are Few

One of the main reasons the revolving door keeps turning is that few criminals are rehabilitated in prison. Despite the pressure to incarcerate them, most drug abusers get no significant treatment behind bars. At least two thirds enter California prisons with a drug problem, but budget constraints mean that fewer than 10 percent get intensive help.

Moreover, few prisoners get training in job skills that would help them after release. Most can land routine maintenance jobs, but only 1 in 10 can obtain the industrial work that is most useful to job seekers after release. At the huge Vacaville prison complex south of Sacramento, for example, only 910 of the 4,121 inmates who are not being treated in a large medical facility do tasks such as bookbinding and manufacturing weight-lifting equipment. State corrections Director James Gomez wants to expand work opportunities, but he argues that many would not volunteer even if more slots were available: "It's not fair to expect us to turn around people of low self-esteem who have spent their lives selling drugs and cheating their friends."

This year [1992] could prove a watershed in the great incarceration debate. Gov. Pete Wilson wants to add 14 institutions in the 1990s. . . . Wilson also wants to stop giving violent offenders "good time," erasing a day from their terms for every day served with good behavior. That change alone could double the $2.5 billion corrections budget, one of the fastest-growing items in state spending.

The Voter Backlash Against Prison Spending

However, Wilson confronts a serious voter backlash against new prison construction. According to the Center on Juvenile and Criminal Justice, a private San Francisco agency that studies justice issues, it costs taxpayers $43,000 to house and monitor a typical California convict—who serves a 14-month term, then is paroled, rearrested and returned to prison for 6 months. Yet even with those high outlays, California runs one of the nation's most crowded prison systems. . . . One harbinger of the sales problem Wilson faces: In 1990, 60 percent of California voters rejected a $450 million prison bond issue, partly because they didn't think it was a cost-effective way to solve the crime problem.

The Criminal Career

Prison terms are usually imposed late in an offender's criminal career when criminal activity, on average, is tapering off.

A criminal career usually begins at about age 14, with criminal activity increasing until the early 20s. Thereafter, it declines until age 30, when the majority of careers terminate. In California, the average age of arrest is 17; the average age of first commitment is 26.

Joan Petersilia, *Corrections Today*, December 1992.

Many voters prefer smarter, cheaper approaches to punishment. In that 1990 referendum, Californians approved a measure requiring the state to try luring businesses inside prison walls—an idea that is getting a slow but promising start. A dozen San Quentin prisoners started earning prevailing wages entering data into computer terminals and assembling medical devices. Working in such programs will allow inmates to save $2,000 or more, giving them a big edge over most prisoners, who get a mere $200 on release.

Other states, though, have been bolder than California in experimenting with alternatives to prison. . . . Arkansas, like more than half the states, now runs military-style boot camps. In addition, many states are letting convicts out into the community—and monitoring them electronically. Florida may start tracking released convicts' whereabouts by satellite. Such programs do save money: An alternative-punishment plan in Mobile, Ala., costs taxpayers less than $1,000 each year per convict, compared with the $14,000 needed to house a state prisoner. But most alternative programs aren't making appreciable dents in the rate of crime.

Looking ahead, the essential choice seems clear. As the teenage population hits a growth spurt in the 1990s, the crime rate will grow. The question is whether politicians will seek to attack the problem at its roots or will continue to argue that the nation can build its way out of the plague of violence.

Periodical Bibliography

The following articles have been selected to supplement the diverse views presented in this chapter.

William P. Barr — "Crime, Poverty, and the Family," The Heritage Lectures Series, July 29, 1992. Available from The Heritage Foundation, 214 Massachusetts Ave. NE, Washington, DC 20002-4999.

Charles S. Clark — "Prison Overcrowding," CQ Researcher, February 4, 1994. Available from 1414 22nd St. NW, Washington, DC 20037.

Don J. DeBenedictis — "How Long Is Too Long?" ABA Journal, October 1993. Available from the ABA, 750 N. Lake Shore Dr., Chicago, IL 60611.

John J. DiIulio Jr. — "A Limited War on Crime That We Can Win," The Brookings Review, Fall 1992. Available from 1775 Massachusetts Ave. NW, Washington, DC 20036.

Barbara Dority — "Americans in Cages," The Humanist, November/December 1993.

Reuben M. Greenberg — "Less Bang-Bang for the Buck: The Market Approach to Crime Control," Policy Review, Winter 1992.

Philip B. Heymann and Jay Apperson — "Is Locking 'Em Up Just Throwing Away the Key to Safety?" The Washington Post National Weekly Edition, March 7-13, 1994.

Wayne R. Inman — "Portland Law Enforcement Officer Poses Challenge to ACA Members," Corrections Today, August 1992.

Vicki Kemper — "Biting the Bullet," Common Cause Magazine, Winter 1992.

Richard Lacayo — "Lock 'Em Up!" Time, February 7, 1994.

Marc Mauer — "Men in American Prisons: Trends, Causes, and Issues," Men's Studies Review, Spring 1992. Available from The Sentencing Project, 918 F St. NW, Washington, DC 20004.

Wilbert Rideau — "Why Prisons Don't Work," Time, March 21, 1994.

Charles E. Silberman — "Truth and Justice: Why the Best Hope in a 'War' on Crime May Be a Stalemate," The New York Times, January 30, 1994.

Jill Smolowe — ". . . And Throw Away the Key," Time, February 7, 1994.

Ben Wattenberg — "Crime Solution—Lock 'Em Up," The Wall Street Journal, December 17, 1993.

Can Controlling Guns Control Crime?

Chapter Preface

Named for James Brady, the White House press secretary who was shot and wounded by John Hinckley Jr. during the attempted assassination of President Ronald Reagan in March 1981, the Brady bill establishes a national waiting period and background check for the purchase of a handgun. Introduced to Congress in February 1987, the Brady bill was signed into law November 30, 1993. Part of the lengthy debate over the Brady bill centered on whether it was consistent with the U.S. Constitution's Second Amendment guarantee of "the right of the people to keep and bear arms."

Sarah Brady, wife of James Brady and chairperson of Handgun Control, Inc., argues that the framers of the Constitution envisioned "a great nation of peace and tranquility . . . a nation free from violence." The Brady bill's waiting period and background check are consistent with the Constitution, in her opinion, because they would reduce violence by keeping guns from those who commit violent acts. Brady asserts, "reasonable laws to protect the public safety, laws to deny easy access to firearms by those who would misuse them . . . are obviously constitutional."

Opposing the Brady bill, Robert Dowlut, counsel for the National Rifle Association, states, "The purpose of the Bill of Rights' guarantees was to enunciate a set of fixed rights that may not be trespassed upon by any branch of government." Dowlut believes the Brady bill trespasses on the rights of law-abiding citizens, and is therefore inconsistent with the Constitution, because it imposes a waiting period on exercising the right to own guns. In his opinion, "Neither oppressive taxes or fees nor waiting periods may be imposed on the exercise of a right."

Much of the debate over gun control in America rests on differing interpretations of the intentions of the framers of the Constitution. A debate on the meaning of the Second Amendment begins the following chapter, which examines the effectiveness of gun control as a means of decreasing violence and crime.

"The Second Amendment protects a state's right to keep a well-organized militia, rather than an individual's right to bear arms."

Gun Control Is Constitutional

Joshua Horwitz

Efforts to adopt gun control legislation in Congress have focused on defeating the National Rifle Association's lobby and its contention that the Second Amendment guarantees an absolute right for Americans to own guns. Citing federal court decisions, Joshua Horwitz argues in the following viewpoint that the Second Amendment guarantees a state's right to maintain a militia, not an individual's right to bear arms. Horwitz is legal counsel for the Coalition to Stop Gun Violence in Washington, D.C.

As you read, consider the following questions:

1. The Second Amendment, quoted in the following viewpoint, mentions "a well-regulated militia." What two other adjectives does Horwitz use to describe this "well-regulated militia"?
2. According to the Supreme Court and other federal court decisions cited by Horwitz, what specific types of guns are not protected by the Second Amendment?

Joshua Horwitz, "The Second Amendment Allows Militias to Have Guns—Not You," *The Philadelphia Inquirer*, December 20, 1991. Reprinted with permission.

Gun violence has reached crisis proportions throughout the United States. Once a problem thought to be confined to large urban centers, gun violence now has spread to smaller, historically safer cities, such as Milwaukee, Wis., and Charlotte, N.C., both of which set firearms fatality records in 1991. Even small towns in rural America are not immune from this violence, as the massacre of 23 people by a crazed gunman in Killeen, Texas, has horribly demonstrated. In 1991, firearms violence accounted for 33,000 deaths and more than 250,000 injuries.

It is clear that a major contributing factor to the violence is the abundance and easy availability of handguns and assault weapons. While most of us abhor this violence and want to do something about the problem, some may be reluctant to advocate tough gun-control laws because they misunderstand and misinterpret the Second Amendment.

A Well-Regulated Militia

This misinterpretation has been fostered by the firearms lobby, which often quotes only the second clause of the Second Amendment, seemingly forgetting that the first clause even exists. Indeed, the second clause is the only part of the amendment inscribed on the National Rifle Association's headquarters building in Washington.

The Second Amendment in its entirety states: "A well-regulated militia being necessary to the security of a free state, the right of the people to keep and bear arms shall not be infringed." This amendment was adopted to assure the states that they would have the right to maintain their own militias to protect against federal and foreign encroachment.

There is no substantial historical evidence for the claim that the amendment was intended to guarantee an *individual* the right to have arms for any purpose other than participation in a state-regulated militia. In fact, there was not even a mention of an individual right to bear arms for hunting or other non-militia purposes. Moreover, what is clear is that in contemporary America the National Guard is the militia.

Judicial Interpretations

Interestingly, the federal judiciary has been remarkably consistent in finding that the Second Amendment protects a state's right to keep a well-organized militia, rather than an individual's right to bear arms. The one modern Supreme Court case concerning the Second Amendment, *United States v. Miller,* found that a regulation outlawing sawed-off shotguns did not violate the Second Amendment. In 1991, the high court vindicated this view by refusing to hear a Second Amendment challenge [*Farmer v. Higgins*] to the federal ban on machine guns brought by the NRA.

Following the lead of the Supreme Court, lower federal courts have never overturned a gun control law on Second Amendment grounds and have been uniform in holding that the Second Amendment does not apply to individuals. For example, the U.S. Court of Appeals for the Sixth Circuit, deciding that the National Firearms Act [of 1934, which restricted certain types of guns associated with organized crime violence] did not violate the Second Amendment, held that "it is clear that the Second Amendment guarantees a collective rather than an individual right" (*United States v. Warin*). The Seventh Circuit Court of Appeals, in *Quilici v. Morton Grove*, found that the Second Amendment did not bar the city of Morton Grove, Ill., from banning handguns. The court said: "Under the controlling authority of *Miller* we conclude that the right to keep and bear handguns is not guaranteed by the Second Amendment."

The National Guard Is the Well-Regulated Militia

The right to bear arms protected in the Second Amendment has to do directly with "a well-regulated militia." Evidence of the connection can be found in the Militia Act of 1792.

"Every free able-bodied white male citizen" (it was 1792, after all) was required by the act to "enroll" in the militia for training and active service in case of need. When reporting for service, every militiaman was required to provide a prescribed rifle or musket, and ammunition.

Here we seek the link of the private and public aspects of bearing arms. The expectation was that every man would have his own firearms. But the aspect that was raised to the level of constitutional concern was the public interest in those arms.

What does this mean for the question of gun control today? Well, for example, it means that Congress has the constitutional power to enact a Militia Act of 1992, to require every person who owns a gun or aspires to own one to "enroll" in the militia. In plain 1990s English, if you want to own a gun, sign up with the National Guard.

Robert A. Goldwin, *The Wall Street Journal*, December 12, 1991.

Legal scholars have also emphasized this interpretation. Retired Chief Justice Warren E. Burger has stated that "the need for a state militia was the predicate of the 'right' guaranteed." Former dean of the Harvard Law School, Erwin Griswold, who was also solicitor general in the Nixon administration, wrote in the

Washington Post: "Indeed, that the Second Amendment poses no barrier to strong gun laws is perhaps the most well-settled proposition in American constitutional law."

Clearly, a proper interpretation of the Second Amendment, free from the gun lobby's rhetoric, protects the state-federal relationship and does not stand in the way of comprehensive gun-control laws. The framers of the Constitution would be shocked to see the Second Amendment being used as a shield to justify the daily roster of shootings in this country. We must realize that the only true barrier to gun-control laws and, hence, an eventual reduction of the level of violence, is the gun lobby and the financial interests it seeks to protect, not the Second Amendment.

"The view that the Second Amendment's guarantee of a right to arms applies only to state militias, not to individuals, is an invention of 20th-Century gun prohibitionists. "

Gun Control Is Unconstitutional

Don B. Kates Jr. and Alan J. Lizotte

Attempts to support or defeat gun control legislation in Congress traditionally have been centered on the constitutionality of gun control. In the following viewpoint, Don B. Kates Jr. and Alan J. Lizotte argue that an historical interpretation of the Second Amendment protects every individual's right to own guns. Kates is a constitutional lawyer in San Francisco and a fellow of the Second Amendment Foundation, an educational and legal foundation in Bellevue, Washington, that works to preserve gun ownership as a civil right. Lizotte is a professor of criminal justice at the State University of New York, Albany.

As you read, consider the following questions:

1. How do the authors interpret the phrases "right of the people" and "a well-regulated militia"?
2. What definition of *militia* do Kates and Lizotte cite? From what source do they draw this definition?

Don B. Kates Jr. and Alan J. Lizotte, "Civilian Defense Is Time-Honored," *Los Angeles Times*, November 29, 1993. Reprinted with permission.

The view that the Second Amendment's guarantee of a right to arms applies only to state militias, not to individuals, is an invention of 20th-Century gun prohibitionists. It was unknown to the Founding Fathers or any 18th- or 19th-Century interpreter of the law. The only interpretations before Congress when it adopted the amendment explained it as guaranteeing people "their own arms," "their private arms."

A modern historian who neither owns guns nor cares about the gun-control debate explains that the amendment's intent embodied "two distinct principles: Individuals had the right to possess arms to defend themselves and their property; and states retained the right to maintain militias composed of these individually armed citizens. . . . Clearly, [the Founders] believed that the perpetuation of a republican spirit and character in their society depended upon the freeman's possession of arms as well as his ability and willingness to defend both himself and his society."

Of 36 law-review articles on the amendment published since 1980, only 4 disagree. Three of them were written by employees of anti-gun groups, one by a politician. All appeared in minor law reviews. In contrast, 12 articles supporting the individual-rights position appeared in top law reviews. Among the authors were leading liberal constitutional scholars who don't own guns and never desired the conclusions the evidence forced upon them.

Defining the "Right of the People"

Basic to interpreting the Constitution's first 10 amendments—the Bill of Rights—is understanding that they were enacted as one document and are judicially interpreted as such. In the First Amendment, the "right of the people" is judicially interpreted as an individual right. How can the same phrase just 16 words later in the Second Amendment mean a right of the state? In the Fourth and Ninth Amendments, the same phrase is always understood and judicially interpreted as an individual right. And the 10th Amendment specifically distinguishes the state's rights from those of the people.

Unable to explain this away, gun prohibitionists point out that the courts have upheld federal laws banning gun possession by some people—felons, minors and the insane; if these are not violations of the Second Amendment, then neither is extending the ban to everyone. This argument is specious. Cases upholding such laws prove only that, like other basic rights, the Second Amendment has reasonable limits. Felons, children and the insane have no more right to arms than to vote. Courts should also uphold licensing requirements, but only those designed to exclude the criminal or irresponsible without delaying or denying access to defensive arms by law-abiding adults. There also should be leeway for local laws targeting local problems that may be more sweeping than national laws.

The Intent of the Framers of the Second Amendment

Of the eight state bills of rights adopted before the federal Constitution, four recognized the right of "the people" to bear arms. None of these were contained in a militia clause, nor was the term "bear arms" limited to war usage. For instance, the Pennsylvania Declaration of Rights, Art. XIII (1776) provided: "That the people have a right to bear arms for the defense of themselves, and the state. . . ."

In *The Federalist* No. 46, James Madison alluded to "the advantage of being armed, which the Americans possess over the people of almost every other nation." Madison continued, "Notwithstanding the military establishments in the several kingdoms of Europe, which are carried as far as the public resources will bear, the governments are afraid to trust the people with arms."

Stephen P. Halbrook, *Journal on Firearms and Public Policy*, Fall 1993.

The Supreme Court's only extended discussion of the Second Amendment's right to bear arms (in *United States* vs. *Miller*, 1939) recognizes that the "militia" it mentions is not some formal military organization like the National Guard, but the colonial system of all trustworthy adult "males physically capable of acting in concert for the common defense . . . bearing arms supplied by themselves." The Court rejected the state's-right theory, which was expressly urged upon it, instead allowing the defendants to invoke the right. While recognizing that some arms of ordinary citizens are protected, the case limits the protection to high-quality militia-type arms. This would include handguns, rifles and, yes, "assault rifles," but not poorly made "Saturday-night specials."

Armed Citizens Resist Crime

Anti-gun arguments reflect baseless, illiberal distrust in the people. It is falsely claimed that murderers are ordinary people who kill in moments of rage. Criminological studies show murderers to be aberrants with life histories of felony, substance abuse, injurious motor-vehicle accidents and violent attacks on those around them. Certainly, these aberrants should be disarmed. But, far from endangering the public, widespread gun ownership by good citizens permits resistance to crime.

With the military overseas, government mustered gun owners to patrol against sabotage during both World Wars. But for anti-

144

gun myopia, properly trained citizens today would routinely receive licenses to carry guns and be mustered to provide services under police supervision (as they do in Israel). Of course, armed citizens cannot substitute for measures alleviating poverty and despair, which are at the root of so much crime. But they can aid police efforts in the short term. Nor can a society that fails to either reduce crime or protect people from it complain about their protecting themselves.

"[Gun control laws] are dressed up as 'anti-crime' measures, but they will affect only those who obey the law, not criminals."

Gun Control Will Not Decrease Crime

Dan Peterson

On February 28, 1994, the Brady bill became national law, establishing a five-day waiting period for handgun purchases. Surrounding the debate and passage of the bill, a flurry of gun control measures was proposed in Congress, arousing gun enthusiasts' fears that gun ownership was under attack. In the following viewpoint, Dan Peterson points out flaws in proposed and existing gun control laws. He contends that while these measures are promoted as crime-fighting tactics, they will keep law-abiding citizens from protecting themselves against criminals. Peterson, an attorney in Washington, D.C., believes that gun control laws violate the constitutional rights of American citizens.

As you read, consider the following questions:

1. According to the National Rifle Association data Peterson cites, what happened to crime rates in states that had waiting periods prior to passage of the Brady bill?
2. Why is the ban on semi-automatics proposed by William Hughes "slippery," according to Peterson?
3. According to Susan Lamson, quoted by the author, why is gun rationing "insidious"?

Dan Peterson, "Our Second Amendment Under Fire," *The American Legion Magazine*, January 1994. Reprinted by permission, *The American Legion Magazine*, copyright 1994.

Resolved by the Senate and House of Representatives of the United States in Congress assembled: "The second article of amendment to the Constitution of the United States is repealed."

The Second Amendment to the Constitution is repealed? What is this, a fantasy? A bad dream?

No, it is House Joint Resolution No. 81, [a 1993-94 bill] in the U.S. Congress. It is one of dozens of bills aimed at severely restricting and ultimately wiping out the constitutional right of law-abiding Americans to buy, own and use firearms.

Generations of American soldiers have endured the hardships of war, suffered wounds, watched companions die and sacrificed their own lives, all for a single cause: to preserve this nation and the freedoms to which it was dedicated.

One of the most basic of all of those freedoms is the right of the people to keep and bear arms—a right enshrined by the Framers of the Constitution in the Second Amendment.

It would have been unthinkable a few decades ago, but power-hungry politicians are working hard right now to disarm you, your children and future generations. Unless these political attacks on our constitutional liberties meet fierce resistance, the walls protecting our historic freedoms will be breached.

Straitjackets on your rights are being proposed at both the national and state levels. They are dressed up as "anti-crime" measures, but they will affect only those who obey the law, not criminals. Some state laws have already been passed, and major battles are under way in Congress.

Waiting Periods

Numerous states have already passed laws requiring waiting periods before a handgun, or in some states any firearm, can be purchased or transferred. The National Rifle Association (NRA) reports that about two-thirds of the population of the United States is currently covered by waiting-period laws.

The effectiveness of waiting periods in reducing crime has been zero. According to data published by the NRA, states with waiting periods have seen increases in homicide or violent crime rates *greater* than the increase for the nation as a whole.

So what is the solution proposed by anti-gun politicians to the increasing anarchy on the streets? Why, pass a national waiting period, of course.

The principal waiting-period bill is the so-called "Brady Bill," [signed November 30, 1993], pushed by Sarah Brady's organization, Handgun Control, Inc. The Brady Bill has two basic parts.

The first part would establish a national five-business-day waiting period before a handgun could legally be transferred from a dealer to a purchaser. During this five-day period, the

147

Brady Bill would allow time for local law enforcement authorities to do a criminal background check.

There are serious doubts as to whether the federal government has the constitutional power to tell local law enforcement authorities to do background checks. Be that as it may, such a requirement would divert police from fighting real crime and give them the unwanted chore of snooping into the backgrounds of American citizens.

WHICH IS A BETTER WAY TO REDUCE CRIME?

(A) **FIVE-DAY WAITING PERIOD**   (B) **FIVE-TO-TEN-YEAR WAITING PERIOD**

Steve Kelley. Reprinted with permission.

If the applicant is turned down by the local police, his only recourse would be to bring suit in federal court to try to get a judge to allow the purchase. Under the Brady Bill, local governments and their employees who did the background check could not be held liable in court. So, even if the police refused an application for a wrong reason, the applicant might have to spend thousands of dollars in attorney fees to vindicate his rights, with no possibility of reimbursement from the government.

In the second part of the Brady Bill . . . the waiting period would be phased out, and instead a national computerized background check would be established. This computerized background check would apply to *all firearms* transferred through a licensed dealer, not just handguns. The computerized system would not apply in states with their own firearms permit systems.

Despite much wrangling, Congress passed the Brady Bill and it was signed, as promised, by President Clinton. After the bill passed, Sarah Brady laughed when asked whether she would now stop her gun-control campaign. All along Brady has said that her bill is only the first step in the gun-controllers' agenda. Next on their agenda: a ban on semiautomatic firearms, which they characterize as "assault weapons."

Bans on Semiautomatics

New Jersey, California and a number of municipalities in other states have enacted bans on the possession or transfer of certain semiautomatic firearms. As men with military experience know, semiautomatic weapons fire one round for each trigger pull. Fully automatic weapons fire a continuous burst with each trigger pull.

Semiautomatics have been with us for a century and have been commonly used for sporting purposes as well as military purposes. There are those who are capitalizing on the public confusion between semiautomatics with a military appearance and fully automatic weapons, which are already strictly controlled. Some politicians in Congress are seeking to ban semiautomatics by redefining them as "assault weapons."

Bills [introduced to] Congress [in 1993] ban possession and transfer of semiautomatics by manufacturer's name and model, and even allow for more guns to be added to the list.

Others are even broader. A bill introduced by Rep. William Hughes of New Jersey would simply delegate to the Secretary of the Treasury the task of compiling the list of banned semiautomatics. He could include on the list any semiautomatic firearm that, in his opinion, is not "generally recognized as particularly suitable for, or readily adaptable to, sporting purposes." That's a pretty slippery test. One man's legitimate sporting arm is another's dangerous assault weapon.

A bill sponsored by Rep. Luis Gutierrez of Illinois is broader yet. It bans all semiautomatics, both pistols and rifles, and even such old stand-bys as the Colt 1911A1 .45 pistol, which served U.S. Armed Forces for over 70 years.

Sen. Dianne Feinstein of California tacked an "assault weapon" ban onto the Senate's version of the [1993] crime bill. Her amendment bans 19 specific semi-autos by name and model. Included is the Colt AR-15, one of the rifles used in the National

149

Matches at Camp Perry each year. . . .

Some jurisdictions, such as New York, New Jersey, Massachusetts and Illinois, already have laws requiring handguns to be registered or forcing owners to obtain a permit. The District of Columbia has, for all practical purposes, banned handguns since 1977. That is why it is so safe to stroll around at night in Washington, D.C., and New York City.

Now some of your congressmen want to make the rest of the country equally "safe" by requiring nationwide registration of handguns.

Rep. Cardiss Collins of Illinois introduced a bill [in 1993] that would require each state to set up a system to register existing handguns.

The Anticipated Attack on Guns

With the passage of the Brady bill and a gun-control psychosis sweeping the country, Americans can expect an even more intense crusade to abolish private gun ownership entirely. Neither the Brady bill, which imposes a national waiting period for buying a handgun, nor other state and local laws will diminish violent crime. Indeed, their failure to do so is a deliberate tactic of the war against guns.

If less restrictive laws don't work, gun controllers will now claim, sterner measures are needed. But the less restrictive laws establish a precedent for the tough stuff. Having granted the premises that guns require control and that legal control is legitimate, lawmakers who supported the lesser laws will have only weak grounds for opposing the outright repression of gun ownership and the criminalization of gun owners that the gun gestapo demands.

Samuel Francis, *Conservative Chronicle*, December 15, 1993.

Penalties are stiff. For example, possession of an unregistered handgun in your home where it would be "readily accessible" would be punishable by 12 years in jail, if the handgun were larger than a .22 caliber.

Bills by Sen. John Chafee of Rhode Island and Rep. Sidney Yates of Illinois don't fool around with mere registration. They would ban possession of handguns outright, except for members of licensed handgun clubs. Under Chafee's bill, members of these federally licensed clubs could possess handguns only while target shooting at the club's range. The guns would have to remain locked up at the club or be stored with the police at all other times.

One of the slickest stratagems—and it looks like it is becoming a trend—is limiting the number of guns that citizens can buy.

South Carolina has had a limit of one handgun per month since 1975. In 1975, its violent crime rate was about at the national average, according to FBI statistics. Since that time, South Carolina's rate has soared far above the national average.

Despite South Carolina's experience, Virginia adopted a limit of one handgun per month in 1993. Bills have been introduced in Congress by Rep. Robert Torricelli and Sen. Frank Lautenberg of New Jersey to do the same thing for the whole country.

I talked with Susan Lamson, director of federal affairs for the National Rifle Association, about the "one gun a month" bills. According to Lamson, "These bills limiting the number of guns that a citizen can acquire in a given time period are among the most insidious laws now being proposed. Their backers ask the seemingly innocent question, 'Why does anyone need to obtain more than one gun a month?' But that's not the real question."

As Lamson points out, "The real question is, 'Why should government be able to abridge the constitutional rights of law-abiding citizens?' Once the principle is established that gun ownership can be rationed by the government, you can bet that there will be moves to limit purchases to one a year, or one a lifetime. Or less."

If you can't ban the guns, maybe you can ban the ammunition. That's apparently the thinking of yet another New York politician, Sen. Daniel Moynihan. Well, not exactly. Moynihan wants to ban guns, too.

Moynihan believes we can solve the crime problem in this country by banning the manufacture and sale of all .25- and .32-caliber cartridges, together with 9mm ammunition—except for sales to the government. If he can't get that bill through Congress, he's got a backup bill that would impose a 1,000 percent tax on ammunition for those calibers.

What if Moynihan's bills actually worked? We'd all have him to thank when the bad guys switched to .357s and .45s instead of those little .25s. But I'm sure Sen. Moynihan would be a step ahead of us, with bans on .357s, .45s, .38s, .44s, 10mms, .380s and .22s.

In his book, *Strategy*, B.H. Liddell Hart popularized the "strategy of the indirect approach," which counsels that direct frontal assaults are to be avoided in war. Some congressmen are taking a page from his book.

Heavy Taxes on Guns and Ammunition

One indirect way to restrict access by citizens to firearms is to make them more expensive. Identical bills introduced in the House and Senate would impose a 25 percent tax on the sale by manufacturers of handguns, assault weapons, large capacity magazines and ammunition used in handguns and assault weapons. The definition of "assault weapon" is so broad that most types of ammunition would be covered.

The bills would also impose a 25 percent tax on subsequent sales of handguns and the other items listed, even between private parties.

Another indirect approach is to attack the American firearms industry. A bill by Sen. Paul Simon of Illinois would increase the annual license fee for federal firearms dealers by 7,500 percent. It would allow an unlimited number of warrantless searches of dealers' premises by federal agents and impose other requirements that would make it more difficult to obtain and keep a license.

The bill would have the greatest impact on small dealers, many of whom would be driven out of business. Perhaps Simon already thought of that.

Illinois Rep. Cardiss Collins has a bill that is even more pernicious. It would allow anyone injured by a discharge of a handgun or assault weapon to sue the manufacturer, importer or dealer who sold the gun.

The bill would hold the sellers "strictly liable." That means that persons injured or their relatives could recover money damages in court possibly running into the millions of dollars.

It also means the sellers would be responsible, even if the gun were not defective and even if the persons were intentionally shot by criminals during crimes.

Essentially, the bill would hold gun manufacturers and dealers liable for all murders and felonious assaults in which a handgun was employed. So long, Colt. Sayonara, Smith and Wesson.

Not every bit of news is bad, however. Sen. Larry Craig of Idaho introduced an alternative to the Brady Bill that would provide for a computerized instant check for handgun buyers. Five states have successfully implemented such point-of-sale systems. Unlike the Brady Bill, Craig's bill would protect the rights of legitimate purchasers.

Better yet, Rep. Roscoe Bartlett of Maryland proposed the Citizens' Self-Defense Act of 1993. It provides that anyone not prohibited by federal law from receiving a firearm "shall have the right to obtain firearms for security, and to use firearms in defense of self, family or home."

A person whose self-defense right was violated could bring suit to halt the violation or to recover damages. Think of the abusive state and local laws that would topple if that bill were enacted.

But on the whole, the Second Amendment rights of American citizens are under attack like never before. Americans have fought overseas to preserve basic freedoms for other countries. Now the fight for constitutional liberties has come home.

"America has far too many guns in circulation; strong measures are needed to restrict them."

Gun Control Will Decrease Crime

Pierre Thomas and the *Los Angeles Times*

On November 30, 1993, the Brady bill was signed into law, establishing a national waiting period for the purchase of handguns. In Part I of the following viewpoint, written before the law took effect, Pierre Thomas, a *Washington Post* staff writer, presents evidence that waiting periods and background checks keep guns out of the hands of criminals. In Part II, the *Los Angeles Times* contends that violent crime in America has grown out of control, and therefore gun control more strict than the Brady bill is necessary. The *Times*, in a series of editorials, has advocated "a near-total ban on the private possession of guns."

As you read, consider the following questions:

1. The Brady bill establishes a waiting period and a background check. According to Jack Killorin (quoted by Thomas), which is more important?
2. What measures does the *Los Angeles Times* describe as "less comprehensive"? What is its assessment of these measures?
3. How many guns does the *Los Angeles Times* say are in circulation?

Pierre Thomas, "Making Felons Bite the Bullet," *The Washington Post National Weekly Edition*, December 6-12, 1993, ©1993 The Washington Post. Reprinted with permission. "Taming the Gun Monster That Is Consuming America," *Los Angeles Times*, October 15, 1993. Copyright 1993, Los Angeles Times. Reprinted with permission.

I

States with waiting periods and background checks for handgun purchases similar to those in the Brady bill have stopped tens of thousands of felons and other prohibited individuals from buying weapons through gun dealers, a random survey of states shows.

Between 1989 and December 1993, computerized background checks or similar waiting period programs in California, Florida, Virginia and Maryland blocked more than 47,000 attempted purchases by persons who at the time were banned from buying firearms. The states are among at least 25 that now have some restrictions on handgun purchases similar to those included in the Brady bill, which President Clinton signed into law November 30, 1993.

States with laws more stringent than the Brady bill can continue to use their current screening methods and waiting periods. . . . But the change in federal gun laws will require states with less stringent restrictions to move quickly to put into place the five-day waiting period and background check that are required under the Brady bill.

The legislation, the most far-reaching nationwide gun control measure enacted in at least a decade, [took effect February 28, 1994]. The bill provides $200 million to help states update and computerize their criminal records so gun dealers can conduct instant background checks.

Successful Background-Check Systems

Although the laws can do nothing to stop illegal street sales of weapons, in Virginia and Florida instant background checks have helped authorities not only screen out prohibited individuals but also hundreds of fugitives wanted for other crimes.

Between 1991 and December 1993, Florida officials say their telephone check system and three-day waiting period stopped 658 people wanted on felony charges from buying handguns, shotguns and rifles. Virginia, which uses a telephone check system to screen prospective buyers, reports 330 such thwarted sales during the same period.

"I don't think it's going to cure the problem, but every time you catch a wanted felon—and we have caught hundreds—trying to buy guns, it's going to help," says John Joyce, spokesman for the Florida Department of Law Enforcement.

"In the long debate about Brady, the focus was always on the waiting period," says Bureau of Alcohol, Tobacco and Firearms (ATF) spokesman Jack Killorin. "The key has always been the background check. The law may have more impact than people think."

According to state officials, 21,168 sales were blocked between

1989 and December 1993 in California under its 15-day waiting period. Virginia blocked 5,879 and Maryland 3,647 during the same period, officials say; Florida has stopped 16,513 between 1991 and December 1993.

©Boileau/Rothco. Reprinted with permission.

Federal and state gun laws generally preclude firearm purchases by convicted felons, certain misdemeanants and those deemed by a court to be mentally incompetent. But many states have had no mechanism for checking criminal records or mental histories when gun purchasers show up at stores. The Brady bill, named for former White House press secretary James S. Brady who was wounded during the 1981 assassination attempt on President Ronald Reagan, imposes a waiting period of five business days for the purchase of handguns, during which police are required to conduct a background check of prospective buyers.

The waiting period is to be dropped after five years, when a national computerized instant-check system is supposed to be operational.

Authorities say the numbers blocked from buying guns represent only a small percentage of more than a million purchase attempts from authorized gun dealers. Federal officials estimate that somewhere between 2 percent and 6 percent of the overall 7.5 million annual firearms sales will likely be stopped under the Brady legislation.

But here, officials say, percentages do not tell the full story. The existing background checks show that thousands of prohibited persons are routinely walking into gun stores and trying to buy guns. Unless some state barrier exists, they are usually successful.

Killorin says the felons and others stopped by state laws represent "people who absent a record check would have bought guns, and then law enforcement would have had to deal with them. Proven crooks. People who have broken their contracts with society."

II

Isn't it obvious that America has strayed terribly far off course, that the gun violence now poisoning our society is nothing less than a threat to our national security and collective sanity?

Isn't it obvious that America has lost more than its innocence when children can't go to school without being shot at, when domestic quarrels increasingly end in deadly gunfire, when young thugs roam the streets more heavily armed than the police, when the mentally disturbed can vent their frustrations in a crowded town square or office building with an automatic weapon?

In 1993, the United States has been debating what to do in Somalia, where more than 30 Americans have been killed. That's a tragedy. But nothing like the tragedy of the District of Columbia, where in 1992 about 15 times as many people, 443, were murdered, or Los Angeles County, where 1,530 were gunshot homicide victims in 1992.

Where are America's priorities? As columnist Gerald F. Seib put it in the *Wall Street Journal*, "The carnage in U.S. cities has become so great that political leaders are simply tuning it out, even as they worry mightily about lesser tragedies."

Isn't it now obvious that the national culture of guns and violence borders on a kind of addiction? That this addiction is a serious danger to the nation's health? And that, as with any addiction, a strong prescription and permanent abstinence will be required?

The time has come for a historic about-face. America has far too many guns in circulation; strong measures are needed to restrict them to either special circumstances or a select group of people. The challenge is enormous and the change will be politically and emotionally difficult, but the long journey back from self-destruction must begin now.

Question: Why should anyone other than police officers possess a handgun? Until recently, it was enough to answer that the Second Amendment to the U.S. Constitution assures private citizens the right to possess guns. Or to say that because so many criminals are now armed—so heavily armed—law-abiding citizens must be allowed to own a gun for self-defense. But those responses are no longer adequate. Indeed, they serve only to raise far more urgent questions: How can we act meaningfully to reduce gun violence? Indeed, can we?

It is our judgment that the Second Amendment offers no real impediment to comprehensive federal gun reform. It's certainly true that many decent and patriotic Americans believe sincerely and deeply that the Second Amendment affords citizens the absolute right to have a gun. We don't agree, and most federal court rulings don't either. On the contrary, the proposition that the Second Amendment does *not* guarantee a right to keep and bear arms for private, non-militia purposes may be one of the most firmly established propositions in American constitutional law. The amendment states: "A well-regulated Militia, being necessary to the security of a free State, the right of the people to keep and bear Arms, shall not be infringed." That's all it says.

Federal Action Is Needed

It is also our judgment that the only way to end the killing and maiming is to impose a near-total ban on the manufacture, sale and private possession of handguns and assault weapons—in effect to restrict their possession to law-enforcement officers. To this end, national policy must work to encourage Americans to turn over their handguns and assault weapons voluntarily to the authorities, as a demonstration of how serious this nation is about dealing with the problem.

A voluntary return program can be designed to work better than most of those already tried, especially if it uses market forces to encourage turning guns in to authorities. If such a program proved to be inadequate, Congress might need to write new laws that restrict the number of guns available.

As for rifles and shotguns, they should remain generally but not unconditionally available. Such weapons should be licensed and their owners should have to submit to background checks and undergo training in their safe use. There are of course legitimate sporting and hunting uses for such firearms.

We are not alone in calling for strong action. A growing number of police experts, including Los Angeles Police Chief Willie L. Williams, now support severe restrictions on weapons possession. These men and women, increasingly the targets of gun attacks, are on the front lines in the battle for America's streets.

Physicians too are on the front lines, practicing what amounts to battlefield medicine in emergency rooms across the nation. They have treated the babies permanently disfigured or crippled after being shot in their homes from passing automobiles. More and more of these doctors are advocating a ban on guns. So too are an increasing number of ordinary Americans. In a 1993 national poll, 52% favored a federal ban on handgun ownership and 63% supported a ban on the sale of automatic and semiautomatic weapons.

Poll: Americans Want Tighter Gun Control

A *USA Today*/CNN/Gallup Poll of 1,014 adults was taken Dec. 17-21, 1993. It found that:

- Six out of 10 people oppose a ban on handguns, but the reverse was true for "cheap" handguns.

- Sixty-seven percent of respondents favor stricter firearms-control laws; 7 percent said they should be less strict. Twenty-five percent said they favor keeping laws as they are.

- Eighty-one percent favor registration; 18 percent do not.

- Eighty-seven percent approve of the Brady law.

- Eighty-nine percent said safety classes should be required before owning a gun, and 69 percent said people should only purchase one gun a month.

- Seventy-seven percent favor an assault-weapon ban.

- Twenty-five percent said they would feel more safe if only police had handguns, 34 percent would feel no difference, and 25 percent would feel less safe.

The Christian Science Monitor, December 31, 1993.

However, many Americans vigorously and righteously disagree. Some contend that there's absolutely nothing wrong with gun ownership and indeed that Americans must retain their relatively easy access to guns in order to protect themselves and their families. Many others believe that far less comprehensive measures would sharply reduce the rate of gun violence, measures such as stiffer penalties for gun-involved crimes and better enforcement of existing gun licensing laws. We agree that these measures could help—but only a little. Without tough and nearly comprehensive national restrictions on manufacture, sale and ownership, the slaughter will continue.

It's true that even a comprehensive approach such as we are urging offers no overnight cure. If there were no National Rifle

Association, with its potent political lobby, there still would be huge obstacles.

For instance, even if all gun manufacturing and sales ceased now, about 200 million guns would remain in circulation—nearly one gun for every man, woman and child in this country. We put these instruments of death on our night tables, in our purses, our closets, our glove compartments. But that's not where they remain.

The Grim Statistics

Guns purchased by law-abiding adults for "protection" increasingly end up in the backpacks of schoolchildren and the pockets of small-time drug dealers and robbers, gang members and professional thugs. Firearms killed two children in Los Angeles high schools in 1993. [Throughout California] they killed an elderly man who stopped at a Chatsworth gas station, a bicycle shop owner in Monrovia, a 2-year-old Santa Ana boy who was resting in his father's arms, a 7-year-old Long Beach boy visiting a friend who was handling his father's semiautomatic handgun, an off-duty security guard who went to investigate why someone had shot the family dog.

[In other California incidents] gunfire killed a Northridge mother waiting with her young son to pick up her daughter at a Bible study class. Gunfire killed an 8-year-old caught in a murderous exchange in a Paramount restaurant. Gunfire killed a retired nurse in South Central Los Angeles who was sitting on her living room sofa. In October 1993, a 19-year-old fatally shot four people at an El Cajon fitness center before killing himself.

There were more than 15,300 gun homicides nationwide in 1992, up from more than 14,200 in 1991. Over the last 25 years, more Americans have died in gun-related murders than were killed in the Vietnam War, the Korean War and World War I combined.

In 1991, 1 in 10 U.S. gun homicides occurred in Los Angeles County. Obviously Los Angeles has a special gun problem. That is why the Los Angeles Times intends to carry forward its campaign for comprehensive gun control . . . for however long it takes to reduce the slaughter.

For even the grim numbers don't tell the whole story. Guns are killing our spirit with fear. The fear of sounds in the night, fear of a dark street or an empty parking lot, even a public park on a lazy afternoon. There is no "safe" part of town anymore. The violence now follows us home; armed robbers lurk in our driveways; our own children tragically shoot each other with handguns we buy to defend ourselves.

It is still provocative to propose that Americans give up their right to own a gun, or relinquish the weapons they have. Yet the notion of comprehensive gun control is far from radical in most other industrialized nations. In Britain, Sweden, Switzerland, Canada, Japan and Australia, for example, private citizens generally must have a license to own a firearm and must submit to a background check. Relatively few licenses are granted, and some of those licensed must store their weapons at a club.

In 1990, handguns killed 291 people in all of these countries; in the same year 10,567 in the United States died from handguns.

No wonder Europeans are incredulous at what they see here. "Why don't you get rid of all those guns?" they ask.

It's a good question, isn't it?

"The strong evidence is that the right kind of gun control legislation can reduce murders, suicides, and accidents substantially in the United States."

Privately Owned Guns Decrease Security

Carl T. Bogus

In the following viewpoint Carl T. Bogus cites a study showing that a higher rate of crime and suicide correlates with a higher rate of gun ownership. Seattle, Washington, has both higher crime rates and higher suicide rates when compared to neighboring Vancouver, British Columbia, Canada. The difference in the two cities' crime and suicide rates, according to the study, can be attributed to the higher number of guns in Seattle. Bogus argues that the risks of gun ownership (crime and suicide) outweigh any benefits (self-protection). Bogus is a visiting professor at Rutgers University School of Law, in New Brunswick, New Jersey.

As you read, consider the following questions:

1. What evidence does Bogus offer that private gun ownership does not deter crime?
2. To what does Bogus attribute the "rising tide of savagery"?

While abhorring violence, Americans generally believe that gun control cannot do much to reduce it. A majority of Americans questioned in a 1992 CBS–*New York Times* poll responded that banning handguns would only keep them away from law-abiding citizens rather than reduce the amount of violent crime. Many serious scholars have accepted the argument that the huge number of guns already in circulation would make any gun control laws ineffective. Until recently, it has been difficult to answer these objections. But in the past few years, new research has demonstrated that some gun control laws do work, dramatically reducing murder rates.

Gun violence is a plague of such major proportions that its destructive power is rivaled only by wars and epidemics. During the Vietnam War, more than twice as many Americans were shot to death in the United States as died in combat in Vietnam. Besides the 34,000 Americans killed by guns each year, more than 60,000 are injured—many seriously—and about a quarter of a million Americans are held up at gunpoint.

Measures that demonstrably reduce gun violence would gain wide public support. But that has been exactly the problem: A public that approves of gun control by wide margins also is skeptical about its effectiveness and even its constitutionality. Both of these sources of doubt can now be put to rest.

A Study of Seattle and Vancouver

Perhaps the most dramatic findings about the efficacy of gun control laws come from a study [by John Henry Sloan et al.] comparing two cities that have followed different policies for regulating handguns: Seattle, Washington, and Vancouver, British Columbia. Only 140 miles apart, the two cities are remarkably alike despite being located on opposite sides of an international border. They have populations nearly identical in size and, during the study period (1980–86), had similar socioeconomic profiles. Seattle, for example, had a 5.8 percent unemployment rate while Vancouver's was 6.0 percent. The median household income in Seattle was $16,254; in Vancouver, adjusted in U.S. dollars, it was $16,681. In racial and ethnic makeup, the two cities are also similar. Whites represent 79 percent of Seattle's inhabitants and 76 percent of Vancouver's. The principal racial difference is that Asians make up a larger share of Vancouver's population (22 percent versus 7 percent). The two cities share not only a common frontier history but a current culture as well. Most of the top-ten television shows in one city, for example, also rank among the top ten in the other.

As one might expect from twin cities, burglary rates in Seattle and Vancouver were nearly identical. The aggravated assault rate was, however, slightly higher in Seattle. On examining the data more closely, the Sloan study found "a striking pattern." There were almost identical rates of assaults with knives, clubs and fists, but there was a far greater rate of assault with firearms in Seattle. Indeed, the firearm assault rate in Seattle was nearly eight times higher than in Vancouver.

The homicide rate was also markedly different in the two cities. During the seven years of the study, there were 204 homicides in Vancouver and 388 in Seattle—an enormous difference for two cities with comparable populations. Further analysis led to a startling finding: the entire difference was due to gun-related homicides. The murder rates with knives—and all other weapons excluding firearms—were virtually identical, but the rate of murders involving guns was five times greater in Seattle. That alone accounted for Seattle's having nearly twice as many homicides as Vancouver.

Guns and Crime

Findings of a national crime victimization survey by the Justice Department:

- Death certificates show that 2,853 teen-agers, aged 16–19, were shot to death in 1992 crimes. Black males accounted for 58 percent, more than 8 times their share of the population group.

- Of 415 law-enforcement officers slain between 1987 and 1992, 378 were shot by guns that were not their own. Of these cases, handguns were used in 73 percent (276 deaths), rifles accounted for 19 percent (72) and shotguns 8 percent (30).

- Guns are in the criminal's possession, although not always used, in an average of 858,000 rapes, assaults and robberies each year.

- Firearms of all types were used in 16,000 homicides in 1992.

- Interviews of 14,000 prison inmates elicited the admission that 14 percent (1,960) carried guns during the offense for which they are serving time. Among those who had prior convictions, 23 percent said they bought the weapon from a retail store.

The Washington Times, February 27, 1994.

People in Seattle may purchase a handgun for any reason after a five-day waiting period; 41 percent of all households have handguns. Vancouver, on the other hand, requires a permit for handgun purchases and issues them only to applicants who have a lawful reason to own a handgun and who, after a careful investigation, are found to have no criminal record and to be sane. Self-defense is not a valid reason to own a handgun, and recreational uses of handguns are strictly regulated. The penalty for illegal possession is severe—two years' imprisonment. Handguns are present in only 12 percent of Vancouver's homes.

The Seattle-Vancouver study provides strong evidence for the efficacy of gun control. Sloan and his colleagues concluded that the wider proliferation of handguns in Seattle was the sole cause of the higher rate of murders and assaults. The study answered other important questions as well.

• *Do handguns deter crime?* If handguns deter burglary, the burglary rate in Seattle—where so many more homes have handguns—should have been lower than the burglary rate in Vancouver. But it was not.

• *How often are handguns used for self-defense?* Less than 4 percent of the homicides in both cities resulted from acts of self-defense.

• Perhaps most important: *If handguns are unavailable, will people merely use other weapons instead?* The answer must be "no." Otherwise, the cities would have had similar total murder rates and Vancouver would have had higher rates of homicide with other weapons. . . .

It's Better Not to Have Guns

The gun lobby is fond of saying, "If guns are outlawed, only outlaws will have guns." What's wrong with this picture?

The National Rifle Association (NRA) slogan leads us to envision two groups—solid citizens and hardened criminals—but the real world cannot be neatly divided into good guys and bad guys. Many people are law-abiding citizens until they become inflamed in a domestic dispute, a drunken argument in a bar, even a fender-bender on the highway. Murder is usually an act of rage; it is more often impulsive than premeditated. In fact, 80 percent of all murders occur during altercations and 71 percent involve acquaintances, including lovers, family members, and neighbors. Only 29 percent of those arrested for murder are previously convicted felons.

Rage can pass quickly, but if there is a gun available, even a few seconds may not be soon enough. Of course, enraged lovers and brawlers use other weapons, but it is better to be attacked with anything other than a gun. Guns are, by far, the most lethal weapons. The second deadliest is the knife, but knife attacks result in death only one-fifth as often as those with guns.

For the same reason that it is better to face a knife than a gun in a lovers' quarrel, it is better to be robbed at knife point rather than gunpoint. There are good reasons to believe that reducing the number of guns in the general population will reduce them in the hands of muggers and robbers. Prison inmates report that they acquired one-third of their guns by stealing them, typically in home burglaries. There are also people at the margin—not yet career criminals but drifting in that direction—who are more inclined to have guns if they are cheap and readily available. And since handguns are lawful almost everywhere, these people do not even have to cross a psychological Rubicon to get a gun.

An Increase of Youngsters with Guns

Many of the people at the margin are youngsters. Nearly 70 percent of all serious crimes are committed by boys and young men, ages fourteen to twenty-four. Many of them are not yet career criminals. They are the children of despair, kids from dysfunctional families and impoverished communities who thirst for a feeling of importance. They are angry, immature, and unstable. In the 1950s, they carried switchblades, but since the early 1960s they have increasingly been carrying handguns. Packing a gun makes them feel like men, and it just takes a little alcohol or drugs, a buddy's dare, or a moment of bravado to propel them into their first mugging or holdup of a convenience store. Many juvenile robbers say that they did not intend to commit a robbery when they went out. The nation will be a less dangerous place if these kids go out without guns.

Guns as a Risk Item

The Violence Policy Center, an advocate of tough gun laws, said in a major study financed by *Rolling Stone* magazine that guns should be treated like other consumer goods that pose risks.

"Toasters, teddy bears, trucks, or guns—which product is virtually unregulated?" asked Kristen Rand on Feb. 17, 1994. She's counsel of the policy center. "The answer, surprising to most people, is guns."

"The conclusion of our study, 'Cease Fire,' is that the time has come to hold the gun industry to the same standards we apply to manufacturers of lawnmowers and lawn darts (a toy)," Ms. Rand said. "The result would be a significant reduction in firearms violence."

The Christian Science Monitor, February 23, 1994.

There is a frightening increase in the number of youngsters carrying guns. The National Adolescent Student Health Survey discovered that by 1987, nearly 2 percent of all eighth and tenth graders across the nation said that they had carried a gun to school within the past year. A third of those said they took a gun to school with them every day, which translates into more than 100,000 students packing a pistol all the time. In just the first two months of 1992, more than a hundred firearms were confiscated in New York City schools.

And kids are not just carrying guns, they are using them. New York City was shaken in 1992 when, moments before Mayor David Dinkins was to give a speech to the students at Brooklyn's Thomas Jefferson High School, a fifteen-year-old pulled out a Smith & Wesson .38 and killed two other students. Had it not been for the mayor's presence at the school, the shootings might not have been front-page news.

A Rising Tide of Savagery

It is somewhat disingenuous to be shocked about youths with handguns. Kids emulate adults. They live in a society that has not attached a sense of gravity to owning handguns. . . . Except in a very few locales, automobiles are regulated far more rigorously than handguns.

There are 35 million handguns in the United States; a quarter of all homes have at least one handgun in them. We can tell a teenage boy that he is really safer if he does not pack a gun. But why should he believe adults who keep handguns in their nightstand drawers, even though they have been told that a gun in the home is six times more likely to be used to shoot a family member than an intruder?

For more than a decade some observers, such as Charles Silberman, have noted a rising tide of savagery. For example, my morning newspaper carries a report about a robbery at a local McDonald's restaurant. A man with a pistol demanded the restaurant's cash, which the manager immediately gave him. The robber then told the manager and two other employees to lie down, and proceeded to shoot two to death while one of the three ran away. Not long ago it would have been extraordinarily rare for a robber—with the money in his hand—to kill his victims gratuitously; now it seems commonplace. We may wonder what impels someone to top off a robbery with a double murder, but whatever the motive, the handgun makes that act possible.

An Increase in Suicides

We are also witnessing a bewildering escalation in suicides. In 1960 there were about 19,000 suicides in the United States; now there are more than 30,000 each year. (This represents a rise in the suicide rate from 10.6 per 100,000 in 1960 to 12.4 per 100,000 in 1988.) Nearly two-thirds of all suicides in the United States are committed with firearms, more than 80 percent of those with handguns. The rising number of suicides is due almost completely to firearm suicides. While the number of suicides with other weapons has remained relatively stable (even slightly declining since the early 1970s), the number of firearm suicides has more than doubled since 1960.

Why should that be so? If someone really wants to kill himself, is he not going to find a way to do so regardless of whether a handgun is available? This is something of a trick question. The rabbit in the hat is the phrase "really wants to kill himself" because suicide, like murder, is often an impulsive act, particularly among the 2,000 to 3,000 American teenagers who commit suicide each year. If an individual contemplating suicide can get through the moment of dark despair, he may reconsider. And if a gun is not available, many potential suicides will resort to a less lethal method, survive, and never attempt suicide again. Nothing is as quick and certain as a gun. The desire to die need only last as long as it takes to pull a trigger, and the decision is irrevocable.

In the Seattle-Vancouver study, the researchers found a 40-percent higher suicide rate among the fifteen- to twenty-five-year-olds in Seattle, a difference they discovered was due to a firearm suicide rate that is ten times higher among Seattle adolescents. Other research reveals that a potentially suicidal adolescent is *seventy-five times* as likely to kill himself when there is a gun in the house.

This is the one area, however, where the type of gun may not matter. While more than 80 percent of all gun-related suicides are with handguns, research suggests that when handguns are not available, people attempting suicide may just as readily use long guns. But many homes only have a handgun, and reducing the number of homes with handguns will therefore reduce the number of suicides.

No one suggests that gun control legislation will be a panacea. Nevertheless, the strong evidence is that the right kind of gun control legislation can reduce murders, suicides, and accidents substantially in the United States.

"The implicit theory of the gun-control movement—that most Americans are too incompetent or mentally unstable to use a gun for defensive purposes—simply is not borne out by the facts."

Privately Owned Guns Increase Security

David B. Kopel

In the wake of the November 1993 signing of the Brady bill into law, there have been calls for even stronger gun control measures. In the following viewpoint, David B. Kopel provides evidence to support his opinion that private gun ownership is a better crime deterrent than police protection. He also faults studies that show gun ownership is dangerous. Kopel is director of the Second Amendment Project at the Independence Institute, a think tank in Denver, Colorado, that, among other causes, supports gun ownership as a civil liberty. He is author of *The Samurai, the Mountie, and the Cowboy: Should America Adopt the Gun Controls of Other Democracies?*

As you read, consider the following questions:

1. Why does the United States have a lower burglary rate compared to other countries, according to Kopel? What evidence does he cite?
2. According to Kopel, what percentage of protective uses of guns was not counted by the *New England Journal of Medicine* study?

David B. Kopel, "Better Safe Than Sorry," *Los Angeles Times*, November 26, 1993. Reprinted with permission.

Early one Sunday morning in November 1993, factory worker Arthur Boone was walking home in Brooklyn after shopping in a neighborhood *bodega*. Carl James, age 15, allegedly came up to Boone, stuck a gun to his head and ordered, "Give it up," while 19-year-old Taz Pell began searching through Boone's pockets. So far, a typical Sunday morning in New York.

Boone then pulled out his .44 magnum and shot both robbers dead.

Each of the assailants had a police record; one had been arrested for robbery just two weeks earlier. The 41-year-old Boone, who had been mugged twice before and pistol-whipped so severely that he required hospitalization, was promptly arrested on weapons charges.

A few days before, in Chicago, a 16-year-old with a burglary record broke into the home of Bessie Jones, a 92-year-old widow confined to a wheelchair. She was wheeled around and ordered to point out everything of value. When the burglar stepped outside for a moment to confer with his lookout, she reached under a blanket, pulled out a .38 Colt revolver, and killed him. Although possession of the revolver was clearly in violation of Chicago's handgun prohibition, the state attorney's office decided not to prosecute.

As the *Los Angeles Times* proposes national gun control even stricter than the Chicago and New York models, some attention is due to the many millions of Americans who, like Arthur Boone and Bessie Jones, possess firearms for protection.

Police Cannot Provide Protection

In all nations that have achieved popular compliance with strict gun-control laws, there has always been one common condition precedent: public safety. That is, before the gun laws were enacted, the public already felt little need to have guns for protection because there was little crime.

Contrast that situation in, say, early-20th-Century Britain with the late-20th-Century United States. Not only does the American government fail to provide effective protection; the government insists it has no legal duty to do so. The courts have concurred, holding that the police have no duty to protect anyone and cannot be held liable, even in cases where the victim was targeted in advance but was denied police protection.

[Former Los Angeles Chief of Police] Daryl Gates earned national notoriety for spending the first hours of the Los Angeles riots at a fund-raiser for himself, while riot victims were left to fend for themselves without police assistance. Even on ordinary days, the people of Los Angeles, like the people of every major American city, are for all practical purposes left to take care of themselves. If a criminal attacks, it is almost certain that a police officer will not be there to help. Until this fundamental reality changes, tens of millions of Americans are going to hold on to their guns, no matter what.

Studies of Guns Used for Protection

But isn't it a fact that guns kept for protection are almost never used? Well, no. In a 1981 survey conducted by pollster Peter A. Hart for the National Alliance Against Violence, 4% of the households polled reported at least one use of a handgun against a person in the previous five years. Even if we assume only one incident per reporting household, that's 645,000 defensive uses of handguns per year. Based on these figures, about 18% of people who owned handguns for protection actually used them for protection.

Canadian criminologist Gary Mauser's research found similar rates of protective uses by Canadian handgun owners despite Canadian laws allowing handgun possession only for sport.

Crime Will Be Safer for Criminals

Gun control measures are ineffective, because criminals are not dependent on the legal purchase of firearms. Attorney General Janet Reno is being disingenuous when she says waiting periods, such as the one in the Brady bill, "keep guns from thousands of criminals."

Any criminal detected during a waiting period—or instant background check—can simply turn around and purchase a gun on the street, disarm a police officer or rob a National Guard armory or gun store.

Paul Craig Roberts, *Manchester [N.H.] Union Leader*, December 7, 1993.

In 1993, Florida State University criminologist Gary Kleck conducted a more in-depth survey. Detailed questioning weeded out respondents who confused merely owning a gun for protection with actually using it. The questions also accounted for persons who had used a gun defensively more than once. The new data show that guns of all types are used defensively between 850,000 and 2.5 million times a year in the United States. Most of the defensive uses involve handguns, and the vast majority of such uses do not involve firing the weapon, but merely brandishing it to scare away an attacker.

The surveys of citizen use of guns for protection are consistent with surveys of criminals. In a National Institute of Justice study of incarcerated felons, 38% said that they had decided not to commit a particular crime out of fear that the victim might be armed.

America has much more violent crime than other industrial nations, yet, oddly, America has a lower rate of burglary of occupied residences than do nations that prohibit gun ownership for protection. The best explanation is that only in America do burglars face a risk of getting shot that is as large as their risk of getting arrested.

As Florida law-enforcement officials have noted, one of the important reasons for foreign tourists being singled out for robbery is that in Florida, licensed, trained citizens (including American visitors) can obtain permits to carry a concealed handgun for protection. But in New York City and Los Angeles (and the rest of the country if the anti-gun lobby gets its way), gun-control laws put everyone in the same position as the tourists in Florida—government-certified defenseless prey.

A rational gun-control policy needs to focus on reducing the crimes that inflict grievous harm while increasing the citizens' ability to protect against such crimes. Most gun-control proposals offer little prospect of reducing criminal use but pose a substantial threat to lawful defensive use.

The implicit theory of the gun-control movement—that most Americans are too incompetent or mentally unstable to use a gun for defensive purposes—simply is not borne out by the facts. Learning how to shoot well is easier than learning how to type. After 40 hours in a combat pistol class, a person will have the skills necessary to stop the vast majority of attackers (by putting two shots into the chest within 1½ seconds). Forty hours of handgun training, by the way, is more than many American police officers receive.

Faulty Studies of Gun Dangers

One problem—perhaps the major problem—in achieving a rational debate on this issue is the news media, which tend to broadcast uncritically any "expert findings" that support gun control. Typical was the "news" that a study in the *New England Journal of Medicine* had found that owning a gun increases a person's risk of being murdered by 2.7 times. The author, a prominent epidemiologist, had taken a set of homicide victims, identified some of their socioeconomic and behavioral variables and matched them to a control group of non-victims.

The very same data that "proved" the risk of gun ownership also "proved" that renting a home, rather than owning it, increased the homicide risk by 4.4. Does this mean that when your apartment goes co-op, and you own it instead of renting it, your risk of being murdered falls dramatically? Of course not. Instead, renters may be more likely to live in a rough neighborhood or unstable circumstances, which puts them in a higher risk category. Similarly, people at risk of being assaulted might simply be more likely to own guns than people in safer circumstances. Getting rid of the gun might not make the renter any safer than buying out the landlord.

Most significantly, the study made no effort to investigate the 99% of protective uses of guns that do not involve a fatality. The folks who got murdered are, after all, the folks for whom protection did not work. A study that ignores survivors, the hundreds of thousands of people who use guns for protection each year, can't say much about the overall protective effect of gun ownership.

Gun Control and the Media

Despite the limitations of the study, almost every news report treated the 2.7 figure unquestionably, as a scientific fact. Many academic criminologists thought the study was worthless, but the only dissent reported was from a researcher for the National Rifle Association.

Other published factoids purporting to show the dangers of gun ownership are similarly vacuous. If the media spent one-tenth as much effort looking into the truth behind these claims as they spend investigating the conflicting stories about President [Bill] Clinton's haircuts, the quality of the gun-control debate would improve considerably.

It's true that in some homes, such as those of alcoholics, the mentally ill or ex-felons, the presence of a gun does substantially increase the risk of a homicide. But here, too, the "facts" can be twisted to the gun-control lobby's favor: The male felon killed by his girlfriend is counted as the victim of a "tragic domestic homicide," not the perpetrator of vicious abuse.

But most households are not violence-prone; rather, most gun owners' concern is about violence directed against them from the outside. They know, intuitively, that the government will not protect them from criminal attack. Arthur Boone and Bessie Jones correctly understood this, and they have the support of the tens of millions of other Americans who own guns for protection.

172

Periodical Bibliography

The following articles have been selected to supplement the diverse views presented in this chapter.

James Bovard — "The Assault on Assault Weapons," *The Wall Street Journal*, January 6, 1994.

Nancy Gibbs — "Up in Arms," *Time*, December 20, 1993.

Stephen P. Halbrook — "The Right to Keep and Bear Arms Under the Second and Fourteenth Amendments: The Framers' Intent and Supreme Court Jurisprudence," *Journal on Firearms and Public Policy*, Fall 1993. Available from the Second Amendment Foundation, 12500 NE Tenth Pl., Bellevue, WA 98005.

Albert R. Hunt — "Gun Control Is Essential to U.S. Crime Control," *The Wall Street Journal*, November 18, 1993.

Arthur L. Kellerman et al. — "Gun Ownership as a Risk Factor for Homicide in the Home," *New England Journal of Medicine*, October 7, 1993. Available from 1440 Main St., Waltham, MA 02254.

Ken Kelley — "An Interview with Joycelyn Elders," *Mother Jones*, January/February 1994.

Raymond W. Kelly — "Toward a New Intolerance," *Vital Speeches of the Day*, March 15, 1993.

C. Everett Koop and George D. Lundberg — "Violence in America: A Public Health Emergency," *JAMA*, June 10, 1992. Available from the AMA, 515 N. State St., Chicago, IL 60610.

David B. Kopel — "Gun Play," *Reason*, July 1993.

Daniel Patrick Moynihan — "Guns Don't Kill People. Bullets Do," *The New York Times*, December 12, 1993.

Daniel D. Polsby — "Equal Protection," *Reason*, October 1993.

Jeffrey R. Snyder — "A Nation of Cowards," *The Public Interest*, Fall 1993.

Peter H. Stone — "Showing Holes," *Mother Jones*, January/February 1994.

Josh Sugarmann and Kristen Rand — "Cease Fire," *Rolling Stone*, March 10, 1994.

Gordon Witkin and Ted Gest — "Gun Control's Limits," *U.S. News & World Report*, December 6, 1993.

4

CHAPTER

How Should America Deal with Young Offenders?

CRIME AND
CRIMINALS

Chapter Preface

Some people believe that young people commit crimes due to bad influences. Citing studies arguing that exposure to violence on television causes aggressive behavior among children, many groups have called for the regulation of violent television programming. "Gangsta rap," with violent themes and images drawn from an inner-city culture of gang life, has come under similar attack. Critics say that lyrics such as these (from Ice-T's song *Cop Killer*, which describes a drive-by shooting) encourage young fans of the music to commit violent acts:

I got my twelve-gauge sawed off
I got my headlights turned off
I'm 'bout to bust some shots off
I'm 'bout to dust some cops off

Pointing to lyrics and videos that portray the use of guns, the abuse of drugs, violence against women, and distrust of police, critics contend that the music glamorizes a culture where committing violent crimes and spending time in prison are marks of status among young people. By glamorizing this violent culture, critics contend, gangsta rap contributes to the perpetuation of youth violence. David Klinghoffer, literary editor of *National Review* magazine, condemns gangsta rap, saying, "It serves as musical accompaniment to the entire underclass culture of violence."

Afficionados of gangsta rap say the harsh lyrics express the legitimate anger young blacks feel. According to rapper Snoop Doggy Dogg—who as a teenager spent time in jail and, shortly after his debut album was released in 1993, was arrested as an accomplice to murder—the music portrays the violence of the inner city, but it does not cause that violence. In a December 1993 *Time* magazine interview, the rapper stated, "Before rap came out, there was violence. When I was nine years old, one of my homeboys got shot in some gang violence. And wasn't no rap music being played then."

With violent crime among young people on the rise, as shown by Federal Bureau of Investigation (FBI) statistics, many people are searching for the causes of such crime. Viewpoints in the following chapter debate some causes of violence among young people and some proposed solutions.

"We need to make a loud and collective statement as a whole community that we will shun those who do violence and those who use guns to commit violence."

Society Should Take Handguns Away from Young People

Roy Romer

A 1993 Harris poll found that 39 percent of U.S. middle school and high school students personally knew someone who had been injured or killed by gunfire. Citing the study, Roy Romer, governor of Colorado, argues that discipline is necessary to straighten out juveniles. In the following viewpoint, from a speech delivered during a special session of the Colorado legislature, Romer proposes stricter laws to get guns out of the hands of Colorado's young people and a "Youth Offender System" for dealing with violent youths in the state. He believes that it is necessary to renew people's sense of community and to reverse America's cultural celebration of violence.

As you read, consider the following questions:

1. What reasons does Romer give for rejecting the idea that there is no distinction between kids and adults when it comes to handguns?
2. What choice do judges and prosecutors currently have in trying children who commit adult crimes, according to Romer?
3. In the author's view, how does American culture celebrate violence?

From "Guns in the Hands of Kids" by Roy Romer, *Vital Speeches of the Day*, November 1, 1993. Reprinted with the author's permission.

Let's define the problem. The problem is violence.
The problem is kids killing kids.
The problem is gangs in our neighborhoods.
The problem is guns in the hands of children.

Events show that the code of conduct among many of our youth has changed. Too often, disputes once settled with a shouting match or a fist fight now are settled with a gun.

In some neighborhoods in Colorado, people are afraid to sit on their front porches at night. Children are forced to ride their tricycles in the basement. Some people are even afraid to help neighbors in need.

This is not just a Denver problem. It's a problem throughout the state—in Colorado Springs, in Pueblo. We even had a drive-by shooting this summer in Lamar.

And this is not just a Colorado problem. It's a national problem.

And this is not just a problem for any particular ethnic group. We are all in this together. Rural, urban, Black, Latino, Asian-American, and Anglo—our whole community is victimized by violence.

Let me say this right up front—this is a tough [violence prevention] package we are about to discuss, and I hear and understand the concerns of parents and others in the communities of color that what we do not be an excuse for the police to harass kids because of the color of their skin.

We're not here to do that. We're trying to get the guns out of the hands of children so that they don't hurt one another, no matter what their color. . . . What we want to do is stop the violence, not harass innocent kids.

The Statistics on Kids and Guns

[There is] a survey of over 2,500 kids from around the country, grades 6 through 12, conducted in 1993 by Lou Harris.

Do you know what it says?

It reports that 15 percent of the kids surveyed said they carried a handgun on their person at some point during the previous 30 days.

Nine percent said they'd shot a gun at someone else.

Eleven percent said they'd been shot at by someone else during the past year.

Thirty-nine percent said they know someone personally who has either been killed or injured by gunfire.

And one in three said they think their "chances of living to a ripe old age are likely to be cut short" because of the threat of a handgun being used against them.

I am not in the habit of questioning Lou Harris, but those are absolutely unbelievable numbers. Cut them in half, cut them in quarters, divide them by 10—they're still shocking.

177

This violence is morally wrong. The fear it imposes on us and our children is morally destructive.

How did we get to this point? No one has the complete answer. I have talked with Coloradans across the state who know and care about this issue. I've met with district attorneys, and sheriffs and police chiefs. I've met with community, neighborhood and minority leaders. I've met with judges. I've met with members of the clergy. I've met with former gang members, and I've met with young people who have faced their problems without joining gangs. . . .

I've been listening hard, and I've learned a lot. I will frankly confess that the problem is worse than I had known. I am convinced that the solution involves both discipline and prevention. We need swift and fair discipline to try to straighten out those youth who break the law. And we need to respond with compassion and support for all of our children, so that they have clear alternatives to a life of violence.

Four Critical Tasks

Our first responsibility is to get the bullets off the streets and the guns out of the hands of our kids. There will be many steps that must follow concerning prevention, but we need to focus on four simple but critical tasks.

One, we must ban the possession of handguns by kids under 18.

Two, we must make the consequences of violating this law immediate and serious.

Three, we must provide more detention space and programs so that those who do violate the law spend time in the strict discipline of detention or a boot camp—instead of immediately being turned back on the streets.

And four, we must provide a special sentencing program for the most hardened and violent young offenders. We call this the Youth Offender System. . . .

Let me describe each proposal in more detail.

First, I propose we make it illegal for anyone under 18 years of age to possess a handgun. I also propose we make it illegal for any adult to provide a handgun to anyone under 18 for an unlawful purpose.

We're not talking about rifles. We're not talking about shotguns. We're talking about handguns.

The law would allow kids to engage in legitimate activities, such as hunting and training and traveling to and from such activities.

Some say we have no right to draw a distinction between adults and kids when it comes to handguns. I disagree. We set age limits for many things in our society. We don't let people drink until they are a certain age. We don't let them drive a car until they are

178

a certain age. We don't let kids hunt big game until they are a certain age. They don't need to be carrying guns, either.

Immediate Punishment and More Prison Space

Second, I propose immediate and serious consequences for those caught violating this law. For punishment to mean something to a youngster, it must be administered as quickly as possible. Unfortunately, our court system often is too slow.

Our proposal requires the immediate arrest and detention of any kid caught carrying a handgun not permitted by this law. It requires that each kid face a hearing within 48 hours. The law would state there is a presumption that offenders are dangerous to themselves and the community if released, which will allow judges to deny bail.

Our proposal also would expedite court deadlines and require that trials be held within 90 days.

Third, I propose we increase juvenile detention space in Colorado.

We all know a law is only as effective as our ability to punish those who violate it.

I spent a Friday evening riding with the Aurora police. We came upon the scene of a routine traffic violation. The police had stopped a car carrying three youths, and as the driver—age 16—got out of the car, two guns—two loaded guns—fell out of his shirt.

Keep Juveniles Away from Guns

We must substantially stiffen laws and penalties for juveniles in possession of guns and for adults who make guns available to juveniles. No loopholes, no exceptions.

A new juvenile justice system would quickly reduce the level of fear we all feel. Over the long term, it would reduce the number of juvenile and adult violent criminals. We need to put reformers to work right away and give them a time limit . . . to produce a framework for a new juvenile justice system. . . .

The reformers should be nonpartisan; this is not about politics. It is about making a safe, desirable place to live.

Gil Garcetti, *Los Angeles Times*, February 7, 1994.

What did the police do? They wrote a ticket and sent him on his way. Why? Because there was no place to put him. The juvenile detention facilities are so crowded that this wasn't considered a severe enough offense to detain him.

179

So we have the guns. We don't have the kid. And all he needs to do is get another gun and he's back in business.

Now, I am as pained as many of you are by spending money on jails rather than schools. . . . But if we are serious about getting guns away from kids, the law has to have teeth and we have to have more space to house those who violate it. . . .

I also believe the strict discipline of a boot camp would help straighten out some of these kids. I therefore support the provision of additional beds by establishing such a boot camp within the Division of Youth Services.

Over the long term, our proposal for a new Youth Offender System, which I will discuss in more detail in a moment, will free up additional beds within the existing juvenile system. . . .

Opposition from the Gun Lobby

Let me emphasize one point. Some municipalities have taken their own steps to combat the problem of kids carrying guns. I am proposing a statewide law because the sanctions we can bring through such a law are important. But we should not prohibit cities, counties and towns from imposing their own ordinances if they find it necessary. Therefore, I oppose adding any local pre-emption to this bill.

Now, as soon as the gun lobby back in Washington heard about this special session and our resolve to pass a gun bill with teeth, it hired an ad agency and high-paid lobbyists to kill the idea. The National Rifle Association has been running ads saying we want to take guns away from "good kids" who want to use guns for legitimate activities.

Apparently, the facts don't matter much to the NRA. They ignore the fact that we aren't talking about hunting rifles or shotguns. They ignore the fact that kids would be allowed to participate in all the legitimate activities they mention in their ad.

Let me say to the NRA—you're dead wrong on this one. Over 80 percent of Coloradans *statewide—80 percent*—believe we should pass a law to get guns out of the hands of kids. Many Republicans—including former President Reagan's press secretary Jim Brady—support taking guns out of the hands of kids. . . . I have heard from responsible gun owners and NRA members who support our proposal.

If the NRA in Washington is so out of touch that it cannot even support the simple proposition that a 14-year-old has no business carrying a loaded gun to school or on the street, then it is part of the problem, not part of the solution, and it needs to get out of our way.

The lobbyists . . . haven't walked our streets, and they haven't gone to the funerals of our children. Good kids are dying. Let's be clear—. . . we cannot allow a special interest, no matter how powerful, to stand in the way of doing what the people say they want and need.

Kids Committing Adult Crimes

So my proposal to deal with kids carrying guns is: One: ban possession of handguns by juveniles and make it illegal for adults to provide these handguns unlawfully to juveniles; Two, expedite the prosecution of cases involving kids and guns; and three, expand the detention space and programs, including a boot camp, for those kids who violate the law.

Finally, fourth, I propose changing the juvenile justice system so that we can deal properly with the most hardened of our youthful offenders.

Our current juvenile system is based on a 1950s model, when truancy, runaways, and other non-violent acts were what we had to worry about. In most cases, the maximum sentence that can be imposed is two years, and little flexibility exists to treat those who commit serious or violent crimes differently than those who do not.

The fact is, the system never contemplated and is totally unprepared to handle the problems we see today—kids shooting kids, kids raping kids, kids terrorizing neighborhoods, kids running sophisticated criminal organizations that deal in drugs.

Some kids are committing adult crimes. And in order to impose the kind of punishment such crimes deserve, increasingly we have had to resort to trying kids as adults and placing them in adult prisons.

I do not believe it is right to deal with increasing youth violence by simply dumping more kids into adult prisons. It is not right to force judges and prosecutors to choose between a juvenile system, on the one hand, that is not prepared to handle such violent offenders, and an adult system, on the other hand, that was never designed to handle youth.

With a bipartisan working group, including the district attorneys, we have developed an intermediate sentencing alternative—a middle tier between the juvenile system and the adult correction system. It combines longer sentences and a very serious, disciplined atmosphere with specialized training and rehabilitation geared toward serious youthful offenders.

An Intermediate Sentencing Alternative

We call it the Youth Offender System. . . .

The Youth Offender System would apply to persons aged 14 to 18 who commit crimes like assault with a deadly weapon, aggravated robbery, manslaughter, and many other crimes of violence.

The accused would be tried in an adult court, and if convicted would be given an adult sentence. But the sentence then would be suspended, conditioned on the youth's successful completion of a 1-to-5-year term in the Youth Offender System. If that system doesn't turn the kid around, he or she would go back to court and serve the remainder of the adult sentence in an adult facility.

I propose we house the system in the Department of Corrections rather than the Division of Youth Services. This is a tough choice, but I think it's the right one. We need to make it very clear to these offenders that there are serious consequences for certain crimes. In addition, by moving the most violent youths to the Department of Corrections, we will allow the Division of Youth Services to return to its original mission of reforming and rehabilitating less-serious offenders. . . .

I believe this Youth Offender System will be a key element in tackling the juvenile violence problem. It will take kids who are at crossroads in their lives and let them know there are profound consequences for the choices they make—will they play by the rules, or will they continue their criminal activities?

Ban handguns in the hands of kids. Provide for swifter punishment. Expand juvenile detention space. And create a new Youth Offender System.

If we can accomplish those four goals, we will have taken a meaningful first step in our efforts to solve this problem.

The Agenda for Prevention

As I said earlier, I am convinced the solution involves both discipline and prevention. [It involves] giving the law enforcement, judicial and correctional systems the tool they need to provide swift and fair discipline and programs of rehabilitation. . . .

When we talk about getting to the root causes of violence, when we talk about our agenda for intervention and prevention, it includes many things.

It includes attention to the problem of teen-age pregnancy.

It includes prenatal care.

It includes helping new parents learn the skills of parenting.

It includes readily available child care, preschool education, and medical assistance for families with small children.

It includes working to keep families together and to make sure kids have positive role models in their lives, through mentoring programs if necessary.

It includes quality public education, effective drop-out prevention, alternative education, apprenticeship programs, assistance in moving from schools to jobs, and job opportunities that are real, with the opportunity to earn a real living wage.

This and more is what we mean by prevention and intervention. . . .

But it is not enough. We know we need to do more.

We need to inventory who is in the field, both public and private, state and local. We need to coordinate better. We need to evaluate those programs that are working and those that are not, and we need to identify where the gaps are and find ways to fill them.

We've got a lot of work to do. . . .

Define Community

When I was a kid in Holly [Colorado], in the 1930s and 40s, we knew we belonged to a community that made us its top priority. If a child was on the street during school, someone grabbed that kid by the collar and marched him back to school. People understood they had a responsibility to every child in that community.

Somehow we have lost that sense of belonging as children and responsibility as adults.

I'm not sure many of us can even define our community anymore. Do we know our neighbors? Do we know the children down the block? Do we know the elderly person living alone across the alley? Do we know the latchkey kid who is alone after school in the apartment down the hall?

Let us resolve—individually and as a community—to join in a renewal. To rebuild and recommit to community. To take back our neighborhoods. To take back our children and make their welfare our first priority.

I suggest that . . . we come together in our neighborhoods to meet one another, to reconnect as communities, to learn the special needs of the neighbors around us, and to commit to one another that we will be there to help. We will take an interest in the welfare of everyone's child, we will be attentive to the latchkey kid down the street, we will intervene in situations of domestic violence—we will do what it takes to renew our community.

Let me tell you what I'm talking about. At a neighborhood meeting, a member of my staff—a working mother—expressed her fear about her son's safety walking to and from school alone. At the end of the meeting, three different couples came up to her and offered to walk her child to school every day. That is what I mean by taking responsibility for each other in community.

In the end, it will be those simple but profound acts by individuals—some of them very courageous acts, but none of them very complicated—that will reclaim our communities.

Our Culture's Tolerance for Violence

Now, it would be easy to conclude here. It would be easy to say that the solution to our problem is to pass laws, rebuild communities, and increase our prevention and intervention efforts. That would be neat and simple.

183

But it would not be honest. We must do all of these things, but it's not enough. If we are honest, we have to admit the roots of the violence run much deeper. They go to our culture's tolerance for and celebration of violence.

Deeper still, the roots of the problem go to the virtues, ethics and character traits we pass on to our children. It is a question of moral character.

I do not believe children are born with the propensity for violence. I believe children learn it from us. Our movies, our television, our music, our video arcades, our children's toys, our cultural heroes all celebrate violence.

I am convinced we must change our attitudes about violence if we are ever to solve this problem for good.

We need to make a loud and collective statement as a whole community that we will shun those who do violence and those who use guns to commit violence.

We've done this in the past. There once was a time when it was acceptable—even funny—to drink and drive. But through concerted action, we've made drinking and driving culturally unacceptable.

We can do the same thing with violence—especially violence among our children. And we can do that by making it clear we will no longer tolerate those who engage in it, those who profit by it, and those who glory in it.

How do we do this? It happens community by community, neighborhood by neighborhood, house by house, family by family.

I tell you, frankly, that if we do not turn this around, we will be left with a society where everyone carries guns. That is not the kind of future we want for children.

We Fail to Convey the Right Message

I therefore ask you to help us create an atmosphere where violence—and particularly violence involving kids and guns—is not tolerated.

We need to examine the cultural messages we send our kids, and how we send them and who is sending them. We cannot teach kids not to engage in violence when we celebrate it daily.

The real problem with these cultural messages is that they are coming at our kids harder and faster precisely when their defenses are lowered. It's not just that we are conveying the wrong messages to them. It's that too often we fail to convey the right messages.

There is a void in too many kids' lives—a void created by the absence of positive role models, the absence of a sense of belonging to something meaningful, the absence of a sense that anyone cares about them—that is too easily filled by gangs and violence and other destructive forces.

When we fortify our youth with a positive sense of who they are and what they can become, when we back them up with community support, when we provide them with a sense of expectations and belonging, then they can more easily sort through the signals they are receiving and reject the violence and the other destructive messages.

In the final analysis, we need to do more. We need to ask again: How do we live in community? How do we treat our neighbors? How do they relate to us? How do we nurture and support our children and convey to them the positive values they need?

We cannot lose sight of the fact that the vast majority of kids are good kids. For every kid who joins a gang, there are many, many more who are going to school and making the grade. Black, Latino, Asian-American, Native-American, Anglo—they all are heroes.

It is to them that we must pledge our best efforts. It is they who will reap the benefits of our success or pay the price for our failure. They are not our enemy. Violence is our enemy. And our challenge is to build communities where we can raise moral children.

It is an insult to the kids and parents of kids who struggle every day with poverty and racism and unemployment to say that these conditions excuse or fully explain criminal violence. I do not believe poverty leads inevitably to violence. I know too many parents who are working hard every day, living from paycheck to paycheck, and too many kids, some of whom come from abusive families and unbearable poverty, who nevertheless manage to play by the rules.

"The problem before us is not getting guns out of the hands of juveniles but rather reducing the motivations for juveniles to arm themselves in the first place."

Society Should Reduce Young People's Need for Guns

James D. Wright and Joseph F. Sheley

According to Justice Department figures, in the United States every day, 100,000 guns are carried to schools by juveniles. James D. Wright, Joseph F. Sheley, and their colleagues asked juvenile offenders and high school students their reasons for carrying guns. They conclude that juveniles who live in crime-ridden neighborhoods carry guns for self-protection. Rather than imposing stricter gun control laws and harsher juvenile justice policies, Wright and Sheley believe it is necessary to convince young people that they can survive without guns by increasing economic and social opportunity. Wright is the Favrot Professor of Human Relations in the Department of Sociology at Tulane University. Sheley is associate professor of sociology at Tulane University and is the author of *Criminology: A Contemporary Handbook*.

As you read, consider the following questions:

1. According to Wright and Sheley, why is it impossible to control the supply of guns?
2. How do the authors define "the inner logic of an arms race"?
3. According to the authors, why do juveniles use drugs?

James D. Wright and Joseph F. Sheley, "Teenage Violence and the Urban Underclass." This essay was taken from the Autumn 1992 *Peace Review*, Peace & Justice Studies, University of San Francisco, San Francisco, CA 94117. Reprinted with permission.

Violence in American inner cities has reached epidemic (not to say epic) proportions. Among young, inner-city non-white males, homicide is now the leading cause of death and the reduction of violence among youth has become a leading public health goal. Incidents that would have been shocking and inexplicable just a few years ago—gang warfare, drive-by slayings, wanton brutality, in-school shootings—have somehow become routine, the day-to-day commonplaces of urban existence.

We and our colleagues have completed a study—entitled *Firearms, Violence and Inner-City Youth*—of where, how, and why urban juveniles acquire, carry, and use guns—the principal means by which inner-city violence is perpetrated. Our research was based on surveys of incarcerated juvenile offenders (mostly between the ages of 14 and 18) in four states, and high school students (both male and female) in five large cities in those same four states. Altogether, more than two thousand young people participated in the study. We focussed on these specific groups because they are popularly thought to experience high rates of violence (both as perpetrators and victims), belong to street gangs, and engage in drug use and trafficking. Ours is not a probability sample of U.S. juveniles, even of inner cities, but it is a very good sampling of the juvenile violence problem, nevertheless.

Concern about juvenile violence has resurfaced periodically throughout the twentieth century, but the situation today seems very different. The juvenile felons we studied are generally better armed, more criminally active, and more violent than were the adult felons of [the early 1980s]. Even at that, one is struck less by the armament than by the evident willingness of these juveniles to pull the trigger. From the viewpoint of public policy, we think it matters less where these juveniles get their guns than where they get the idea that it is acceptable to kill. The problem before us is not getting guns out of the hands of juveniles but rather reducing the motivations for juveniles to arm themselves in the first place.

The Urban Underclass

Owning and carrying guns were common behaviors in both our samples. About nine of every ten inmates had owned a gun at some time; one in five male students had a gun at the time they were surveyed; one in three carried a gun at least occasionally; 12 percent carried guns routinely, often to and from school. In the inner-city neighborhoods from which our respondents are drawn, firearms are among the many cheerless realities of daily existence. Violence and the means by which it is perpetrated have become endemic in the new subculture of the impoverished inner city—key elements in what has come to be known as the American underclass.

The social, economic, and structural conditions that have created the urban underclass are by now well known. The national poverty rate has been increasing since about 1980, and so the number of the poor has increased, especially in the central cities. The gap between affluence and poverty has also widened. Public schools are in disarray; drop-out rates are increasing; joblessness among young central city non-white males now routinely exceeds 50 percent. Conventional routes of upward mobility have been narrowed; the life chances of the children of the poor have grown progressively dimmer. The situation has degenerated to the point where, for many youth in the inner city, the odds of going to prison are higher than the odds of completing high school. Life in the urban underclass has truly become a life with no future.

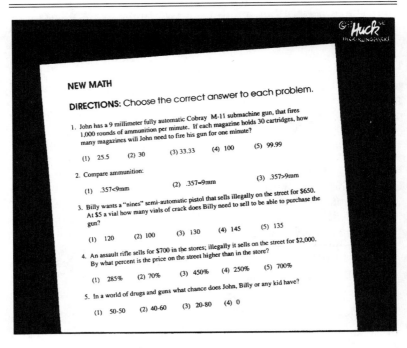

Gary Huck/UE/Huck/Konopacki. Reprinted with permission.

With no legitimate prospects for the future, life quickly becomes a quest for immediate gratification. Weighing the consequences of present behavior against their future implications thus becomes a meaningless exercise. Given a larger culture that increasingly defines personal worth in terms of one's ability to consume, and a social and economic situation where one's ability to consume often depends on being able to take what one wants, any sense of personal merit (or self-esteem) rather quickly comes to imply being stronger, meaner, and better-armed than the next person. Blood flows where life has no purpose.

The Logic of an Arms Race

We were struck especially by the quality of the firearms these juveniles possess. Theirs were not lesser weapons, Saturday night specials, homemade zip guns, or anything of the sort. Many of our juvenile felons were at least as well-armed as the police. Whether a matter of accessibility or preference, the most likely owned hand weapon in either sample was a revolver of at least .357 caliber.

Given the conditions of the inner city, the general ineffectiveness of conventional social control agents, and the pervasive atmosphere of violence and desperation, the preference for high-quality, high-firepower small arms is altogether understandable. Whether to protect what one has or to take by force what one wants, success depends on being adequately armed. The inner logic of an arms race seems to apply. No military force willingly enters battle with inferior weapons, and likewise, no central city resident would willingly carry anything other than the best small arms available.

We also learned that guns are easily and cheaply obtained by juveniles, and rarely through legitimate channels. Most of our respondents looked to family members and friends to sell, loan, or swap firearms to them. Street sources—drug dealers and junkies, primarily—were the next most common suppliers. Handguns of all sorts are typically bought for $100 or less, and even military-style rifles can be had for less than $300.

It is sobering that most of the methods used by our juvenile offenders to get guns are already against the law. It is illegal for juveniles to purchase handguns through normal retail channels. It is illegal to cross state lines to obtain guns. Theft of guns from homes, cars, and shipments is against the law; transferring or selling stolen property is also illegal. Transferring a firearm to a person with a criminal record is against the law. Possession of guns by persons with histories of alcohol or drug abuse is against the law. Street sources and friends who deal firearms to juveniles or who make proxy purchases for them are surely contributing to the delinquency of minors. The problem, clearly, is not that the appropriate laws do not exist. The problem is that the existing laws are not comprehensive, are not or cannot be enforced, and have little influence on people involved in firearms transactions with juveniles.

The total number of firearms now in circulation in the United

189

States is somewhere on the order of 200 million guns; half of all U.S. families possess them. The idea that new laws or stricter enforcement of existing laws would somehow prevent juveniles from getting their hands on some of these hundreds of millions of guns is fatuous. Efforts to control the supply of guns, in short, are essentially doomed; the extant supply is more than ample to satisfy every conceivable criminal purpose for several centuries. The only hope is therefore to reduce the demand for guns, which implies addressing the inner-city problems for which guns have become the solution.

Can Youths Survive Without Guns?

The potential for violence by some youths in certain neighborhoods is great, said [a 1993] report conducted by the Office of Juvenile Justice and Delinquency Prevention. The question, the report concludes, is not whether these young people will get guns—but whether society can "convince youths they can survive in their neighborhood without them."

An overwhelming number of juveniles who were students and inmates stated that they believed guns were needed for self-defense.

"For the majority of the respondents, self-protection in a hostile and violent world was the chief reason to own and carry a gun," the report states. About 45 percent of the 758 students interviewed at 10 inner-city public high schools said they had been threatened with a gun or had been shot at on the way to or from school during the previous few years. Nearly the same number said they had friends "who routinely carried guns."

Pierre Thomas, *The Washington Post National Weekly Edition*, December 20-26, 1993.

For the majority of youth we surveyed, inmates and students alike, self-protection in a hostile, violent and dangerous world was the chief reason to own and carry guns. The perception that so many other people are armed combines with the reality of frequent victimization, with routine transit through precarious places (including schools) and with routine involvement in dangerous activities (such as drug deals, gang ventures, and crimes)—creating a siege mentality among individuals, and a subculture of fear and desperation for inner-city youth as a whole. More than two-thirds of the inmates, for example, said they had fired guns in self-defense.

The perceived need for self-protection means that these juveniles are strongly, not weakly, motivated to own and carry guns. In neighborhoods ruled by predation, there is a weighty incentive not to become prey. Once a person has decided that his or her ability to survive depends on a gun's protection and power, the arguments against guns become unpersuasive. That many of our juveniles seek protection from one another does not diminish the point; if the issue is survival, then weapons are a bargain at any price.

Convincing inner-city juveniles (or adults) not to carry and use guns relies on convincing them they can survive in their neighborhoods without being armed, that they can come and go in peace, and that being unarmed will not subject them to victimization, intimidation, or death. It requires people to believe that customary social control agents can provide personal security. Short of this, gun carrying in the inner city will remain widespread.

Gangs, Drugs, and Gun Violence

The media have stressed the role drugs and gangs play in gun-related violence among juveniles. Our findings suggest a greater complexity to the relationships than is ordinarily assumed. While many of our juveniles used alcohol and drugs at least occasionally, few were heavy, regular users. Only about 5 percent each of the male students had ever used heroin, cocaine, or crack. At 21 percent, 43 percent, and 25 percent each, the inmates used these drugs more, but still only a minority of them. The popular image of inner-city youth (especially those involved in crime) as drug addicts, one and all, was not supported. But when drug use of any kind increased, so also did criminal behavior, gun possession, and gun use.

Drugs have certainly worsened inner-city crime and violence, but drugs per se are not the ultimate cause. Drugs are primarily attractive because they provide immediate gratification; arguments against using drugs—that one might become an addict or eventually destroy one's physical health—all require an orientation towards the future, a concern about tomorrow's consequences for today's behaviors. The structural conditions of the inner city have ground out precisely this sort of orientation among its youth. Drugs are not the cause of crime and violence so much as the symptoms of the general unraveling of the norms, values, and expectations that would otherwise constrain behavior. A subculture has arisen in the central city where anything goes, a hostile subculture estranged from the larger society's behavioral norms.

The drug epidemic has become a convenient scapegoat for the central city's ills. Yet drug use is only symptomatic of more basic problems. Central city youth have come to inhabit a moral universe that ascribes no particular value to a human life, counsels no hesitancy in pulling the trigger, and insists on immediate gratification—for the simple reason that tomorrow may never

191

come. Central city juveniles carry guns, use and deal drugs, join gangs, and commit crimes and violence all for the same reasons: they have no discernible future to which they might aspire and therefore nothing better to do.

The same holds for gangs; they too provide an easy but false explanation for inner-city afflictions. As a form of social organization, gangs do not spring ex nihilo from the minds of the wicked; they exist for certain purposes. In the context of the contemporary urban underclass, they provide safety in numbers and some degree of control in what are otherwise disorganized neighborhoods. Urban gangs have assumed the *social control* function no longer effectively performed by customary agents of social control; they are the lawless equivalent of law enforcement. They give estranged youth something meaningful to which they can belong, an identity otherwise lacking. Gangs express the pathology of inner-city life and the new urban culture of violence, but are the consequence of these developments, not the cause.

Addressing Urban Conditions

Many of the terms of contemporary debate about juvenile violence—drugs, gangs, even guns themselves—are epiphenomenal [secondary problems]. They provide a method of restating the problem but cannot suggest a solution. Guns, drugs, gangs, crime, and violence express a pervasive alienation of inner-city youth from the conventions of larger society. We—the larger society—can try to impose our will, pass new regulatory legislation, and promote harsher punishments for those who defy our rules. But until we rectify the conditions that breed hostility, estrangement, futility and hopelessness, whatever else we do will come to little or nothing.

Every major U.S. city could make a substantial short-term dent in its crime and violence problems by imprisoning several hundred of its most notorious juvenile offenders. But so long as conditions themselves remain unchanged, there would soon be several hundred new offenders to take their place. Shall we continue this process until we have incarcerated an entire class of the urban population? Keeping guns from juveniles poses exactly the same problems as keeping them from adult felons. As we have stressed, juveniles are strongly motivated to carry guns, and their sources are inherently difficult to regulate. If economists are right that demand creates its own supply, then approaching the problem of guns and violence from only the supply side would fall short of a solution. The only solution is to address the conditions that cause people to want guns in the first place.

The central cities have become remarkably unsafe because decades of indifference to their social and economic problems have bred an entire class of people with no stake in their own

192

futures. Isolation, hopelessness, and fatalism, coupled with the steady deterioration of stabilizing social institutions and the police's inability to maintain security, breed an environment where *success* implies predation, and survival depends on one's ability to defend against it. Widespread joblessness and few opportunities for upward mobility are the heart of the problem. Stricter gun control laws, more aggressive enforcement of existing laws, a crackdown on drug traffic, police task forces directed at juvenile gangs, metal detectors at the doors of schools, periodic searches of lockers and shake-downs of students, and other similar measures are inconsequential compared to the true need: the economic, social, and moral resurrection of the inner city. Just how this might be accomplished and at what cost can be debated; the urgent need to do so cannot.

"Since the [1967] Gault *decision provided every juvenile with an attorney, the idea has been to beat the system. Kids view it as a game."*

Violent Juvenile Criminals Should Be Tried As Adults

Rita Kramer

The 1967 *Gault* decision by the Supreme Court extended to juveniles in delinquency proceedings the same constitutional rights as adults, including the right to counsel. In the following viewpoint, Rita Kramer argues that the *Gault* decision, along with rules that protect the confidentiality of the names and records of juvenile offenders, enables young criminals to evade serious punishment and commit repeated crimes. Kramer advocates removing the secrecy from juvenile criminal proceedings and instituting mandatory sentencing so that violent, repeat offenders and potential career criminals can be identified and diverted into the adult criminal justice system. Kramer is author of *At a Tender Age: Violent Youth and Juvenile Justice.*

As you read, consider the following questions:

1. According to Kramer, what idea is the juvenile justice system based on?
2. According to the author, what are the traits of potential career criminals? What does she think can be done for them?
3. What are the possible benefits to juveniles of trying them in adult courts, according to Kramer?

Throughout the country, district attorneys are naming juvenile crime as the number-one crime problem and reform of the juvenile justice system as their top priority.

According to the FBI's Uniform Crime Reports, of those arrested between 1987 and 1992 for the most violent crimes, 29% were under the age of 18. A study released by Northeastern University's College of Criminal Justice last year [1992] reported that between 1985 and 1991 the number of 17-year-olds arrested for murder increased by 121%, the number of 16-year-olds by 158%, and the number of 15-year-olds by 217%. Most shocking of all, the number of arrests of boys 12 and under doubled.

The juvenile justice system, based on the 1950s profile of the delinquent and codified in the early 1960s, is still based on the idea that bad boys deserve another chance and can be reformed by the efforts of psychologists and social workers. It keeps the names and records of juvenile offenders confidential while providing juveniles with attorneys whose job it is to help them beat the rap. The result is a revolving-door pattern that repeatedly sends dangerous youths back to the streets. The four teenagers charged with the murder of a British tourist in Florida in September 1993 were no strangers to the court. They all had been arrested before. The 13-year-old in fact, had been arrested 15 times on more than 50 charges. At the time of his first arrest he was 7 years old.

Open Juvenile Criminal Records

It is clear that the present system of juvenile justice has failed either to deter violent crime by the young or to rehabilitate young criminals. And so public prosecutors have been considering ways to change things. First on many of their agendas is transferring violent juvenile recidivists to the adult system and getting rid of the secrecy in juvenile court that prevents the public from knowing how often a juvenile offender commits a crime.

Gus Sandstrom, district attorney in Pueblo, Colorado, and chairman of the juvenile committee of the National District Attorneys Association, predicts that by 1996 every state will be reexamining its juvenile policies and programs. "For the first time in years," he says, "prosecutors are being listened to. There is a growing public demand to know who's doing all this, to do something about the victimizers. And the media is claiming the right to know. Confidentiality is going out the window. The trend is toward looking at consequences as opposed to treatment." Colorado has already passed legislation allowing the release of the names of juveniles charged with violent offenses or with illegal possession of a handgun.

Other states are following suit. Efforts are under way to rewrite the juvenile justice codes in Minnesota, Michigan, Florida, Utah,

Oregon and Kansas, and prosecutors are taking a hard look at the laws in Pennsylvania, South Dakota, Hawaii and Texas.

Speed Up the Justice System

Another problem is the slowness of the criminal justice system. Too many teenagers wait weeks or even months for a court appearance. By the time they come to court the incident that prompted their arrest has become a vague memory. In many cases they've already committed other crimes. And the case is often dismissed, leaving the juvenile with no sense of any consequences following from his behavior. The system in New York City is particularly slow, which might explain why almost a quarter of the nation's arrests of youths under 16 for robbery go through New York's Family Court.

Peter Reinharz, who heads the Family Court Division of New York City's Law Department, says: "The state assembly continues to reject proposals to do away with the rules whereby the names and the records of anyone in Family Court under 16 are confidential information. There is no way of telling how many times a kid carrying a loaded weapon has been picked up before on the same charge. And the kids all know it." New York appears to be one of the last holdouts, as other states press for change in a juvenile justice system that doesn't work.

The Cost to Society Is the Same

Moving juveniles into adult courts might be an effective strategy for all juvenile cases—particularly cases involving repeat juvenile offenders. Since the cost to society is the same regardless of the age of the criminal, why should juvenile offenders receive lighter sentences than adults? After all, it is no secret that juvenile courts are considerably more lenient than adult courts. And it stands to reason that the threat of spending more time in prison rather than less time in a juvenile detention center would have a significant deterrent effect. Since the vast majority of states do not gain jurisdiction over young offenders in criminal courts until the age of 18, it is not surprising that criminal activity is so prevalent among the young, since they pay such a low "price" for it.

Robert L. Sexton, *Conservative Review*, November/December 1993.

Another focus of reform is early intervention, which becomes possible when violent juveniles are prosecuted as adults. Eliminating the secrecy surrounding juvenile court deliberations makes it possible to take into account a history of violent criminal acts.

"There should be more emphasis on intervention and prevention, the earlier the better, where there is a clear pattern," says Michael Tranbarger, special assistant to the Los Angeles district attorney. He points to the Orange County, California, probation department, which has come up with a solution that is becoming a model for others around the country.

Identify Career Criminals Early

Orange County's 7-year study of thousands of youths in juvenile institutions or on probation showed that about 70% of first-time offenders were never arrested again. Around 8% became chronic offenders, responsible for more than half of the repeat appearances in the juvenile system. Analysis of that 8% revealed traits that make it possible to spot a potential career criminal the first time he is charged.

These teenagers, typically 15 or younger at the time of their first offense, had problems at school (failure, truancy, suspensions or expulsions), problems at home (parental death or divorce, family conflict, child abuse or neglect, criminal relatives), a history of drug or alcohol abuse, or a pattern of delinquency (history of running away, stealing, gang membership). Identifying first-time offenders with these warning signs makes it possible to focus efforts on turning them around before it's too late.

Says Mr. Tranbarger: "We've been taking a hard look at intervention and prevention programs for that small group of recidivists who commit the most violent crimes so that prosecutors and social service agencies can concentrate their efforts on the most at-risk. It's a form of triage."

Programs based on early intervention are under consideration in many states. David Quantz, chief counsel for the division of child advocacy of the Pima County attorney's office in Tucson, Arizona, says, "Instead of a judge guessing whether a kid will be a repeat offender or not, we are trying to create legislation that will provide an objective basis for automatic transfer of violent recidivists to the adult criminal system."

Try Juveniles in Adult Court

There would be clear criteria for sentencing, based on the type of offense, the age of the offender and the number of offenses he's committed. Those transferred to the adult court would be given the due process protections of a jury trial. If the verdict is guilty, the judge will have the options of suspending the sentence, putting the juvenile on probation or remanding him to a youth center. If he gets into trouble again, the judge can revoke the earlier decision and sentence him as an adult, both for the earlier crime and the new one. That means prison (in which he would be separated, however, from the adult prisoners). "We would no longer have to guess which kids will turn out to be chronic and violent offenders," says Mr. Quantz. "It will be decided by the kid's own behavior."

Not only will the new rules attempt to identify the potentially dangerous at an early stage in their criminal activities, they will be aimed at a younger and younger group, the 8-, 9- and 10-year-olds, whom Colorado's Mr. Sandstrom calls "the fastest growing segment of kids committing crimes." On the basis of recent studies of urban violence by juveniles, the optimal age for intervention has been revised downward to age 8. Not surprisingly, burglary has replaced truancy as the number-one indicator of future criminal activity.

In Chicago there is automatic transfer to the adult system of 15- and 16-year-olds charged with murder, armed robbery with a gun, aggravated criminal sexual assault, possession of drugs on school grounds or selling drugs within 1,000 feet of a school. But Assistant State's Attorney Cheryl D. Cesario, family issues coordinator for Cook County, Illinois, says that efforts to transfer 13- and 14-year-old serious offenders to the adult system still meet with resistance on the part of juvenile-court advocates. "Since the [1967] *Gault* decision provided every juvenile with an attorney, the idea has been to beat the system. Kids view it as a game."

It's too early to tell whether efforts to divert the very youngest of the young troublemakers before they become habitual criminals will prove effective. But mandatory sentencing might serve to send the message to repeat offenders that they'll no longer get a free ride from a system without serious sanctions. It might even turn some young criminals around. At the very least, it should help make our cities safer by taking some violent offenders off the streets.

*"The 'waiving' of juveniles into adult courts
protects neither the public nor the children."*

Juvenile Criminals Should Not Be Tried As Adults

Alex Kotlowitz

According to a poll cited in the following viewpoint, three-quarters of Americans think children who commit violent crimes should be tried as adults. Alex Kotlowitz counters that juveniles should not be tried as adults because they are not mature enough to make adult decisions. Kotlowitz argues that adult trials for juveniles do not deter other juveniles from committing crimes as they are intended to. Kotlowitz is the author of *There Are No Children Here: The Story of Two Boys Growing Up in the Other America.*

As you read, consider the following questions:

1. According to Kotlowitz, what premise were juvenile courts founded on?
2. How are children developmentally different from adults, according to the author?
3. According to Kotlowitz, what assumption does the law-and-order approach make?

Jacqueline Ross has handled upward of 3,000 cases in her five years as a public defender, all in Chicago's imposing Criminal Courts building. She represents mostly young men, many of whom have been in prison before. But one case still haunts her—that of Pauletta R., who, at the age of 14, was charged with first-degree murder. Pauletta and three girlfriends schemed to lure a man into an alley for sex where another companion, a man in his 20's, waited with a handgun. The robbery went sour and the young man shot the intended robbery victim.

During the trial, Ross recalls, Pauletta would sit at the defense table, her head buried in her hands, her thumb in her mouth. At other times, during particularly tense moments, she would rock in her chair, childlike.

"She had very little idea what was going on," Ross recalls. "She should have been tried in juvenile court."

Pauletta is one of thousands of children who, accused of violent—and in recent years nonviolent—crimes are transferred to adult court, where retribution rather than rehabilitation is the result, if not the objective. This, according to a *USA Today/ CNN/Gallup* Poll, is what the public wants. Three-quarters of those polled said children who commit a violent crime should be treated as adults.

The "Adultification" of Children

As more and more juveniles are arrested for murder, rape and armed robbery—arrests for violent crimes went up 27 percent in the decade between 1980 and 1990—politicians, partly out of desperation, partly out of fear (for their jobs), are cracking down on kids. It is a frenzy that child advocates have labeled the "adultification" of children. In 1993 alone, the Colorado, Utah and Florida Legislatures passed laws making it easier to try certain youth offenders as adults. A number of other states are considering similar legislation. Senator Carol Moseley-Braun, the freshman Illinois Democrat, has introduced a measure calling for the automatic transfer of juveniles as young as 13 who are accused of Federal crimes.

The juvenile courts were founded on the premise that they could be more flexible in working with children; there the accused would be defined less by their offenses than by their youth and their need for adult guidance and care. In juvenile court, the judge—in consultation with probation officers, psychologists and social workers—has great leeway as to what kind of treatment and punishment to impose. Children, because their personalities are still in the process of formation, are thought to be more open to rehabilitation than adults. The "waiving" of juveniles into adult courts protects neither the public nor the children. Consider Pauletta's case.

200

On the night of July 27, 1991, Pauletta drove around the streets of a tough neighborhood on the North Side of Chicago with three girlfriends and a young man named Michael Brandon. They stopped to chat with a neighborhood gang leader whom Pauletta's sister owed $100. He told Pauletta that if she didn't come up with the money, he'd hurt her. Pauletta and her friends, one of whom was also in debt to the gang leader, then drew up a plan. They'd pose as prostitutes and rob a customer.

The Serious Nature of Pauletta's Crime

In the early hours of the next day, the four girls primped and posed on a street corner when a young man approached them for sex. They told him he could have his pick. He chose Pauletta's friend, Robin, also 14. Robin and her prey walked into a nearby alley where Brandon lurked in the shadows with a pistol. A struggle ensued, and Brandon shot once, killing his victim. Pauletta heard the gunshot as she walked toward a friend's house. Within hours, the police arrested Pauletta—as well as the four others. All five were charged with first-degree murder.

The Worst of Both Worlds

America's juvenile justice system was envisioned to be a humane process of rehabilitating wayward kids rather than merely punishing them. Not only has that mission failed, it may be scrubbed.

Echoing the language of the U.S. Supreme Court, . . . some legal experts charge that juveniles still get the "worst of both worlds"— neither the due-process safeguards guaranteed adults . . . nor the solicitous care intended for children.

Critics charge that there is neither funding for juvenile programs nor attention from the rest of the legal community to solve fundamental problems. Congressional reforms also have had limited success. At the same time, many states have weakened juvenile judges' authority through new "get-tough" laws that funnel youths directly into criminal courts.

Paul Marcotte, *ABA Journal*, April 1990.

Given the serious nature of the crime, the prosecution asked the courts to try this eighth grader as an adult. The court psychologist, Nancy Feys, testified that Pauletta, who lived on welfare with her mother, had "serious problems with depression" and functioned "like a small child" with wide mood swings, including suicidal impulses. Pauletta had told the psychologist, "I just don't like the world," according to court documents.

Feys urged that Pauletta be placed in a long-term residential treatment center; both she and Pauletta's probation officer recommended that Pauletta remain in the juvenile system. The judge, though, sent her to adult court where she was found not guilty of murder, but guilty of armed robbery. She received a six-year sentence that insured she would spend her formative teen-age years behind bars.

The crackdown on children has gone well beyond those accused of violent crimes. In Florida, for example, between October 1990 and June 1991, 3,248 children were transferred to adult court for offenses as serious as murder and as trivial as possession of alcohol. And Florida is not alone.

Automatic Transfer to the Adult System

In November 1993, I met Brian H. and his father, Leon, a supervisor at an electrical company, in Courtroom 301 of the same Criminal Courts building where Pauletta's case was heard. Brian, dressed in a gray suit and tasseled brown loafers, sat erect on the bench, nervously clenching his hands as he awaited the judge's arrival. His father leaned over to straighten his tie.

Brian is 15. He had been arrested and charged with possessing 1.9 grams of cocaine with the intent to deliver. This would be Brian's first offense, but because he was accused of selling drugs on the sidewalk near a local elementary school, he will be tried in the adult courts. Under Illinois law, any child charged with dealing narcotics within 1,000 feet of a school or public housing property is automatically transferred into the adult system.

"What does a kid know at 15?" asks his father. "How can you hold a kid at that age responsible for adulthood? There's got to be another way."

Children like Pauletta and Brian live in neighborhoods that don't allow much room for adolescent mistakes. They experience more than they should. In the summer of 1993, for instance, Brian saw a friend shot in the forearm; another schoolmate was killed in a gang shoot-out. Pauletta came from a family shattered by alcohol and domestic violence. Still, despite the wreckage caused by astronomical unemployment, daily gunfire and inadequate schools, they are just children. They hunt for snakes, ride bikes, play video games and go on dates. They are also impulsive and silly. They often make wrongheaded decisions. They're easily swayed by peers.

A Child in the Wrong Place

Treating adolescents as adults ignores the fact that they are developmentally different. "We can't rewire them," says Dr. Katherine Kaufer Christoffel, a pediatrician and director of the Violent Injury Prevention Center at Children's Memorial Medical Center in Chicago. "It seems like we're saying, 'Don't be a child in the wrong place.'"

Dr. Christoffel argues that preventing youth crime requires changing the child's environment. She cites studies indicating that the greatest impact on diminishing drunken driving among teen-agers comes from changes like curfews, alcohol-free proms and raising the driving age to 17.

Dr. Christoffel is concerned about what she perceives as a backlash toward children. "To the extent that parents and community fail, society has to back them up," she says. What has society done to back up urban children and their parents? Not much.

Juvenile-Court Judges Oppose Get-Tough Approach

New laws . . . lower the age at which teenagers can be prosecuted as adults for certain violent or repeat offenses.

This get-tough approach, a National Council of Juvenile and Family Court Judges (NCJFCJ) statement says, "means that juveniles who commit violent crimes should not be treated as individuals who can be rehabilitated, but rather as individuals who should be temporarily warehoused for public safety."

The judges cite studies indicating that they impose punishments on youth just as stiff as those criminal courts do, and that juvenile courts are more likely to impose sanctions on young criminals than criminal courts—which dismiss many of the cases transferred from the juvenile-justice system.

The NCJFCJ statement insists that "protection of public safety remains the paramount goal of the juvenile court in dealing with violent juvenile crime.". . . The juvenile-court judges acknowledge the need to transfer some hard-core cases to the adult criminal courts, but they oppose the mandatory transfer provisions for violent offenders contained in many federal and state bills.

James H. Andrews, *The Christian Science Monitor*, March 3, 1994.

Brian's situation is illustrative. When he first showed signs of trouble—coming home late, failing classes, being suspended for fistfights at school and wearing expensive jewelry—his parents sought help. The assistance Brian could receive at his school is limited; there's only one full-time social worker and one part-time psychologist for 1,700 students. His parents called the juvenile detention center to ask if Brian could visit the facility. They hoped that might shake him up. Officials there don't give tours and had no suggestions for referral. His father then called the local police station to ask if an officer would come to their house to talk with Brian. But the police, according to his parents, said they couldn't do anything until Brian got into trouble.

"We wanted to frighten him," Brian's mother says. "We wanted him to get back on track. I was under the impression that as a parent if you were willing to work within the system you could get help."

Transfer Laws Don't Deter Crime

Children need to face consequences, particularly if they're involved in criminal activity. They cannot be absolved of responsibility. Moreover, the painful truth is that some children need to be locked up for a long time, if for no other reason than to assure public safety. But a blanket policy of sending children like Pauletta and Brian into the adult courts is a grievously misguided policy. This law-and-order approach assumes that trying kids as grown-ups will deter crime. But longer sentences haven't necessarily reduced adult crime. Worse, these transfer laws often have an unintended consequence. The criminal courts are already so overburdened that some adult-court judges have shown a propensity to give children lighter sentences than they might receive in juvenile court.

The debate over treating juvenile offenders as adults is more than a debate over youth crime; it gets to the fundamental question of what it means to be a child, particularly in an increasingly violent world. Children need help navigating through what can be a treacherous adolescent maze. That is why children can't marry without permission of their parents, why children can't buy liquor—and why society created Juvenile courts.

"What's so disturbing," says Felton Earls, a professor at the School of Public Health at Harvard University, "is to see a legal process that's lowering the age of adulthood rather than seeing this as a failure of social structures and policy towards our children."

When I met Brian and his father at court, their case was continued to another date. In the hallway, they huddled with their lawyer.

"Is it very serious?" Brian asked, his hands buried deep in his pants pockets, his eyes riveted on his tasseled shoes.

"It doesn't get much more serious than this," his attorney told him.

Because of mandatory-minimum sentencing, if found guilty, Brian—tried as an adult—will receive a sentence of at least six years. Moreover, he will carry for life the stamp of a convicted felon, making it difficult to find employment.

"I'm scared to go back," Brian told me. (He spent three weeks in a detention facility for juveniles.) "I got plans to do with my life." He says he wants to be an electrical engineer, just like his dad.

As for Pauletta, she's due to be released from the Illinois Youth Center at Warrenville in July 1994, at which time she'll be a month away from turning 18. She will re-enter society without a high-school diploma and without the kind of intense counseling the court psychologist said she needed.

Pauletta and Brian made mistakes. Were they big enough that society should snatch away their childhoods?

"[Boot camps enforce] the human qualities of dignity and self-respect that are fostered by hard work and accomplishment."

Prison Boot Camps Can Reform Young Offenders

Dennis E. Mack

Military-style boot camps for young, first-time offenders are a popular trend and have been advocated by President Bill Clinton. In the following viewpoint, Dennis E. Mack describes a boot camp program in New York City and outlines the theory behind it. In support of boot camps, he cites statistics to show the success of the New York State program. Mack, who has taught in the New York City school system, is currently an educational instructor at the Rikers Island High Impact Incarceration Program, New York City's program for first-time offenders.

As you read, consider the following questions:

1. The author states that boot camp drill instructors may demand push-ups for any infraction of the rules. What is his view of the benefits of this sort of punishment?
2. What are the five objectives of shock incarceration programs and how does the author say they are met?
3. According to Mack, why do boot camp inmates "squeal" on each other?

Dennis E. Mack, "Rikers Boot Camp," *American Jails*, May/June 1992. Reprinted (without footnotes) by permission of the American Jail Association.

It's 5:00 a.m. at Rikers Island, in New York City, in the yard of the Correctional Institution for Men, one of nine Rikers facilities that incarcerates youths and adults (50,000) for up to eighteen months. Make no mistake about it, what is happening in this yard is diametrically opposed to media images perpetuated by movies such as *Bad Boys, An Innocent Man, Lock-Up, Penitentiary,* or countless other films. In this yard, inmates don't have to "play the dozens" (an insult game), "diss" (disrespect) each other, or otherwise strut their stuff in order to avoid being physically and/or emotionally victimized by other inmates.

In the High Impact Incarceration Program (HIIP), first piloted in October 1990, inmates between the ages of 19 and 35, sentenced to terms of more than 90 days for a nonviolent crime, undergo a strict 60-day boot camp program where they receive strict disciplinary guidance, intensive physical activity, military precision drills, substance abuse [treatment], educational classes in G.E.D. [General Educational Development—a high school diploma program], Pre-G.E.D. and Data Entry, and career and educational counseling.

A Program That Stresses Teamwork

The drill instructor, who adopts a mean-looking, no-nonsense demeanor, who is wearing a sharply pressed brown uniform, a Stetson campaign hat and black boots, barks out commands to a company of Alpha Teammates (inmates).

"To the left . . . to the left . . . to the left . . . right . . . left . . ."

He growls at Alpha because a teammate has turned in the wrong direction.

"Do you teammates know the difference between your left and right?"

Alpha Company stares into the distance, eyes straight ahead, bodies locked and cocked, in drill instructor lexicon. They look straight, turn, and answer.

"Sir . . .Yes, Sir . . ."

The drill instructor barks back, "Then one of you is acting like an individual."

In a program that stresses teamwork being called an individual is tantamount to being "dissed" in front of your peers. In the High Impact Incarceration Program, the brainchild of former New York City Correction Commissioner Allyn R. Sielaff, inmates call each other teammates because they're being molded into a community. They drill in formation, participate in meetings where they're prodded into admitting their failures, and attend remedial classes and drug counseling sessions.

In a traditional Rikers setting many inmates believe in a code which contains behavioral expectations of conduct. This code adheres to the principle that the best prisoner is pro-prisoner, and thus anti-administration. Thus, a squealer, rat, or weakling can be victimized physically, materially, and sexually.

In 1990 and 1991 more than 8,000 inmates were stabbed and eight homicides occurred on the rock [Rikers Island].

Rikers inmate terminology makes reference to "chickens," "ducks," "guerrillas," "maytags," and "new jacks." A "chicken" is young, tender, inexperienced, and, if space considerations permitted it, would greatly benefit from being placed in protective custody. A "duck" is an easily intimidated person often unfamiliar with jailhouse inmate hierarchy. A "guerrilla" intimidates others and a "maytag" is coerced into washing another's clothes.

A "new jack" who arrives in a New York City correctional facility with any possession may have to "play the corner" to protect his bounty. "New jacks" must often fight in order to establish their dominance and avoid "being played for a sucker."

Clinton Administration Support for Boot Camps

Thirty states and the federal government have experimented with boot camps to address an ongoing national problem: too few prison cells and tougher mandatory sentences that will only aggravate overcrowded prisons.

In some ways, boot camps are a practical solution. [Clinton] administration officials say they free up space by allowing judges to sentence first-time nonviolent offenders to temporary incarceration rather than longer jail stays, and they curb crime by placing offenders in an environment free of career criminals where discipline, respect for authority, and hard work are taught.

"If you put more first-time offenders into boot camps, then you free up space for hard criminals in state and federal penitentiaries," said Bill Adams, Senate Judiciary Committee press secretary. "And, simultaneously, you're keeping these new offenders away from the criminal culture of prisons."

Angela E. Couloumbis, *The Christian Science Monitor*, March 2, 1994.

In high impact incarceration, an alternative to regular incarceration, participants are obligated to follow ten general orders. The second general order is, "I will refrain from the use of violence and the threat of violence." Other general orders demand that teammates "Follow All Orders Given by All Staff at All Times," "Will Not Use Drugs or Alcohol," "Will Tell the Truth with Compassion," "Will Speak and Act with Good Purpose," "Will Remain Alert and Participate in Network (Counseling) at All Times," "Will Adhere to the Network Group Contract at All

Times," "Will Maintain Military Bearing at All Times," "Will Maintain a Positive Attitude at All Times," and "Will Remain Alert and Participate in All Classroom and Outdoor Sessions."

Inmates Have Little Time for Mayhem

Since the inception of the program there have been no stabbings or slashings, which, given the violent nature of many New York City inmates, is no small accomplishment. Inmates, who begin their day at 5:00 a.m., are closely supervised to the point where their bathroom time is limited, and must be in bed with lights out by 10:00 p.m., have little time or inclination for violence or mayhem.

Drill instructors demand push-ups for talking out of turn, eyeballing staff, any infraction of the rules, or simply because they're trying to make an example out of someone.

High impact incarceration confers the same disciplinary powers on civilians as it does on drill instructors. A teacher who catches a student sleeping in class can force that individual to do push-ups. In a traditional correctional setting a teacher would have to refer that sleeping student to a correctional officer; a teammate caught sleeping will do at least 25 push-ups, and more often than not apologize to the instructor for "losing focus."

Teammates are required to wear their hair short-cropped, aren't allowed to watch television, and cannot wear flashy jewelry. Those who don't conform often participate in a "learning experience." These "experiences" could include wearing a children's bib or walking around with a degrading sign around the neck. Their reward for successfully completing the program is the opportunity for early release, parole, or work release as well as the reduction of as much as three months off their period of confinement.

HIIP represents an innovative, although not unique, form of rehabilitation. Former Commissioner Sielaff maintains that "perhaps the most compelling benefit of HIIP is the rehabilitative effect of enforcing the human qualities of dignity and self-respect that are fostered by hard work and accomplishment. Through HIIP, inmates are given an opportunity to help themselves begin a new life, with a sense of hope and determination."

Five Objectives for Boot Camps

Today's shock incarceration can be traced to the 19th century practice of affording young offenders the option of joining the military or serving time. The New York State Reformatory at Elmira utilized a military training model, including the execution of the manual of arms and five to eight hours a day of marching, from 1888 to 1920.

Five objectives are characteristic for boot camp programs: specific deterrence, general deterrence, rehabilitation, incapacitation and reduction of overcrowding, and cost savings [for the state]. An extremely structured period of incarceration is theoretically supposed to engender a strong disincentive for an individual to commit behavior leading to a return to prison (specific deterrence).

The punishment aspects of boot camp, such as early wake up, constant exercise, quick punishment for minor rules infractions, are supposed to have a deterrent effect on the general population.

Two types of rehabilitation are supposed to take place in shock incarceration: rehabilitation by transference and rehabilitation by treatment. Hopefully, the structured lifestyle and personal disciplines inculcated in boot camp will create behaviors that are transferable to the outside world. These behaviors include self-control and self-esteem and the ability to cope with stress. The treatment model encompasses programs designed to deal with aggressive behavior and substance abuse, and improve job skills.

Boot camp provides a structured, physically demanding environment which quenches the public's desire for retribution.

Even though shock incarceration inmates are incapacitated for relatively short amounts of time, they are still off the street and cannot commit other offenses (incapacitation).

Most prison systems are filled to capacity, and shock incarceration programs can reduce overcrowding by diverting inmates from longer prison terms.

How Boot Camps Differ from Prison

If a man is successfully recruited for the HIIP, he lives in one of seven structures built around the Correctional Institution for Men. If he flunks out of HIIP, he returns to the general population, a sanction that the drill instructors hope will be taken seriously.

Teammates in the high impact program will sometimes "squeal" on each other to drill instructors because many of them embrace the general orders of the program. They also don't have to be concerned about the often general rule of thumb concerning the fate of squealers, "Snitches get stitches."

HIIP teammates are able to purchase only basic toiletries and cigarettes from commissary, thus eliminating a significant amount of the hustles that take place in a general population setting.

Boot camp enrollees perform landscaping, painting, and other housekeeping responsibilities. During the last two weeks of the program, supervised work crews do community service work in various neighborhoods under the auspices of the Environmental Protection Agency and the city's Department of Parks and Recreation and Sanitation.

One staff member claims, "Let us have a knucklehead, and

we'll instill discipline and self-respect or die trying."

As staff members and teammates readily agree, "Just because you can talk right and walk right doesn't mean you'll do right in New York." Shock incarceration is often viewed as a rehabilitation panacea which can provide retribution, deter crime, cut prison costs and overcrowding, and reduce recidivism through rehabilitation.

A New York State program first created in 1987 claims many successes. On a "positive adjustment scale," measuring recidivism with variables such as steady employment and participation in employment programs, shock incarceration graduates scored 33 percent higher than those incarcerated with the general population, [according to the New York State Division of Parole].

A positive adjustment scale also compared shock graduates with general population inmates in relation to work, family, community, and reclamation. Boot camp graduates scored 56 percent higher than the control group in attaining vertical mobility in education, employment, or vocational training. In addition, a 107 percent increase was observed over the control group in participation in self-improvement and therapy programs. Meaningful advantages were also recorded in attaining financial stability (28 percent), keeping a job for at least six months (24 percent), and supporting family members (10 percent).

New York State statistics on recidivism showed that one year after graduation from the program only 23 percent of the six platoons analyzed had been reincarcerated, while 28 percent of a comparison group released from traditional incarceration had been reincarcerated.

One must consider the fact that these positive statistics have been generated because New York has maybe the most strict eligibility standards in the country. The criteria include no previous incarcerations. In contrast to the state inmate boot camp population, the vast majority of inmates on Rikers have been previously incarcerated.

If New York City's HIIP can be half as successful as New York State's Shock Incarceration program, HIIP should be viewed as an overwhelming success. This type of incarceration can benefit inmates, employees, corrections systems, and government budgets. If boot camps continue to serve a function among an array of sentencing alternatives such as electronic monitoring, intensive supervision, community service, parole, and others, we can take the first step on the long road toward saving the inner city.

"No one has shown clearly that this approach to punishment [boot camps] actually helps turn young lawbreakers away from crime."

Prison Boot Camps May Not Reform Young Offenders

Frank Bentayou

President Clinton's 1993-94 crime bill included a proposal to expand the use of shock incarceration, the increasingly popular boot camp programs for first-time offenders. In the following viewpoint, Frank Bentayou gives an account of a boot camp program in Ohio and offers some reasons why these programs are becoming so popular. Bentayou cites critics of such programs, who argue that boot camps are more expensive than traditional prisons and that the brutal treatment of young prisoners may instill hostility in volatile youths. Further, these critics contend that boot camps employ rehabilitative techniques that could reform young offenders if used in traditional prison settings. Bentayou is a freelance writer from Ohio.

As you read, consider the following questions:

1. What is the possible danger of arbitrary discipline, according to the author?
2. According to Ralph Coyle, as quoted by the author, what is the appeal of shock incarceration for the American public?
3. Ronald Powell, quoted by Bentayou, believes that shock incarceration can reduce recidivism. How do critics respond?

From Frank Bentayou, "The New Chain Gangs," *The Progressive*, August 1992. Reprinted with permission from *The Progressive*, 409 E. Main St., Madison, WI 53703.

Shift-change time at Ohio's Southeast Correctional Institution: Guards are laughing as Sergeant J.A. Jeff Scudder, a short bull of a man, struggles to fold up the sleeves of his black uniform. The coarse fabric barely stretches over his upper arms, which are thick as hams.

Scudder's first job today is showing nine new prisoners how to "make a tight rack"—straighten up their beds, he politely explains—and stow their gear. But first he girds himself for battle. After wrestling with the sleeves, he slips a stiff-brim drill-instructor's hat onto his head, bristling with stubble from a close cut.

"You have to teach these guys everything," he says. Calm and neat in his starched uniform, Scudder strolls toward a group of men wearing tattered white jumpsuits and clutching laundry bags. As he approaches, he suddenly explodes and shoots out his hands to grab two prisoners, jerking them toward a wall.

"All right, you pigs, maggots!" Scudder shouts. "Get over here at attention! Now!" A few croak a hasty, "Sir, yes sir!" as they scramble to comply, but Scudder swirls and seizes a youth by the collar.

"What's a matter with you, puke?" Scudder yells in his face, his voice breaking, eyes popping from their sockets. "Haven't you learned how to talk to a guard?"

"Sir, no sir! Yes, sir—" the man stammers.

"You disgusting maggot!" Scudder screams. "Gimme twenty pushups." He hurls him to the floor, then whirls and snatches two laundry bags. In a rage, he dumps them on the floor, too, and kicks the limp garments repeatedly as the prisoners stare at him.

Scudder's dramatic transformation might amaze anybody who hasn't spent time around an institution like this one. It was my second day visiting Camp REAMS, so I understood that the young guard behaved as he is paid to do and that the facility he works for is not like most other prisons.

A Fast-Growing Trend

In fact, REAMS—the acronym stands for Respect, Education, Attitude, Motivation, and Success—is one of at least thirty-four boot camps launched by U.S. prison systems between 1983 and 1992. State corrections officials and lawmakers are so impressed with them that they're planning at least ten more. Aimed at young, usually first-time offenders convicted of nonviolent crimes, they embody military-style discipline, chain-gang labor, and often the kind of brutal treatment Scudder displays. To the chagrin of earnest prison reformers, it is just those features that have made "shock incarceration" the fastest-growing trend in penology, applauded in middle America and embraced by recent Administrations.

According to specialists at the U.S. Justice Department's National Institute of Justice, the new boot camps have sucked up tens of millions in state and Federal corrections dollars for construction and millions more for operations. Yet no one has shown clearly that this approach to punishment actually helps turn young lawbreakers away from crime.

Lowe. Reprinted by permission: Tribune Media Services.

In fact, the strategy of battering and demeaning young offenders to "scare them straight" may do the opposite. Some warn that it may instill dangerous resentment in volatile youths and send them a message that such violent behavior as their guards routinely practice has a place in our society. Still, savaging prisoners, working them hard, and subjecting them to strict—and arbitrary—rules seem to appeal to the same public that, in 1988, responded favorably to George Bush's Willie Horton campaign ads [television ads that publicized the case of a black inmate in Massachusetts who committed two murders while on a day pass from prison].

"I think this approach is what people want," says Major Ralph Coyle, the Camp's thirty-three-year-old commander. "They're tired of driving by and seeing a prisoner sitting on a $6,000 John

Deere tractor mowing the lawn. I'm tired of it, too. So these guys work hard. And when they mow a lawn, it's with one of those little push-type reel mowers over there. People want to see these guys working."

Hard Labor at Boot Camp

At boot camps, they work. They clear brush, saw logs, build fences, bust up rocks—all by hand. They also suffer the insults and capricious abuse of tough guards whom they must treat with exaggerated respect.

At REAMS, hard labor starts a few days after inmates arrive; the authoritarian rule starts the moment they step into camp. On Wednesday, intake day, a van stops in a yard surrounded by a tall fence looped with razor wire. The ten passengers, first-time felons recommended for the program, have agreed to work here for three months, followed by time in a halfway house and then probation, in exchange for the shorter sentences.

"They've been briefed on what it's like here," Coyle tells me with a smile. "But they don't really know what to expect."

The guards, like Scudder done up in black drill-instructor uniforms, hats low over their eyes, stand and wait a moment for effect. Then they rush the van. Screaming orders, they throw open the door and begin hurling prisoners out onto the gravel yard.

"Get outta there, you damn maggot!" "Move it, slime!" they shout.

A slender guard with a narrow mustache shoves a prisoner toward the fence, thrusting his chin to within an inch of the youth's cheek. "If I see that smirk on your face again," he growls, saliva flying, "I'm gonna put you through that goddamn fence." He pulls back and yells at the group, "Now we're gonna teach you some damn courtesy."

The Popularity of Boot Camps

During the first two days, guards do just that. They shout conflicting orders, march the inmates, shave their heads, belittle them, scream epithets—"fat boy," "crackhead," "geek," and "peter puffer." One drops out, begging to be sent to prison for his full eighteen-month term. Standing in a corner with his hands cuffed behind him, Julius Cheney, a twenty-five-year-old drug dealer, tells me, "I can't take it. I'm just gonna do my time." Then he cries.

"One or two or three will drop out," Coyle says, "usually in the first couple of days. We're not for everybody. But I warn them about what happens to the young guys up the hill," he says, waving vaguely toward Southeast Correctional [Institute (SCI)], the 1,600-inmate medium-security prison on whose ground Camp REAMS is located.

No one has proved prisoners at vast correctional warehouses like SCI are more apt to return to crime than boot-camp alumni, but the bandwagon for shock incarceration keeps rolling. In addition to the thirty-four like REAMS, juvenile systems have opened camps, and there are also camps for women. New York has five boot camps with a population of more than 1,500, and the state plans more. An Ohio guard jokes that "the job market for former Marine DIs [drill instructors] has never been better."

The media have covered shock prisons in a mostly supportive and uncritical manner. Some articles in newspapers and magazines focus on success stories of inmates who, in the course of boot camp, take control of their lives. Others emphasize how caring guards are beneath their rough facades. Jerome G. Miller, a prison reformer, laughs and says, "These places make great TV." In fact, all the positive media coverage, he says, "is one reason politicians love them so much. Of all the human services—if you can call corrections a human service—it's the one most likely to be run by sound bites."

Regular Prisons Are Not Successful

Miller, who heads the Virginia-based National Center for Institutions and Alternatives, a nonprofit organization that develops alternative sentencing options mostly for criminal-defense teams, has been tracking boot camps since their emergence. The former sociology professor, correctional administrator, and author of *Last One Over the Wall*, a book about juvenile corrections, says, "This movement is just the latest corrections fad. I don't think it's necessary. If you treat people in prison decently, you can get good results."

Miller considers good results to be something better than the grim recidivism rate of felons in the United States, where at least 40 per cent return to criminal behavior, many ending up back behind bars. The national prison population has been growing at a rate of almost 7 per cent a year, according to the Washington-based Sentencing Project, a private research group. Whatever prisons are doing today is not wildly successful.

A visit to any large state institution shows why: Rehabilitation plays virtually no role. Prisoners mostly laze around in their cells or the yard, pump iron, or socialize—if you can call it that. Inmates, particularly young ones, who seek what educational programs are available find themselves shunned, intimidated, and bullied by their more cynical peers.

Prison officials hope shock incarceration will improve things. "We aim everything here at getting these kids to change," Coyle explains. "All of this discipline you've seen and the rough treatment, the hard labor, that's part of it. You have to get their attention to get them to change. Then they can feel positive about

216

having gotten through something challenging."

If the hard work and discipline were all there is to the approach, it might represent just another vengeful response to crime. The rise in both numbers of prisoners—there are 1.1 million felons locked away in the United States, a total that doubled between 1980 and 1990, that tripled between 1970 and 1990—and the toughness of sentences reflect an increasingly harsh public attitude. To Ohio's and some other states' credit, many boot-camp planners also fold in a measure of rehabilitation aimed at these eighteen- to twenty-five-year-olds.

Rehabilitation and Recidivism

"This is the way we envisioned shock-incarceration camps from the beginning," says Ronald Powell, head of the New Hampshire prison system. "They're aimed at a high-risk population and must combine intensive rehabilitation services with the military boot-camp approach." He believes they need education programs, like the high-school equivalency classes REAMS offers, peer tutoring by inmates who have degrees, drug rehab, and what Powell calls "character-building sessions." Without such features, he predicts, "we'll see some notable failures in the coming years."

Boot Camps Increase Crowding

It turns out that boot camps may actually *increase* demand for prison beds. Critics say that to ease overcrowding, camps would have to include those headed for prison. Yet the majority of shock-incarceration programs (both juvenile and adult) are designed for offenders who would otherwise be on probation. Many ex-boot-campers end up in jail for minor infractions of their own strict, post-camp probation—further swelling penitentiaries. Some young offenders may already be beyond reform by the time they reach camp.

Peter Katel, *Newsweek*, February 21, 1994.

In 1983, Powell helped set up the first prison boot camp in Dodge County, Georgia. "Crime, in my mind, is more related to character disorders than to the broader sociological trends some people cite," he says. "We try to get back to individual values. The hope is that we can take a young man with these disorders and produce, well, a man. With a few reservations, I think it works."

Critic Jerry Miller, on the other hand, has many reservations. "Yes, if you include this expensive after-care, maybe there's a possibility the recidivism rate for shock prisons will improve, but who's to say a traditional prison wouldn't have the same effect if it had all these programs, halfway houses, and probationary terms?"

The point, Miller says, is that "we should concentrate on what we know works—provide rehab programs to inmates, provide alternative sentencing to many of them, get them into community-service projects." All this shouting and shoving only sends young run-amoks the wrong message, he believes: "You get all this sadism from the guards in this situation, and who knows what can happen?"

That's an issue Powell says he considered in New Hampshire. His fear was that guards could too zealously harass a particularly unstable prisoner and cause an incident, even a riot. Someone could get badly hurt or killed. Powell says that in New Hampshire, he has structured his program differently from, say, the camp in Ohio: "We tolerate no physical or verbal abuse of any kind." Coyle, however, thinks of harsh verbal commands and physical prodding as important elements of Camp REAMS.

A Lack of Guidelines

Some policy-makers and scholars, in their search for answers, are applying standards to corrections that seem to work with other social problems. Much of what they've learned has strengthened the skeptics' position: Shock prisons do some of what the zealots claim—but only when they're set up and operated with tremendous care, a level of care that's hard for a corrections system to approach, let alone sustain.

By being selective about admissions, for instance, a corrections system might save some money, though boot camps can be costly. Oklahoma gave its 1991 boot-camp per-bed cost at $23,500, while beds at its regular prisons cost $17,800. The advantage was that the ninety-day program processes more inmates per bed each year.

"Unfortunately," says Doris MacKenzie, "the planning and training aren't always the best. A system might put offenders who otherwise would get probation or parole in a boot camp, and that would cost quite a lot more." A professor and criminologist at the University of Maryland, she has offered to help the Corrections Institute develop guidelines for operations. So far, no one can tell policy-makers what works. The lack of guidelines hasn't stopped corrections systems from buying drill-instructor hats and sharp uniforms, hiring some guards, and diving in.

"As it stands now," MacKenzie explains, "we've got county and city systems setting up boot camps. There are juvenile systems, too. Some of them don't have any idea what they're doing. What we want from a prison is to prompt some attitude change on the part of these young offenders. We frankly don't yet know if this is the way to get it."

Of the prison guards he's seen, Jerry Miller says, "The closest they've ever gotten to a real boot camp is *Gomer Pyle*. And I don't see much sign that the training is getting better.". . .

Possibly prison boot camps, as they now operate around the country, may actually help some troubled kids change. But no one knows in what direction or for how long. Considering the kind of model such guards as Jeff Scudder present to the young men whom they pummel and excoriate, we may be unhappy with the outcome.

Back at Camp REAMS, Scudder finishes his hour-long performance playing bad cop, showing new inmates how to make a tight rack and precisely tuck away all personal belongings into a foot locker. Wiping his damp head and neck, he begins to transform himself back into the earnest and friendly young man he was when we first met.

"I feel I'm on a mission," he says. "These guys have lost control, and it's my mission to try to show them how to put some order in their lives."

Scudder has been masterful as a raging DI, and his intention seems laudable. Still, questions hang in the air: What is the shock camp's real effect on prisoners, and what will be its effect on society?

Periodical Bibliography

The following articles have been selected to supplement the diverse views presented in this chapter.

George M. Anderson
"Punishing the Young: Juvenile Justice in the 1990's," *America*, February 29, 1992.

D. Stanley Eitzen
"National Security: Children, Crime, and Cities," *Vital Speeches of the Day*, March 1, 1993.

Barry C. Feld
"Juvenile (In)justice and the Criminal Court Alternative," *Crime and Delinquency*, October 1993.

James Alan Fox and Glenn Pierce
"American Killers Are Getting Younger," *USA Today*, January 1994.

Sarah Glazer
"Juvenile Justice," *CQ Researcher*, February 25, 1994. Available from 1414 22nd St. NW, Washington, DC 20037.

Ronald Henkoff
"Kids Are Killing, Dying, Bleeding," *Fortune*, August 10, 1992.

Barbara Kantrowitz
"Wild in the Streets," *Newsweek*, August 2, 1993.

Michele Magar
"Kids and Crime," *Media Studies Journal*, Winter 1992. Available from Columbia University, 2950 Broadway, New York, NY 10027.

Lance Morrow
"Childhood's End," *Time*, March 9, 1992.

Carol Moseley-Braun and Laura Murphy Lee
"At Issue: Juvenile Justice," *ABA Journal*, March 1994. Available from the ABA, 750 N. Lake Shore Dr., Chicago, IL 60611.

Janet Reno
"How to Save Our Children," *USA Today*, January 1994.

Richard Rodriguez
"Gangstas: Hard Truths from the Streets of East L.A.," *Mother Jones*, January/February 1994.

Holly Sklar
"Young and Guilty by Stereotype," *Z Magazine*, July/August 1993.

Gordon Witkin et al.
"Kids Who Kill," *U.S. News & World Report*, April 8, 1991.

James D. Wright, Joseph F. Sheley, and M. Dwayne Smith
"Kids, Guns, and Killing Fields," *Society*, November/December 1992.

How Is Fear of Crime Affecting America?

Chapter Preface

A January 1994 *Los Angeles Times* poll showed that crime was, at that time, the top concern of Americans nationwide. Dan Lewis, a criminologist at Northwestern University in Evanston, Illinois, calls it a "moral panic [that] is almost completely unrelated to underlying reality." In fact, Federal Bureau of Investigation (FBI) statistics show that America's crime rate has remained stable since the early 1970s, which leads some to debate why concern over crime peaks at certain times.

Some criminologists—noting that the actual crime rate does not govern when fear of crime tops opinion polls—place the blame on shifting media attention. They believe that when there are no other issues for the media to focus on, such as the economy, foreign policy, or scandal, they will often sensationalize crime stories. According to reporter Keith Henderson, "the statistics don't justify the public outcry over crime." Henderson quotes Jerome Miller of the National Center on Institutions and Alternatives: "This hysteria around crime is created" by the media.

According to other criminologists, it is the lulls in concern about crime that are misleading, not the peaks. Crime should always be at the top of the list of concerns, they believe, but people become complacent at times about the high crime rate. Though statistics show that the crime rate has remained steady, they argue, it has remained at what ought to be considered an intolerably high level. As New York City police commissioner Raymond W. Kelly said in a speech in February 1993, "In New York City there has somehow arisen a new benchmark for homicides. Over 2000 homicides a year is considered bad; up to 2000 is somehow expected or acceptable."

Most criminologists would agree that the average American's perception of crime and safety is important, since it affects not only quality of life but also the response to the perceived danger. The viewpoints in the following chapter debate the effects of perceptions of crime on American society.

"We are getting used to a lot of behavior that is not good for us."

American Society Accepts Too Much Deviant Behavior

Daniel Patrick Moynihan

Daniel Patrick Moynihan notes that crime often tops public opinion polls of the concerns of Americans. In the following viewpoint, Moynihan cites sociological theories which propose that certain behavior is defined as deviant in order to distinguish what is normal. In Moynihan's opinion, however, too much behavior previously considered deviant has now become accepted as normal. The result, he believes, is that truly shocking murders have become so routine that they no longer merit much attention, as a survey of newspaper articles shows. Moynihan is a Democrat who has served as a U.S. senator from New York since 1977 and is currently chairman of the Senate Finance Committee.

As you read, consider the following questions:

1. According to Moynihan, what accounts for the "cultural war" proclaimed at the 1992 Republican National Convention?
2. How would today's crime peaks have been viewed thirty years ago, in the author's opinion?
3. According to Moynihan, at what level have motor vehicle deaths been normalized?

From Daniel Patrick Moynihan, "Defining Deviancy Down." Reprinted from *The American Scholar*, vol. 62, no. 1, Winter 1993, by permission. Copyright ©1993 by the author.

In one of the founding texts of sociology, *The Rules of Sociological Method* (1895), Emile Durkheim set it down that "crime is normal." "It is," he wrote, "completely impossible for any society entirely free of it to exist." By defining what is deviant, we are enabled to know what is not, and hence to live by shared standards. This aperçu appears in the chapter entitled "Rules for the Distinction of the Normal from the Pathological." Durkheim writes:

> From this viewpoint the fundamental facts of criminology appear to us in an entirely new light. . . . [T]he criminal no longer appears as an utterly unsociable creature, a sort of parasitic element, a foreign, inassimilable body introduced into the bosom of society. He plays a normal role in social life. For its part, crime must no longer be conceived of as an evil which cannot be circumscribed closely enough. Far from there being cause for congratulation when it drops too noticeably below the normal level, this apparent progress assuredly coincides with and is linked to some social disturbance.

Durkheim suggests, for example, that "in times of scarcity" crimes of assault drop off. He does not imply that we ought to approve of crime—"[p]ain has likewise nothing desirable about it"—but we need to understand its function. He saw religion, in the sociologist Randall Collins's terms, as "fundamentally a set of ceremonial actions, assembling the group, heightening its emotions, and focusing its members on symbols of their common belongingness." In this context "a punishment ceremony creates social solidarity."

The matter was pretty much left at that until seventy years later when, in 1965, Kai T. Erikson published *Wayward Puritans*, a study of "crime rates" in the Massachusetts Bay Colony. The plan behind the book, as Erikson put it, was "to test [Durkheim's] notion that the number of deviant offenders a community can afford to recognize is likely to remain stable over time." The notion proved out very well indeed. Despite occasional crime waves, as when itinerant Quakers refused to take off their hats in the presence of magistrates, the amount of deviance in this corner of seventeenth-century New England fitted nicely with the supply of stocks and whipping posts. . . .

Defining Deviance to Meet Demand

Erikson was taking issue with what he described as "a dominant strain in sociological thinking" that took for granted that a well-structured society "is somehow designed to prevent deviant behavior from occurring." In both authors, Durkheim and Erikson, there is an undertone that suggests that, with deviancy, as with most social goods, there is the continuing problem of demand exceeding supply. Durkheim invites us to imagine a society of saints, a perfect cloister of exemplary individuals. Crimes, properly so called, will there be unknown; but faults which appear venial to the layman will create there the same scandal that the ordinary offense does in ordinary consciousness. If, then, this society has the power to judge and punish, it will define these acts as criminal and will treat them as such.

Recall Durkheim's comment that there need be no cause for congratulations should the amount of crime drop "too noticeably below the normal level." It would not appear that Durkheim anywhere contemplates the possibility of too much crime. Clearly his theory would have required him to deplore such a development, but the possibility seems never to have occurred to him.

Erikson, writing much later in the twentieth century, contemplates both possibilities. "Deviant persons can be said to supply needed services to society." There is no doubt a tendency for the supply of any needed thing to run short. But he is consistent. There can, he believes, be *too much* of a good thing. Hence "the number of deviant offenders a community *can afford* to recognize is likely to remain stable over time." [Author's emphasis]

Three Categories of Redefinition

Social scientists are said to be on the lookout for poor fellows getting a bum rap. But here is a theory that clearly implies that there are circumstances in which society will choose *not* to notice behavior that would be otherwise controlled, or disapproved, or even punished.

It appears to me that this is in fact what we in the United States have been doing of late. I proffer the thesis that, over the past generation, since the time Erikson wrote, the amount of deviant behavior in American society has increased beyond the levels the community can "afford to recognize" and that, accordingly, we have been redefining deviancy so as to exempt much conduct previously stigmatized, and also quietly raising the "normal" level in categories where behavior is now abnormal by any earlier standard. This redefining has evoked fierce resistance from defenders of "old" standards, and accounts for much of the present "cultural war" such as proclaimed by many at the 1992 Republican National Convention.

Let me, then, offer three categories of redefinition in these regards: the *altruistic*, the *opportunistic*, and the *normalizing*.

The first category, the *altruistic*, may be illustrated by the deinstitutionalization movement within the mental health profession that appeared in the 1950s. The second category, the *opportunistic*, is seen in the interest group rewards derived from the acceptance of "alternative" family structures. The third category, the *normalizing*, is to be observed in the growing acceptance of unprecedented levels of violent crime. . . .

225

Defending the Values of Civilization

Somebody said every civilization is only a generation away from barbarism. What throws the switch is when the older generations lose their courage and their will to defend the values of their civilization.

One defends a value by first of all practicing it. One defends a value by holding up examples for public praise and—this is absolutely necessary—by condemning those who reject those values. One defends a value by being intolerant of those who oppose it.

Today, too many Americans are afraid. They are afraid to defend even courtesy. They are afraid not to laugh at vulgarisms. They are afraid to defend their own cultural values. Some are even afraid to assert that they believe in anything. Admittedly, the deck is stacked. Most of the elite is on the side of the barbarians.

Charley Reese, *Conservative Chronicle*, July 7, 1993.

Our *normalizing* category most directly corresponds to Erikson's proposition that "the number of deviant offenders a community can afford to recognize is likely to remain stable over time." Here we are dealing with the popular psychological notion of "denial." In 1965, having reached the conclusion that there would be a dramatic increase in single-parent families, I reached the further conclusion that this would in turn lead to a dramatic increase in crime. In an article in *America*, I wrote:

> From the wild Irish slums of the 19th century Eastern seaboard to the riot-torn suburbs of Los Angeles, there is one unmistakable lesson in American history: a community that allows a large number of young men to grow up in broken families, dominated by women, never acquiring any stable relationship to male authority, never acquiring any set of rational expectations about the future—that community asks for and gets chaos. Crime, violence, unrest, unrestrained lashing out at the whole social structure—that is not only to be expected; it is very near to inevitable.

The inevitable, as we now know, has come to pass, but here again our response is curiously passive. Crime is a more or less continuous subject of political pronouncement, and from time to time it will be at or near the top of opinion polls as a matter of public concern. But it never gets much further than that. In the words spoken from the bench, Judge Edwin Torres of the New York State Supreme Court, Twelfth Judicial District, described how "the slaughter of the innocent marches unabated: subway riders, bodega owners, cab drivers, babies; in laundromats, at cash machines, on elevators, in hallways." In personal communication, he writes: "This numbness, this near narcoleptic state can diminish the human condition to the level of combat infantrymen, who, in protracted campaigns, can eat their battlefield rations seated on the bodies of the fallen, friend and foe alike. A society that loses its sense of outrage is doomed to extinction." There is no expectation that this will change, nor any efficacious public insistence that it do so. The crime level has been *normalized*.

Consider the St. Valentine's Day Massacre. In 1929 in Chicago during Prohibition, four gangsters killed seven gangsters on February 14. The nation was shocked. The event became legend. It merits not one but two entries in the *World Book Encyclopedia*. I leave it to others to judge, but it would appear that the society in the 1920s was simply not willing to put up with this degree of deviancy. In the end, the Constitution was amended, and Prohibition, which lay behind so much gangster violence, ended.

A St. Valentine's Day Massacre Every Weekend

In recent years, again in the context of illegal traffic in controlled substances, this form of murder has returned. But it has done so at a level that induces denial. James Q. Wilson comments that Los Angeles has the equivalent of a St. Valentine's Day Massacre every weekend. Even the most ghastly reenactments of such human slaughter produce only moderate responses. On the morning after the close of the Democratic National Convention in New York City in July [1992], there was such an account in the second section of the *New York Times*. It was not a big story; bottom of the page, but with a headline that got your attention. "3 Slain in Bronx Apartment, but a Baby Is Saved." A subhead continued: "A mother's last act was to hide her little girl under the bed." The article described a drug execution; the now-routine blindfolds made from duct tape; a man and a woman and a teenager involved. "Each had been shot once in the head." The police had found them a day later. They also found, under a bed, a three-month-old baby, dehydrated but alive. A lieutenant remarked of the mother, "In her last dying act she protected her baby. She probably knew she was going to die, so she stuffed the baby where she knew it would be safe." But the matter was left there. The police would do their best. But the event passed quickly; forgotten by the next day, it will never make *World Book*.

Nor is it likely that any great heed will be paid to an uncanny reenactment of the Prohibition drama a few months later, also in the Bronx. The *Times* story, page B3, reported:

9 Men Posing as Police Are Indicted in 3 Murders
Drug Dealers Were Kidnapped for Ransom

The *Daily News* story, same day, page 17, made it *four* murders, adding nice details about torture techniques. The gang members posed as federal Drug Enforcement Administration agents, real badges and all. The victims were drug dealers, whose families were uneasy about calling the police. Ransom seems generally to have been set in the $650,000 range. Some paid. Some got it in the back of the head. So it goes.

The Press Gives a Quick Glance

Yet, violent killings, often random, go on unabated. Peaks continue to attract some notice. But these are peaks above "average" levels that thirty years ago would have been thought epidemic.

LOS ANGELES, AUG. 24 [1992]. (Reuters) Twenty-two people were killed in Los Angeles over the weekend, the worst period of violence in the city since it was ravaged by riots earlier this year, the police said today.

Twenty-four others were wounded by gunfire or stabbings, including a 19-year-old woman in a wheelchair who was shot in the back when she failed to respond to a motorist who asked for directions in south Los Angeles.

["The guy stuck a gun out of the window and just fired at her," said a police spokesman, Lieut. David Rock. The woman was later described as being in stable condition.

Among those who died was an off-duty officer, shot while investigating reports of a prowler in a neighbor's yard, and a Little League baseball coach who had argued with the father of a boy he was coaching.]

The police said at least nine of the deaths were gang-related, including that of a 14-year-old girl killed in a fight between rival gangs.

Fifty-one people were killed in three days of rioting that started April 29 after the acquittal of four police officers in the beating of Rodney G. King.

Los Angeles usually has above-average violence during August, but the police were at a loss to explain the sudden rise. On an average weekend in August, 14 fatalities occur.

Not to be outdone, two days later the poor Bronx came up with a near record, as reported in *New York Newsday*:

Armed with 9-mm. pistols, shotguns and M-16 rifles, a group of masked men and women poured out of two vehicles in the South Bronx early yesterday and sprayed a stretch of Longwood Avenue with a fusillade of bullets, injuring 12 people.

A Kai Erikson of the future will surely need to know that the Department of Justice in 1990 found that Americans reported only about 38 percent of all crimes and 48 percent of violent crimes. This, too, can be seen as a means of *normalizing* crime. In much the same way, the vocabulary of crime reporting can be seen to move toward the normal-seeming. A teacher is shot on her way to class. The *Times* subhead reads: "Struck in the Shoulder in the Year's First Shooting Inside a School." First of the season.

The Public Health Approach

It is too early, however, to know how to regard the arrival of the doctors on the scene declaring crime a "public health emergency." The June 10, 1992, issue of the *Journal of the American Medical Association* was devoted entirely to papers on the subject of violence, principally violence associated with firearms. An editorial in the issue signed by former Surgeon General C. Everett Koop and Dr. George D. Lundberg is entitled: "Violence in America: A Public Health Emergency." Their proposition is admirably succinct.

> Regarding violence in our society as purely a sociological matter, or one of law enforcement, has led to unmitigated failure. It is time to test further whether violence can be amenable to medical/public health interventions.

> We believe violence in America to be a public health emergency, largely unresponsive to methods thus far used in its control. The solutions are very complex, but possible.

The authors cited the relative success of epidemiologists [researchers who study the incidence of diseases within populations] in gaining some jurisdiction in the area of motor vehicle casualties by redefining what had been seen as a law enforcement issue into a public health issue. Again, this process began during the [Averell] Harriman administration in New York in the 1950s. In the 1960s the morbidity and mortality associated with automobile crashes was, it could be argued, a major public health problem; the public health strategy, it could also be argued, brought the problem under a measure of control. Not in "the 1970s and 1980s," as the *Journal of the American Medical Association* would have us think: the federal legislation involved was signed in 1965. Such a strategy would surely produce insights into the control of violence that elude law enforcement professionals, but whether it would change anything is another question.

Defining Handgun Violence Down

For some years now I have had legislation in the Senate that would prohibit the manufacture of .25 and .32 caliber bullets. These are the two calibers most typically used with the guns known as Saturday Night Specials. "Guns don't kill people," I argue, "bullets do."

Moreover, we have a two-century supply of handguns but only a four-year supply of ammunition. A public health official would immediately see the logic of trying to control the supply

229

of bullets rather than of guns.

Even so, now that the doctor has come, it is important that criminal violence not be defined down by epidemiologists. Doctors Koop and Lundberg note that in 1990 in the state of Texas "deaths from firearms, for the first time in many decades, surpassed deaths from motor vehicles, by 3,443 to 3,309." A good comparison. And yet keep in mind that the number of motor vehicle deaths, having leveled off since the 1960s, is now pretty well accepted as normal at somewhat less than 50,000 a year, which is somewhat less than the level of the 1960s—the "carnage," as it once was thought to be, is now accepted as normal. This is the price we pay for high-speed transportation: there is a benefit associated with it. But there is no benefit associated with homicide, and no good in getting used to it. Epidemiologists have powerful insights that can contribute to lessening the medical trauma, but they must be wary of normalizing the social pathology that leads to such trauma.

The hope—if there be such—of this [viewpoint] has been twofold. It is, first, to suggest that the Durkheim constant, as I put it, is maintained by a dynamic process which adjusts upwards and *downwards*. Liberals have traditionally been alert for upward redefining that does injustice to individuals. Conservatives have been correspondingly sensitive to downward redefining that weakens societal standards. Might it not help if we could all agree that there is a dynamic at work here? It is not revealed truth, nor yet a scientifically derived formula. It is simply a pattern we observe in ourselves. Nor is it rigid. There may once have been an unchanging supply of jail cells which more or less determined the number of prisoners. No longer. We are building new prisons at a prodigious rate. Similarly, the executioner is back. There is something of a competition in Congress to think up new offenses for which the death penalty is deemed the only available deterrent. Possibly also modes of execution, as in "fry the kingpins." Even so, we are getting used to a lot of behavior that is not good for us.

As noted earlier, Durkheim states that there is "nothing desirable" about pain. Surely what he meant was that there is nothing pleasurable. Pain, even so, is an indispensable warning signal. But societies under stress, much like individuals, will turn to pain killers of various kinds that end up concealing real damage. There is surely nothing desirable about *this*. If our analysis wins general acceptance, if, for example, more of us came to share Judge Torres's genuine alarm at "the trivialization of the lunatic crime rate" in his city (and mine), we might surprise ourselves how well we respond to the manifest decline of the American civic order. Might.

"Nearly all people violate some laws, and many people run afoul of dozens without ever being considered, or considering themselves, criminals."

American Society Criminalizes Too Many Behaviors

Stephen J. Adler, Wade Lambert, and Richard Morin

In early 1993, in the face of public outrage over her having hired and failed to pay taxes for undocumented child-care help, Zoe Baird withdrew her name from nomination for U.S. Attorney General. In Part I of the following viewpoint, Stephen J. Adler and Wade Lambert argue that Americans frequently ignore laws that prohibit commonly accepted behavior, such as the ones that tripped up Baird. When politics breathes new life into laws, Adler and Lambert argue, the law seems capricious and becomes unsettling. In Part II, Richard Morin argues that overblown media attention to crime creates the impression of a crime wave, even though crime rates are relatively stable. Adler and Lambert are staff writers for the *Wall Street Journal*. Morin is a staff writer for the *Washington Post*.

As you read, consider the following questions:

1. According to Delbert Elliott, cited by Adler and Lambert, how widespread is lawbreaking?
2. According to Maxwell E. McCombs, quoted by Morin, how might agenda-setting by the media be both good and bad?

I

We are a nation of lawbreakers.

We exaggerate tax-deductible expenses, lie to customs officials, bet on card games and sports events, disregard jury notices, drive while intoxicated—and hire illegal child-care workers.

The last of these was the crime of the moment in early 1993, and Janet Reno wouldn't have been in the position to be confirmed unanimously as attorney general if Zoe Baird had obeyed the much-flouted immigration and tax laws. But the crime of the moment could have been something else, and next time it probably will be.

This is because nearly all people violate some laws, and many people run afoul of dozens without ever being considered, or considering themselves, criminals. . . .

Our Willingness to Break Laws

Why do we break the law? Is it, as some psychologists suggest, because the law is our symbolic parent, whom we both adore and abhor and whom we enjoy disobeying? Or is it, more prosaically, that many laws seem too foolish, unfair, burdensome or intrusive for even the most law-abiding to obey slavishly? Or is it simply that we know we can get away with it?

Some people who deal with serious crime scoff at these questions, arguing that routine, nonviolent infractions are too trivial to worry about in a nation threatened by murder, rape, armed robbery, gang warfare and drug trafficking. But other social scientists take seriously the phenomenon of lawbreaking among the ostensibly law-abiding. They say our willingness to break laws undermines respect for ourselves, for one another and for the rule of law.

As a practical matter, laws that are often broken with impunity make it difficult for people to predict the consequences of their acts. In the 1970s, Douglas Ginsburg smoked marijuana, as did many of his contemporaries; in 1987 he lost the chance to be a Supreme Court justice as a result. Perhaps a young lawyer who now tosses soda cans into the garbage will be next: In the year 2001, failing to recycle could disqualify someone for the cabinet.

Lawbreaking among the mostly law-abiding isn't new, of course. Tax evasion dates back to biblical times. Avoiding jury duty has been common sport at least since the 17th century. Millions drank liquor during Prohibition. People have been driving while intoxicated since the invention of the automobile. Criminologists say they believe that there are more such crimes than there used to be, but there are no figures to back up that claim.

Academic studies do show how widespread lawbreaking is today. University of Colorado sociologist Delbert Elliott has tracked a group of young adults since 1976, when they were junior-high and high-school age. The tally thus far: 90% of the group has broken the law at some time. Other studies yield similar results.

One reason for so much lawbreaking, criminologists say, is that there are so many laws, with new ones being added every year. A state's statutes, including regulations of businesses, can fill 40 volumes or more. State criminal codes average about 1,000 pages each. And on top of the state tomes sit the U.S. laws: Federal criminal provisions fill some 800 pages. Town and city ordinances add to the list.

"There are so many things legally one can get in trouble for breaking, it would be difficult not to be a lawbreaker in our society," says Paul Fromberg, an Episcopal priest at Christ Church Cathedral in Houston. "If you don't know what the rule is, how do you follow it?" wonders Jack Greene, a criminal-law professor at Temple University.

Also, in a nation that is increasingly multicultural, many laws don't represent shared values. Laws restricting gambling, drinking, fortunetelling, extramarital sex, sexual behavior and the use of fireworks, for example, are more acceptable in some communities than in others. In many states, adds James Fyfe, a criminal-justice professor at Temple University, the legislature is still dominated by rural lawmakers whose laws "reflect the values of the farms but not of the urban areas."

Who Is the Victim?

Under the circumstances, people who seek to maintain high moral standards often make sharp distinctions between laws they will break and those they won't. Some people who steal, for example, do so only when they believe they have a moral right to what they are taking. "Just because something is against the law doesn't mean it's wrong," says San Francisco author Timothy Ferris. "I've stolen legal pads from every office I've ever been in. But I use those legal pads to write books. That's a good use of the legal pad."

Crimes that are seen as victimless, or as invasions of privacy, are often broken without much soul-searching. "There is a huge number of people who violate drug laws because they believe it is their own private business," says Arnold Trebach of the Drug Policy Foundation in Washington, which advocates decriminalization of some illegal drugs. "To a large number of drug users, the law is an ass."

But people differ as to which crimes are victimless and which victims merit concern. Who is the victim when one cheats on one's taxes or lies to the insurance company or makes illegal home repairs? Whoever the victim is, it is nameless, faceless and too distant to concern many people. This may be why people so readily cheat the Internal Revenue Service, even though the economy may suffer as a result. "We would have no national debt if people would pay the taxes they owe," says Todd Clear, a criminal-justice professor at Rutgers University in Newark, New Jersey.

Certainly, the more distant or abstract the victim, the less incentive there seems to be to respect or protect that victim. Kenneth Lenihan, a professor at John Jay College of Criminal Justice in New York, says he witnessed this phenomenon a few years ago when he employed several ex-prisoners. After one apparently stole the professor's checkbook and forged some checks, two of the others indicated that they would cooperate with the bank's investigation. But when they learned the loss would be the bank's and not Mr. Lenihan's, they changed their minds, he says.

An Under-the-Table Ideology

Another obstacle to good citizenship is that lawbreakers are often admired, both for taking a risk and for profiting from doing so. Says Professor Greene of Temple: "There's an under-the-table ideology in this country. People want a good deal."

This attitude seems to be particularly prevalent in the workplace, where competition dictates straddling a fine line between shrewd and shady. "What a lot of people do is, they hang their ethical hat at the door," says Michael Daigneault, whose Falls Church, Virginia, firm, Ethics Inc., teaches ethics to businesspeople.

But some law-and-psychology specialists say something far deeper is at work in lawbreaking. "Our emotional stance toward the law isn't one of unequivocal respect, but one of ambivalence," says Martha Grace Duncan, a professor at Emory University's law school.

"From a psychoanalytic perspective, it makes sense that this should be so," she adds, "for the law represents the parent (and) thus serves as a repository of powerful feelings from early childhood—complex feelings of affection and disdain, attraction and repudiation."

It Is Easier to Pass a New Law

If so, the national parent may need a lesson from Dr. Spock in the virtues of consistent discipline. Civil libertarians warn that when too many rules exist, and only some are enforced, the law becomes capricious and unsettling. The legal system starts to resemble a lottery.

One solution is to repeal or amend laws that don't make sense to a lot of people. Indeed, the Zoe Baird flap seems likely to result in more sensible rules for paying Social Security taxes for domestic employees. But most of the often-disobeyed laws are likely to stay on the books, either because they are sound public policy or because it is easier to pass a new law than to repeal an old one. Particularly when morals are thought to be an issue, many legislators don't want to appear to be on the side of sin. Even some people who admit to occasional lawbreaking say they are happy the laws are there "just so people don't get really out of hand," as Los Angeles teacher Janie Teller puts it.

MacNelly. Reprinted by permission: Tribune Media Services.

Inevitably, then, some long-dormant law will awaken periodically and, like a B-movie monster, wreak havoc for a time. But fear of the consequences probably won't increase adherence to the law. Just ask Los Angeles architect Steven Wallock. Some of the prohibited acts "are just too much fun" to resist, he explains. And, like most of us, he doesn't expect to get caught. "Why would somebody doubt me?" he asks. "I'm a good guy, and I look honest."

II

In the last few months of 1993, crime soared to the top of the country's short list of most important problems, replacing the economy in most surveys as the single most important problem facing the country.

Yet some serious students of public opinion view this increase with a disquieting sense of déjà vu. They wonder if concerns about crime aren't being driven by the media, rather than by the reality of crime.

These doubters recall a similar spike in public concern about drugs that occurred in the 1980s. Scholars now convincingly argue that this hyper-concern about drugs was largely the result of the media's sudden interest in the subject, rather than an increase in the prevalence or use of illicit narcotics. They note as evidence that when the media lost interest in the drug story, it fell like a rock from the top of the polls.

Although it is too early to tell, we may be just starting a similar roller-coaster ride over crime.

First, a bit of statistical history. In January 1989, 19 percent of those interviewed in *Washington Post*–ABC News polls named drugs as the "most important problem" facing the country. In August, the proportion who listed drugs as the top problem more than doubled to 44 percent. In October, more than half of those interviewed—53 percent—said drugs were the country's biggest problem. And the pattern was just as apparent in other major media polls.

But just as quickly, the bottom fell out. In January 1990, 40 percent named drugs as the most important problem but by September, only 16 percent named it the country's biggest problem. In 1994, drugs received a single-digit response in the polls.

As it turned out, both the boom-and-bust pattern of public concern about drugs was dramatically out of step with reality. Data from a number of large-sample surveys taken during those years, including the University of Michigan's annual survey of high school seniors, suggested that drug use during this period was, if anything, flat or perhaps even going down slightly—anything but up. And even if drug use were in fact really increasing, what was to be made of the precipitous fall in public concern after October 1989?

What had increased and then dropped off the table during this period was the media's attention to drugs as a social issue. "The *New York Times* discovered drugs and thereafter many news organizations discovered it," says Maxwell E. McCombs, a professor of communication at the University of Texas and a pioneer in the subject of agenda-setting by the media. "The reality was that nothing had changed regarding the incidence or use of drugs. The high spike of public concern was very much driven by media concern."

Suddenly There's a Crime Wave

Concerns about crime may be following a similar pattern, perhaps for identical reasons. The percentage naming crime as the most important problem rocketed from 5 percent in June 1993 to 21 percent in the November *Washington Post*–ABC News poll, and similar spikes have been captured in other surveys. Significantly, during 1993 the national media focused on gun violence, the Brady bill, and violent juvenile crime, McCombs notes. Crime also has emerged as the top political issue. . . . In statewide political surveys done by the *Washington Post* in Virginia, Maryland and the District of Columbia, crime topped the issues list in each of these very different jurisdictions, a pattern currently being seen in state and local polls elsewhere. But nationally and in most states, the overall crime rate has been essentially flat or rising at an incremental rate. McCombs says he was discussing the recent surge in public concern about crime in Texas with the director of the Texas Poll. "It is interesting that she was noting that roughly the same time of this increase in public concern in crime that the crime rate in the state was going down," he says. "There may be less crime, but maybe within the media they do not know it."

"You know the old saying, put together all the day's police reports and suddenly there's a crime wave," he says. "There's a fair chance this may be a media creation. But one could get into a debate whether that's good or bad. One could take the position that this is pro-social agenda setting, we really need to deal with the problem."

The Media and the Public Agenda

McCombs says there always is some reality behind the public's concerns: "These things are never made up out of whole cloth." In the mid- to late-1980s, for example, crack cocaine exploded on the scene, and crack's emergence was always viewed by this writer to be at least partially responsible for the spike in public concerns about drugs. And the emergence of drive-by shootings and urban gang wars have sent homicide rates soaring in recent years, notably right here in the nation's capital. (In fact, when questioned in *Washington Post* polls, four out of five respondents who name "crime" as their biggest concern will volunteer violent crime or murder when asked to be more specific.)

And certainly part of the reason crime has emerged as an issue is the apparent health of the nation's economy. As economic worries recede, the vacuum appears to have been filled, at least in part, by concerns about drugs. "That's a likely scenario," McCombs says. "It very much seems to be a zero-sum game. It could well be as the economy moves off the agenda, then in effect it opens the door to another issue to move on stage, and crime may be it." (In fact, the decline of the drug issue in the late 1980s coincided with the souring of the economy and a sharp increase in the percentage of Americans who named an economic issue as the country's biggest problem, suggesting that drugs may not have "gone away" as much as they were swamped by economic concerns.)

Although journalists don't like to talk about it, the media play a huge role in ordering the public agenda. "It doesn't matter much what the media do when people's jobs are disappearing and their houses are getting repossessed. They'll figure out there's an economic problem," McCombs says. "I would estimate roughly that about half the time it's due to things that are really going on, but there are quite a few instances it's the extra play or the discovery of the issue" by a previously inattentive media that boosts a problem to the top of the public's agenda.

"The public's willingness to make a separate peace with crime by altering behavior [is] 'abetting our own enslavement.'"

Fear of Crime Harms the Quality of American Life

Linda Lichter and Froma Harrop

In Florida during 1993, a string of murders of foreign tourists drew worldwide media attention. The American Automobile Association (AAA), among others, responded by advising tourists to avoid certain areas of Florida and take precautions against crime. In Part I of the following viewpoint, Linda Lichter describes how self-defensive habits, adopted to protect lives, rob people (particularly women) of time. In Part II, Froma Harrop argues that middle-class Americans are too quick to adopt these self-defensive habits; they ought to be outraged over crime, she contends, and should demand government action. Lichter is codirector of the Center for Media and Public Affairs in Washington, D.C. Harrop is a writer for the *Providence (Rhode Island) Journal.*

As you read, consider the following questions:

1. According to Lichter, what are some habits "that save your skin but steal your time"?
2. What does Harrop mean when she criticizes our "willingness to make a separate peace with crime"?
3. In Harrop's view, why are the mainstream media no help to residents of poor city neighborhoods trying to fight violent crime?

The costs of crime are usually measured in mortality rates, hospital visits and property loss. But, as I discovered, there is a pervasive cost of crime that goes largely unnoticed. Upon returning from shopping at a suburban shopping mall, having found the perfect gift at the very first store, I was surprised to see how late it was. Then I realized that all the routine safety measures I employed to avoid being raped, robbed or murdered had doubled the length of the trip.

I was cheated of time even before entering the mall, since I dared not park in the most convenient lot—a covered concrete structure filled with menacing shadows where one woman had been attacked and another carjacked. Instead I parked in an open area adjacent to a busy bus stop. This safety in numbers cost me an extra 10-minute walk each way.

Habits That Steal Time

Once inside, I thought better of using the nearest restroom, which was placed at the end of a dark hallway. Crisscrossing the mall in search of a well-lit facility took another 10 minutes (that felt like hours).

Leaving the mall seemed an even riskier venture. Exiting the store, I noticed a suspicious looking man (in this hair-trigger world, any male wearing a wool hat on a balmy day qualifies as suspicious) who was dancing among the cars near mine while thrusting his arms toward heaven as if praying for rain. Being alone and unarmed, I felt it was the better part of valor to wait until this shabby hoofer two-stepped his way to the other side of the parking lot—another five minutes stolen.

Add a few miscellaneous moments to check for predators underneath and inside the car, as a police pamphlet suggested, and my "bargain" shopping trip cost nearly 40 minutes of irretrievable crime-prevention time.

A quick survey of family and friends revealed a lengthy list of similar habits that save your skin but steal your time: the zigzagging back and forth across downtown streets to avoid aggressive panhandlers, the hours spent ferrying children to and from schools to shield them from perverts and kidnappers, the eternal commutes from dangerous cities to semi-safe suburbs, the constant locking of columns of bolts on house and apartment doors.

Then there are the time stealers that are imposed on us, such as metal detectors in schools and airports. Several women mentioned that they always wait for another elevator rather than ride one alone with a strange man, no matter how well-dressed. One recounted a dinner where she and several female friends spent their last half hour discussing the logistics of how to group together to safely escort each other home. She finally exclaimed,

"Did D-day take this much planning?" For obvious reasons, women are more likely to take time-draining security measures. But since they live longer than men, perhaps this is nature's way of balancing the score.

The Hidden Cost of Self-Defense

Many people seem oblivious or resigned to the incalculable hours the routine avoidance of crime thieves from their lives. Even a [December 1993] assessment by *Business Week* of the true costs of crime—including not only police protection and running the criminal justice system but property loss, urban decay, the price of security devices, the medical treatment of victims and their lost income—did not include the loss of time. But in an age of 12-hour workdays, overburdened two-career families and "cuisine" cooked in microwave minutes. we can ill afford this hidden cost of self-defensive living. Even if we had time to stop and smell the roses, we would probably get our pockets picked while bending over them.

"I DON'T WORRY ABOUT GETTING ROBBED ANYMORE. NOW THAT I CARRY MY MACE, PEPPER SPRAY, SONIC ALARM, AND REVOLVER, THERE'S NO ROOM IN MY PURSE FOR MONEY!"

Gorrell/Copley News Service. Reprinted with permission.

Criminologists frequently attribute the escalating violence of our nation's youth to a decreasing respect for life. In the days before we needed such explanations, polite people often refused some offer of assistance by saying, "I wouldn't dream of imposing on your time," a response that links respect for life with the precious moments that constitute a life. The decline of civility and the rise in crime might be more than a curious coincidence.

Unfortunately, the adjustments we must make to avoid becoming Federal Bureau of Investigation statistics are sapping our lives. The war on crime won't be won until the term "stolen moments" rightfully regains its romantic connotations.

II

For every problem, there is said to be a solution. Thus, when Barbara Jensen Meller of Berlin became the sixth foreign tourist murdered in Miami since December [1992], the city and the state of Florida sprung into action.

The Sunshine State quickly replaced license plates that identified automobiles as rented (that is, a tourist, easy prey, unarmed, maybe carrying lots of cash).

The city fathers of Miami put up new signs pointing visitors to the beaches (that is, away from the dangerous inner city). The local tourist boards issued brochures instructing visitors what to do when their automobiles are purposely bumped by a car full of criminals (that is, how to avoid getting robbed, and, as in the case of Mrs. Meller, run over in front of one's children).

It Helps to Keep Perspective

Of course, tips on how to avoid becoming another corpse in Miami are less necessary for the natives. They already know about barricading streets, erecting barbed wire fencing around their homesteads and running for indoor cover after sundown.

Some of the more naive Miamians complained that the authorities get worked up over crime only when it jeopardizes the state's $30-billion-a-year tourism industry. Residents are permanently conscripted into the army of victims.

Follow these tips, one and all, and you'll be all right, asserted the alarmed authorities. It also helps to keep things in perspective. So shortly after the Meller homicide, the Travel Industry of America's president, Edward Book, offered this comforting thought to Miami visitors and their travel agents: "I don't know if more tourists are being murdered than residents. I suspect not. I think what happens is, when an incident like this takes place, we all kind of jump on it."

I think we may be going insane.

The real problem is that murder has ceased to shock us, let alone infuriate us enough to take the imperative steps to end this mad state of affairs. Even children killing other children in the sanctity of the schoolhouse is regarded as a tragic, but no longer a freak, incident. When we concede that homicide is an inevitable fact of American life, we surrender our will to maintain our civilization and more basically to look after our self-preservation.

"A society that loses its sense of outrage is doomed to extinc-

tion," said New York State Supreme Court Justice Edwin Torres.
If every homicide were regarded as hugely traumatic, the public would demand government action to reverse the growth of criminal violence, never mind the cost.

But the mass of middle class Americans still regard murder as a problem of impoverished urban ghettos over which they have no control. While many try to divert attention abroad by deploring the Europeans for not acting to stop the bloodshed in Bosnia, these same Europeans are stunned by our acquiescence to appalling levels of violence at home.

Vicarious Victimization and Fear

Some criminologists use the term "vicarious victimization" to explain the escalating fear of crime.

Dan Lewis, a professor of social policy at Northwestern University, said high-profile violence, such as the shooting deaths of more than a half-dozen Florida tourists in 1993, dramatically increase anxiety about crime when they take place at locations familiar to millions of Americans.

"Anytime you see something happening where you can see yourself in the shoes of the victim, it's going to increase your concern," Lewis said. "Vicarious victimization can have a big effect on fear rates."

Michael Rezendes, *The San Diego Union-Tribune*, December 25, 1993.

Instead of regarding crime as the result of social policy that must be changed, we view it as a natural force, like a hurricane or tornado that can be coped with but not eliminated. This resignation alarms law enforcement officials. New York City Police Commissioner Raymond Kelly, for example, calls the public's willingness to make a separate peace with crime by altering behavior "abetting our own enslavement."

And our "enslavement" is spreading. Inevitably, the havoc caused by violent crime has moved beyond a particular city or place. Troubled youth in suburbs and rural areas have ominously begun emulating the violent acts of their urban counterparts. Clever management of crime is becoming less and less effective.

Stop Evading the Crisis

Until recently, the middle class American felt some security by placing two tons of automobile between himself and Them Out There. It was perhaps ingenuous to believe that modern highwaymen would pass up such easy pickings for long. Carjackings are the quintessential automobile-culture crime. The Los Angeles area now averages one fatal carjacking a week. But remember the chief reaction when a Maryland woman was dragged to her death by assailants after her arm got caught in a seat belt? It was a desperate slew of new tips:

When approaching your car in the mall parking lot, always have your keys ready. Fumble and you could be dead. Look all ways when getting out of your car. Your own driveway is particularly dangerous because criminals know that is where you let your guard down. When approaching a red light, always stop several feet behind the car in front so you can make a quick getaway if attacked. Tell your children that if a stranger suddenly leaps into the car, they should slide out the other side.

Since the rest of society is trying to survive by managing and isolating murder and mayhem, the beleaguered residents of poor city neighborhoods must face the challenge head on. It is undeniably difficult to overcome fear and summon up the wrath necessary to change a situation in a place where daily exterminations take on a dulling regularity. And the mainstream media will not help. For an inner city homicide to catch a news producer's eye these days, the deed must be truly gruesome, and the threshold for gruesomeness continues to rise.

There are well-known right-wing and left-wing solutions to the madness. But until good people stop evading the crisis, there will be no genuine efforts to put an end to it. We acted with far more urgency when our oil supplies in the Persian Gulf were threatened.

We must recognize that domestic crime has become a national threat greater than an economic squeeze or present foreign danger. Until we do, remember to park in well-lighted areas, keep your keys handy, don't get off at the wrong exit.

"White suburbanites, rather than black ghetto residents, tend to drive the crime debate because they have access to the means to do so."

Middle-Class Fear of Crime Is Exaggerated

Michel McQueen

The following viewpoint was written during the 1992 presidential race between then-president George Bush and then-governor of Arkansas Bill Clinton. According to Michel McQueen, both candidates promoted similar campaign themes on the issue of crime. She argues that middle-class suburbanites have more political influence on the crime issue than lower-class urban residents, regardless of their respective vulnerability to actual crime. McQueen is a staff writer for the *Wall Street Journal*.

As you read, consider the following questions:

1. According to David Bositis and James Fyfe, quoted by McQueen, why are economic issues more important than crime to urban residents?
2. With higher rates of crime in urban areas, why are suburbanites more concerned with crime, according to George Gerbner, cited by the author?
3. Why do middle-class suburbanites support measures that aren't really effective in fighting crime, according to Guy Sapp, quoted by McQueen?

From Michel McQueen, "Political Paradox: People with the Least to Fear from Crime Drive the Crime Issue," *The Wall Street Journal*, August 12, 1992. Reprinted by permission of *The Wall Street Journal* ©1992 Dow Jones & Company, Inc. All rights reserved worldwide.

Once again, crime is bubbling to the surface of presidential attack politics. . . .

This happens every four years, from Richard Nixon's "law-and-order" [campaign theme] to George Bush's own Willie Horton. But there's an inherent irony in the issue: The people it is designed to appeal to are, in fact, the people with the least to fear from crime.

Suburban vs. Urban Concerns

They are people like Craig Stabler, a 30-year-old white computer technician. He had his first and only brush with crime in Summer 1992: A neighbor's purse was stolen from her home at the city's [Wilmington, Delaware] affluent northern edge.

The offender was caught by police 20 minutes later. But the incident made a strong impression on Mr. Stabler. He has installed a steel security door and now always makes sure his doors are locked and his car is secure. He has become "more defensive, more careful," he says.

"I'm pro–law enforcement," he says. "As far as the city goes, crime is a big thing." And he adds: "I would never vote for [Bill] Clinton, never in a million years."

Despite Mr. Stabler's fears, crime is more likely to touch people like Jerome Edwards, a 33-year-old black janitor who lives across town in East Wilmington. He says he feels perfectly safe on his block in his blue-collar neighborhood because "it's more calm around our way." But a check of police records shows his block had the same number of service calls in 1991 as a notorious drug market a few blocks away; a murder took place just two blocks from his house. Still, Mr. Edwards insists he isn't concerned about street crime because "I know how to defend myself." And if you ask him what the most important issues are, he says: "Getting some jobs out here and something for these kids to do."

Politicians Are Talking About Crime

The riots in Los Angeles highlighted the crime problem in the public mind. Scenes of young black men beating a white truck driver, of people looting stores and talking openly about a war on the police, have raised the specter of a season of unrest and violence. And national and local politicians are once again talking about crime.

In July 1992, Democratic presidential candidate Bill Clinton took a page from the GOP [Republican] playbook and surrounded himself with dozens of police officers to make a speech critical of the [Bush] administration's record on crime. He called for the hiring of 100,000 new police officers and bans on some so-called assault weapons. Mr. Bush's political advertisements also sounded the crime theme. In an ad on many local and cable channels, Mr. Bush says, "We must increase respect for the law. We must pass strong legislation to help the fight against crime and to back up our police officers."

But despite this renewed attention, law enforcement personnel and crime experts say the public's perception of crime and the reality of crime remain far apart. "The way this is being framed as a political issue doesn't jell with the reality," says Katherine McFate, a political scientist who has been studying urban crime at the Joint Center for Political and Economic Studies, a research institute in Washington, D.C.

For example, Ms. McFate says there is a widespread perception that blacks commit most of the violent crime in America. And she worries that events in Los Angeles may reinforce the fears of many whites who think they are the likely targets. That attitude doesn't always show up in public opinion polls, she says, because "people know the politically correct answer to these questions." But when a 1989 ABC/*Washington Post* poll asked whether it was "common sense" or "prejudice" for white people to avoid black neighborhoods out of fear of crime, three-quarters of the whites answered: common sense.

Socio-Economic Factors vs. Race

In fact, in 1990, whites committed 54% of all violent crimes, while blacks committed 45%—although that figure is still far above the 12% of the total population represented by blacks. And while the incidence of violent crime has risen sharply over the past decade, the rate of increase has been the same among blacks and whites alike.

Moreover, violent crimes between races are by far the exception, not the rule. In 1990, a full 72% of violent crimes committed against whites were committed by other whites, while 84% of violent crimes committed against blacks were committed by other blacks.

Political appeals on the crime issue all too often are also subtle appeals based on race. Many whites and blacks, including a number of black Republicans who served in the Bush administration, continue to see the [1988 presidential campaign] ad about Willie Horton—a black man who attacked a white couple while out on a prison furlough—as a way to stir racial fears rather than as an attack on [Massachusetts governor and 1988 presidential candidate] Michael Dukakis's lax crime policies, as Mr. Bush said it was.

But perceptions of crime don't break down neatly along racial lines; instead, socio-economic factors are often key. A 1992 survey by the Joint Center for Political and Economic Studies and Home Box Office found that upper-income black voters were more likely to see crime as a critical issue than were lower-income blacks, although they report experiences with it less often, according to David Bositis, a senior analyst at the Joint Center. "I think it is more of a voting issue for whites, especially as it pertains to race," Mr. Bositis says. But even within racial groups, crime is "more important to higher income than lower income," he says. "It is more of a suburban fear."

Crime in Election Years

A *New York Times* article by Richard L. Berke on the front page of the Sunday, January 23, 1994, edition stated: "The sharp rise in concern about crime helps assure that it will be a front-line issue in this election year." But the sentence could just as truthfully be restated as "the sharp rise in concern about this being an election year helps assure that crime will be a front-line issue." The article, which reports on a mid-January nationwide *New York Times*/CBS News poll, indicated that "crime has filled the vacuum" left by diminished fears about the economy. "Asked to cite the single biggest problem facing the nation, 19 percent said crime or violence, with an additional 2 percent saying guns." After health care (15 percent), the economy (14 percent), unemployment or jobs (12 percent), came the deficit (remember that?) at 5 percent, and drug abuse at a lowly 3 percent.

Stephen Leiper, *Propaganda Review*, Spring 1994.

Television promotes another common misperception: One study found women of any race were far more likely to be portrayed as the victims of crime than men. In fact, black males are by far the most frequent victims of violence. According to figures compiled by the federal government in 1992, for every 1,000 black males over the age of 12, 53 have been victims of a violent crime. That compares with 35.5 white males, 28.2 black females, and 21.3 white females.

Crime vs. Economic Concerns

The impact of violence on the life expectancy of black males has been so great that [former] Health and Human Services Secretary Louis Sullivan declared homicide one of the greatest risks to inner-city public health. Murders "are sort of an occupational hazard of living in the ghetto," says James Fyfe, a [former] professor of Justice, Law and Society at American University in Washington, D.C. and a former New York City police officer. "White, middle-class people are at very little risk."

Mr. Fyfe, like Mr. Bositis, believes that white suburbanites, rather than black ghetto residents, tend to drive the crime debate because they have access to the means to do so. They are more likely to be consistent voters and vocal activists, and to demand attention from their elected officials on such issues, while poorer citizens are more preoccupied with individual economic survival. In the Joint Center survey, for example, all black voters identified jobs and the economy as the No. 1 concern, but poorer respondents were even more firm about it.

Messrs. Fyfe and Bositis also cite the ambivalent relationship that has long existed between law-enforcement officials and many black communities, whose residents often complain they are targeted for harassment even as they complain of being underserved by police.

And Mr. Bositis also suggests that many black voters have concluded that the government's repeated "wars" on crime don't work or that they produce alarming results—such as high rates of incarceration of black men—so they are more interested in government efforts on things such as creating jobs.

Television vs. Real-Life Violence

Television may also serve to exaggerate the fears of suburbanites by its frequent portrayal of crime. "Violence on television is vastly exaggerated compared to real life and has a totally different demography," says George Gerbner, a professor of communications at the University of Pennsylvania, who has collected more than 20 years of research into television and movie violence.

Mr. Gerbner says that, in all networks combined, there are an average of six to eight acts of violence per hour in prime time, and an average of two murders each night. More than half of all major characters in network prime-time shows get involved in some violence every week.

Mr. Gerbner theorizes that this is important not because television violence stimulates real-life violence—he says there's no proof of that—but because it encourages "feelings of insecurity, dependence and fear" in heavy viewers of television who don't have much direct experience with crime. In contrast, he contends, such portrayals of violence have little impact on inner-city residents, who have enough experience with real-life crime to separate reality from fantasy.

Suburban Fear of Crime

A visit to Wilmington and its suburbs shows just how deeply misperceptions about crime run. In the suburbs of New Castle County [Del.], which includes the high-income "Chateau Country" that is home to several du Pont heirs as well as the city's top business executives, the biggest crime increases have not been in violent crime, but in auto theft. Compared with city residents, those in New Castle County "are probably very, very secure," says [Col.] Thomas Gordon, the county's chief of police. But, he adds, "they are living in fear of crime." And perception of crime, he adds, "is more important in some cases than crime itself."

Melissa Eissner, who is Craig Stabler's fiancée, lives in New Castle County. She has never personally experienced crime, although she knows of a neighbor who was murdered by a boyfriend. Still, crime, she says, "is an issue. Being a girl on my own I have taken care of that." She was careful to select an apartment in a high-security building with a guard, and always uses her door locks. "When you're younger you don't really think about what can happen to you," she says, "but now that I'm on my own, I really try to be more careful," especially since she believes that women are far more likely to be victims of crime than men.

A handful of burglaries left Ms. Eissner's neighbors in the nearby Chateau Country in an uproar, with heavy demands for police action. No one was hurt, but five burglaries resulted in an average loss of $44,000. Col. Gordon decided to add a police substation to an area known as Westover Hills. While some might call that an overreaction, Col. Gordon believes it is necessary. "What happens in these areas like the county is they're going to private security," he explains. "I think that's very dangerous." A reliance on private security tears at the social fabric, he says, and heightens public perception of an unequal justice system. To prevent that, he wants to take actions that will reduce fear—even if it isn't clear that those actions will actually reduce crime.

Col. Gordon has also begun doing things like using his new police recruits to take door-to-door neighborhood surveys. Each month, his sergeants call randomly selected residents who have come in contact with the police for any reason—even those who have been arrested—to see whether they feel they were fairly treated. And he has substantially increased foot patrols, believing they allow officers and residents to get to know each other. "What you have is a lot more participation, and that makes people feel safe," he says. "It's important to reduce fear, because fear is related to quality of life."

The Most Important Police Role

Many crime experts agree. Lynn Curtis, executive director of the Eisenhower Foundation, a Washington research organization on crime and urban problems, says that even in depressed areas, the most important police role is "reducing fear."

Adds Guy Sapp, chief of the Wilmington police: "It's funny. Some of the things that are analytically least effective in combating crime are the most popular with the public, things like mounted patrols and walking patrols. People feel safer, I guess."

East Wilmington, a depressed area just outside downtown Wilmington, shows what can happen when that fear is not calmed: At some point, people become far too sanguine about crime. Psychologist Alvin Turner, who counsels young offenders as well as drug and alcohol abusers and their families, says many ghetto youths have "learned as part of their development to not respond to fear."

Dr. Turner says that despite the much higher rate of crime in the predominately black and lower-income neighborhoods where he practices, compared to the university areas where he teaches, "I hear white people talking about [crime as an issue]. I don't hear black people talking about it. It's almost a non-issue for us."

Hasan Carter, 29 and unemployed, has been robbed twice in recent years. In one case he was beaten so badly that he suffered broken ribs. He never reported the incidents.

"What would I say?" Mr. Carter asks, since he says the first time it happened he was attacked by drug dealers whom he had tried to rob earlier. The second time he was held up in a bathroom at a concert. Mr. Carter says he isn't involved in crime now and doesn't carry a weapon, but he insists he isn't afraid to walk the streets of his East Wilmington neighborhood. "It's going to happen to every black male, black female," he explains with a shrug.

New Castle County Police Maj. Sherry Sczubelek says "you have to re-educate people it's not OK" to be a victim of crime. "You can go to a high-crime area and they don't think it's that bad of an area."

Not all inner-city residents deny their fear. Waiting at a bus stop with her two small children, 22-year-old Shatana Richards says crime in her neighborhood is "bad. Nothing ever happened to me in particular but I have two friends over the past couple of years that's been killed. A lot of kids are getting guns." Nevertheless, she doesn't believe there is much to be done about it—except, she says, "move."

"The best way to reduce racism real or imagined is to reduce the black crime rate."

Fear of Black Crime Is Justified

James Q. Wilson

On March 3, 1991, four Los Angeles Police Department officers were videotaped beating Rodney King. On April 29, 1992, the four officers were acquitted of eleven of the twelve indictments brought against them; a weekend of rioting, looting, and burning followed in Los Angeles. In the following viewpoint, first published shortly after the rioting, James Q. Wilson argues that fear of black men is a legitimate response to fears of crime; to reduce this apparent racism, black men should reduce their criminal conduct. Wilson is the Collins Professor of Management at the University of California, Los Angeles, and is the author of *The Moral Sense*.

As you read, consider the following questions:

1. What do you think Wilson means when he says that certain "expectations now govern what we say" and do?
2. What is the relationship, according to Wilson, between fear and police brutality?
3. According to the author, how is fear sustained by ignorance? What does he mean by ignorance?

James Q. Wilson, "To Prevent Riots, Reduce Black Crime," *The Wall Street Journal*, May 6, 1992. Reprinted by permission of *The Wall Street Journal* ©1992 Dow Jones & Company, Inc. All rights reserved.

Sometimes understanding causes doesn't help in finding solutions. There is no doubt that black rage at white racism brought scores of blacks onto the streets of Los Angeles after the four police officers were acquitted [in April 1992] of illegally beating Rodney King. From this some will conclude that if we are to improve the police, reduce the anger and prevent more riots, we must end racism. That conclusion, while not entirely wrong, is misleading and, worse, futile.

In 1965, when riots erupted in Watts [a neighborhood in Los Angeles], racism by any measure was greater than it is today. Then, most whites knew no blacks and, whether they knew them or not, would speak of them in often contemptuous stereotypes. It was almost inconceivable that whites would vote for black candidates or take jobs in places with many black workers. Blacks bold enough to move into white neighborhoods were often met with organized resistance. Racial disturbances almost invariably consisted of whites assaulting blacks.

Today, there is far more contact between the races. Every survey of opinion has shown a sharp decline in racist sentiments among whites. Though it may be objected that these polls only measure what people believe others expect them to say, it is remarkable that these expectations now govern what we say and even what we do.

It Is Not Racism, But Fear

But if racist thinking has declined, why are relations between the races so bad? Why has Los Angeles, like many other cities, become more segregated residentially today than it was in 1965? Why do so many whites who cannot be called racists in any fair meaning of the word so often treat blacks warily or react to their proposals with neglect or unease?

Fear. Whites are afraid of young black males (and of young Latino males). It is not racism that keeps whites from exploring black neighborhoods, it is fear. It is not racism that makes whites uneasy about blacks moving into their neighborhoods, it is fear. It is not racism that leads white parents to pull their children out of schools with many black students, it is fear. Fear of crime, of drugs, of gangs, of violence.

The fear is not confined to whites; many black women fear black men as well, and their fear is doubly corrosive because they have fewer avenues of escape and less reason to think the police will help them than do white women.

There was fear in 1965, too, but it was more mythic than real. The rate of violent crime was one-third of what it is now, gangs were armed with zip-guns and not Uzis, heroin (a sedative) rather than crack (a stimulant) was the drug of choice, and society faced far fewer legal or political constraints in directing state power against domestic threats.

What the four officers did in subduing Rodney King was, in my view, wrong. They should be punished; in fact, they were punished; the rookie was summarily dismissed and the three veterans were relieved of duty without pay, pending the outcome of a Board of Rights hearing. Whether what they did was illegal beyond a reasonable doubt is unclear. The racist bigotry directed at the Ventura County jurors by people who did not sit through the trial or read the transcript is appalling. Are those people who explain an unpopular verdict by referring to the race of the jurors prepared to use the same explanation when black jurors vote to acquit a black defendant or convict a white one?

Nothing More Painful

There is nothing more painful for me at this stage in my life than to walk down the street and hear footsteps and start to think about robbery and then look around and see it's somebody white and feel relieved. How humiliating.

The Rev. Jesse Jackson, in a Chicago speech decrying black-on-black crime, November 27, 1993.

It is not to excuse the officers to suggest that fear explains much, though not all, of the tensions that exist between the police and the citizenry. I have been riding around in squad cars with police officers since the early 1960s. The average big-city cop is much less prejudiced today than he was three decades ago, but he (and now she) is more fearful. When police stop a young black male they expect defiance rather than submission; when they enter a housing project, they expect taunts, not thanks; when they encounter a gang, they fear a fusillade of bullets instead of just sullen complaints.

Fear can produce behavior that is indistinguishable from racism. Fear, like racism, can make an officer seek to intimidate a suspect or use excessive force to subdue him; fear creates tensions that lead to the telling of jokes identical to those told by people motivated by pure racism. Responding to the fears of others, police officers are more likely to stop and question black men than white men; statistically the former are more suspect than the latter, with the result that innocent black men are more likely to be stopped than innocent white men.

The Problem Runs Deeper than Poverty

Fear is sustained by ignorance. We don't know how to reduce the crime and violence, or break up the gangs. The Great Society produced some good things: Head Start, the Job Corps, various civil-rights laws. But it did nothing about crime, and especially nothing about the predatory behavior of young males who inseminate women, abandon children, join gangs, deal drugs and shoot innocent people.

We can, of course, try more of the same—more Head Start, more Job Corps. That is probably desirable. We can add to the mix a more community-oriented style of policing. That is happening in Los Angeles and it will continue under the new chief [Willie Williams]. We can try to think of ways of bringing jobs to unemployed people and training those people for the jobs that exist, but the only big new idea around for doing that—Enterprise Zones [a proposal to allow tax deductions for businesses located in designated inner-city areas]—is at best a question mark. I can't imagine many new factories will open in South Central Los Angeles even if their owners are given tax breaks. The owners will look at what happened to the Korean merchants who started businesses in black areas without tax breaks: They were bombed, burned and looted.

We can provide cheaper transportation so that blacks can travel to job sites, but I doubt that transportation is the key problem. Every day there are thousands of Latino men waiting on street corners 20 miles or more from where they live, hoping to be hired as day laborers by contractors and home owners. Many are hired. They all get to these street corners by bus. There are no black men on these corners.

Reducing poverty, ending racism, creating jobs and improving schooling are all good things to do, whether or not they prevent crimes or riots. But the problem our big cities face runs far deeper. There is an underclass, and though many races are found among it and it accounts for only a small fraction of the black community, it is perceived to be a black phenomenon. So long as black men commit violent crimes at a rate that is six to eight times higher than the rate found among whites, that perception will persist. And as long as that perception persists, fear will heighten our anxieties and erode our civility.

The Riot Was Not a Protest

As we obtain a greater perspective on the events in Los Angeles, it will become clear that much of what happened had nothing to do with protest and everything to do with greed, high times and the settling of old scores. Of the 5,438 people arrested by the LAPD from midnight April 30 [1992] until the morning of May 4, 568 were white, hardly any of whom, it seems safe to say, were social activists protesting injustice. Hispanic arrestees outnumbered black ones, 2,764 to 2,022. Anger triggered the riots, but once the mechanisms of social control had been overpowered, rapacity took over.

And consider who was not arrested. No minority in California has been treated worse than Japanese-Americans. They were excluded from juries, prevented from voting, and in 1942 torn from their homes and confined for many years in relocation camps in the desert. They were the objects of racism pure and simple. Of the 5,438 people arrested, none was Japanese. One was Chinese. Three were Filipinos.

The best way to reduce racism real or imagined is to reduce the black crime rate to equal the white crime rate, which, God knows, is high enough. (I assume no one favors the alternative, namely, raising the white crime rate to equal that of blacks.)

To do this may require changing, in far more profound and all-encompassing ways than anything we now contemplate, the lives of black infants, especially boys, from birth to age eight or ten. We have not yet begun to think seriously about this, and perhaps never will. Those who must think about it the hardest are those decent black people who must accept, and ideally should develop and run, whatever is done.

"The unwillingness to confront its racial component head-on has warped and stymied the political debate over crime."

Fear of Black Crime Has Racist Undertones

Marcus Mabry, Evan Thomas, and Scott Minerbrook

In the rioting that followed the April 1992 acquittal of four Los Angeles Police Department officers for the beating of Rodney King, 54 people were killed, 2,383 were injured, and some 5,200 buildings were destroyed or damaged. In Part I of the following viewpoint, written shortly after the riots, Marcus Mabry and Evan Thomas argue that racial feelings underlie Americans' fear of crime. In Part II, Scott Minerbrook argues that fear of black men has produced inequity in the criminal justice system. Mabry is an editor of *Newsweek*; Thomas is assistant managing editor of *Newsweek*'s Washington bureau. Minerbrook is the New York correspondent for *U.S. News & World Report*.

As you read, consider the following questions:

1. According to Mabry and Thomas, what unspoken fear is behind the "conspiracy of silence"?
2. For Mabry and Thomas, how can fear bridge the gap between blacks and whites?
3. According to Minerbrook, what is the message blacks heard when the jury "fully approved the police conduct"?

I

The fear of young black men. It's not something most people like to talk about, at least not in public. Crime routinely shows up in public-opinion polls as one of the two or three issues that voters worry about most. But left unspoken is the fact that, for most Americans, crime has a black face.

The motives for this conspiracy of silence are by no means all bad in a society that is already split along color lines. But the unwillingness to confront its racial component head-on has warped and stymied the political debate over crime. For years liberal Democrats were afraid to talk tough on crime, lest they be branded racist. As a result, Democratic leaders were accused of coddling criminals. Republican politicians have pandered to white fear, but they have been deliberately coy about it, using code words and thinly veiled messages like the GOP's [Republican] infamous Willie Horton ad in 1988 [a presidential campaign ad which featured a black man who killed two whites while in a prison furlough program].

White Middle-Class Fear

The political gamesmanship masks a fear that is real and deep. To many TV viewers, the scariest image of the [April 1992] L.A. riots was the live film of white truckdriver Reginald Denny being dragged from his truck by black youths and repeatedly bashed on the head. It brought home a primitive nightmare of many middle-class whites, that their cars and homes and families could be invaded by marauding black men.

The fear is greatest of inner-city youths, in high tops and gang colors. But all blacks are tarred to some degree. Legal experts argue that this may account for higher conviction rates and harsher sentences for black defendants. In 1991 a University of Chicago study found that 56 percent of whites believed that blacks were "prone to violence." In focus groups conducted by business consultants, whites characterize a black man speaking forcefully at a meeting as "hostile" or "threatening," while they see a white man behaving the same way as "aggressive" or "determined." Black men are familiar with the chill. Women hug their pocketbooks closer when a black man passes by; taxicabs routinely refuse to pick up black men, even well-dressed ones. Hollywood is not above using white fear to titillate. In [the movie] *Boyz N the Hood*, director John Singleton intended to portray real life in the ghetto, but the aim of film distributors may have been to attract white audiences by giving them a good scare.

Black Fears

To be sure, there is a basis for the fear of black inner-city youth. They commit a vastly disproportionate amount of crime.

Nationally, about a quarter of all African-American males between 20 and 29 are in jail, on parole or on probation. But the fear can cut the other way as well. The most law-abiding black teenager fears the police, and often with reason.

Fear and Danger for Black Men

People are afraid of my husband. He's six-four, 240 pounds. Let's put it this way: The last time he had a flat, he walked seven miles home from work. You wouldn't stop to give him a ride. And when he stops to help you with your flat, you're terrified. He's black. He's big. People cross the street, clutch their purses, avert their eyes.

He works crazy shifts at his job. Sometimes he leaves before sunrise, and then he stops to get gas in the dark. A nervous attendant steps on the silent alarm and seven police cars surround him, gun barrels aimed. I've been with him, seen his hands pressed against a brick wall, the circle of metal close to his ear. Walking down the wrong street is dangerous. A malfunctioning turn signal is dangerous. He never speeds.

Susan Straight, *Utne Reader*, March/April 1993.

And, of course, most of the victims of black crime are black. African-Americans are 70 percent more likely than whites to be victims of violent crimes. . . . Few whites have to worry about drive-by shootings on their block. In fact, contrary to conventional wisdom—and the paranoia of some white homeowners—suburban crime has declined slightly since the early 1970s. In 1973 almost 3 percent of suburbanites suffered a violent crime; in 1988 (the last year for which statistics are available) just over 2.5 percent were victimized.

Law-and-order sentiments run just as strong, if not stronger, in black neighborhoods as they do in white ones. In Chicago in 1991, white civil libertarians wrung their hands when the city's public-housing authority conducted random police sweeps to drive out gang members and drug dealers who had taken over vacant apartments. The projects' tenants, on the other hand, cheered loudly.

Playing on Paranoia

But the realities of race and crime can be easily obscured in an atmosphere where only the extremists speak out. David Duke, a Klansman with a face-lift, became a national figure by playing on white paranoia [during his unsuccessful 1992 campaign to become Louisiana's governor]. Black charlatans like the

Rev. Al Sharpton attract TV cameras wherever they go by posing as victims of a vast white conspiracy to exterminate the black race. It's not surprising that some African-Americans, even middle-class blacks, believe that the white power structure has cooked up something called The Plan to wipe out black men with drugs and AIDS.

Fear will only worsen matters if it drives whites deeper into the suburbs. But fear may be the only way to get whites to pay attention to the wretched conditions of the inner city. In an age of "compassion fatigue," white voters aren't likely to want to do much about the plight of poor blacks unless they feel personally threatened. Denying that fear exists only leaves the field open to exploitation by politicians and extremists. It may seem ironic to suggest that fear could help bridge the gap between the races. But it could—if only we admit it.

II

For months, the 81-second burst of official violence on the body of Rodney King seemed the essence of tragic racial drama. There was a *frisson* of moral outrage and bad conscience. Even President [George] Bush was briefly sickened by what he had seen. But suddenly, with [the April 1992] acquittal of the four officers charged in the attack, the entire event took on a meaning more frightening to many Americans than the event itself: What had seemed a quasi lynching, the official verdict declared, was really not criminal behavior at all. As one juror put it: "Not much damage was done." King's offense, apparently, was that even in the prone position, while protecting his head, he might attack the officers who nearly killed him.

The key question is this: How is it possible for a jury of comfortable, concerned, educated folks from the suburbs, who represent all that is supposedly decent and right about America, to deny the horror of a beating they witnessed with their own eyes? There are two ways to answer the question. The first is that the verdict was confirmation of the fall from grace black people have suffered in recent years. Blacks have lost the moral high ground. They are no longer the brave soldiers of conscience. In the span of a single generation, young black men like Rodney King have come to be seen as violent, predatory, out of control.

Few white people will admit in public to this reversal of perspective, but many seem haunted by black people in general and by black young men in particular, often terrified of "danger" that exists only in the imagination. As riots exploded after the verdict, at least one of the jurors in Simi Valley said: "These people would have rioted anyway." They were, she suggested, only waiting for an excuse. In this environment of racial intolerance, it is a short leap to the idea that the rights of a black man like King are secondary to what he symbolizes—a danger to white society that must be suppressed. Few recalled Martin Luther King Jr.'s great summary of violence: "A riot," he said, "is the language of the unheard."

Police Serve White Fear First

The second answer about this verdict is more disturbing and, to black people, more obvious. There is a growing perception among blacks I know that the jury acquitted the officers because they were *not revolted* by the police beating, described as "careful police work" by one of the defense attorneys. This jury, in fact, fully approved the police conduct. This is the message black people have heard.

It doesn't help that some young black men of south-central L.A. reacted by playing to stereotype and scorching their own communities. Part of the tragedy of the King verdict is that it seems to set back so much of the stubborn work of a generation of hard-won civil-rights victories. A crucial lesson has been lost on black youth: Revolt rarely travels to places like Simi Valley. Many black neighborhoods have never recovered from the 1965 [Watts] riots. Tragically, another lesson hasn't been lost at all: The main reforms of the past generation—changes that gave Los Angeles a black mayor, a black police chief, much greater black representation on the police force and a host of minority legislative leaders—still were not enough to block the King beating or the acquittal.

The Rhetorical Wink

There are certain code words that allow you never to have to say *race*, but everybody knows that's what you mean—and *crime* is one of those rhetorical winks. So when we talk about locking up more and more people, what we're really talking about is locking up more and more black men. That's what everyone means, . . . and you can see it happening all over the country. You're not supposed to mention race, of course, and if you do you're being divisive, but that's what it's all about.

Jerome Miller, quoted in *The Humanist*, January/February 1994.

In the end, this outcome confirms the worst fears of black men. The police are not your friends. Always, it is the fear of white people that they serve first. They stop you when you ride through white neighborhoods, including the one you may live in. They respond to the calls of clerks if you object to not being buzzed into a store. They, or their proxies in a private security force, might be the ones to show up at your tableside in a nice restaurant if you demand to see the maitre d' because your service has not been good.

So, the polarization grows. The people of Simi Valley may truly believe justice has been served. By contrast, more blacks now believe that equal justice doesn't exist. Such disparities will not make American life safer for anyone. The verdict won't help those white officers who courageously came forward to testify against their fellows. It won't help black and white relations in corporate suites, in schools, in courts. And the officers who beat King might have won at their trial, but they have helped elevate King to a moral symbol with power great enough to inspire throngs to turn parts of America's urban landscape into rubble.

Periodical Bibliography

The following articles have been selected to supplement the diverse views presented in this chapter.

Russell Baker	"All Shook Up," *The Wall Street Journal*, November 9, 1993.
Simon Barber	"Crime, Fear, and Panaceas," *World Press Review*, January 1994.
Patricia Chisholm	"Crime: The Fear Index," *Maclean's*, January 4, 1993.
Charles S. Clark	"Suburban Crime," *CQ Researcher*, September 3, 1993. Available from 1414 22nd St. NW, Washington, DC 20037.
Sara Collins	"Cost of Crime: $674 Billion," *U.S. News & World Report*, January 17, 1994.
Charles Colson	"Crime, Morality, and the Media Elites," *Christianity Today*, August 16, 1993.
Stanley Crouch	"Our Color but Not Our Kind," *The Wall Street Journal*, November 17, 1993.
Barbara Dority	"Anti-Crime Hysteria," *The Humanist*, January/February 1994.
Alan Farnham	"U.S. Suburbs Are Under Siege," *Fortune*, December 28, 1992.
Jesse Jackson	"Stopping Violence Means Pulling Together," *Liberal Opinion Week*, December 27, 1993. Available from 108 E. Fifth St., Vinton, IA 52349.
Paul Johnson	"Crime: The People Want Revenge," *The Wall Street Journal*, January 4, 1994.
Michael J. Mandel et al.	"The Economics of Crime," *Business Week*, December 13, 1993.
Scott C. Matthew	"The First Civil Right Is Safety," *Lincoln Review*, Fall/Winter 1991-1992.
Daniel Patrick Moynihan	"Toward a New Intolerance," *The Public Interest*, Summer 1993.
Mary Nemeth	"Hot Off the Presses," *Maclean's*, January 24, 1994
Jennifer Reese	"How Crime Pays," *Fortune*, May 31, 1993.

Murray N. Rothbard   "Coping with Street Crime," *Chronicles*, May
                            1992. Available from 934 N. Main St.,
                            Rockford, IL 61103.

Rick Szykowny   "No Justice, No Peace: An Interview with
                            Jerome Miller," *The Humanist*,
                            January/February 1994.

Kenneth T. Walsh   "The Voters' Cry for Help," *U.S. News &*
and Ted Gest   *World Report*, November 15, 1993.

Richard Zoglin   "Manson Family Values," *Time*, March 21,
                            1994.

Mortimer B. Zuckerman   "War on Crime, by the Numbers," *U.S. News
                            & World Report*, January 17, 1994.

For Further Discussion

Chapter 1

1. Peter R. Breggin and Ginger Ross Breggin oppose biological-psychiatric research on the grounds that its findings potentially will lead to abuses. They compare such research to infamous experiments conducted in Nazi Germany. How would James K. Hughes respond to this comparison? What other reasons do the Breggins give for opposing bio-psychiatric research? How would you respond?

2. Post Traumatic Stress Disorder has been used successfully as a criminal defense by battered women who have maimed or killed their abusers. If you were on a jury, would you accept such a defense for a battered woman? Why or why not? Francis Flaherty describes crimes committed by a teenager who grew up in a violent family and neighborhood. Would you accept PTSD as a defense in this case? Why or why not?

3. Carl F. Horowitz argues that crime leads to the failure of the public sector, which in turn perpetuates conditions of poverty. How does Philippe Bourgois describe the relationship between crime, poverty, and the failure of the public sector in East Harlem? How do Horowitz and Bourgois differ?

4. Both Elliott Currie and Myron Magnet argue that American culture nurtures criminals. How does each describe American culture? How does each describe the relationship between rich and poor Americans? In your opinion, which author provides a more accurate picture of American culture? Explain.

Chapter 2

1. While Carl F. Horowitz favors community policing as effective in reducing fear of crime, Nicolas Alexander describes it as a failure in reducing fear of crime. How does each distinguish between reducing crime and reducing fear of crime? What evidence does each present that community policing is a success/failure?

2. Mary Kate Cary argues in favor of mandatory minimum sentencing, while Chi Chi Sileo argues against it. How does each author define the purpose of sentencing, parole, and rehabilitation? What is each author's view of deterrence? Do you believe that mandatory sentencing will deter criminals? Why or why not?

3. Eugene H. Methvin argues that the crime rate has dropped as America has built more prisons. Ted Gest argues that the crime rate has remained unchanged despite the building of more prisons. What statistical proof does each author provide to support his argument? What types of crime does each look at? Do you feel that it is worthwhile spending tax money on prison construction? Explain your answer.

Chapter 3

1. Joshua Horwitz argues that "a well-regulated militia" should be interpreted to mean a "state-regulated militia" and a "well-organized militia." Would Don B. Kates Jr. and Alan J. Lizotte agree with those interpretations? Why or why not? Do you agree with these interpretations? Explain.

2. Dan Peterson argues that proposed gun-control measures should not be passed because they are flawed. The editors of the *Los Angeles Times* support gun control measures despite the flaws. What flaws does each point out in the proposed measures? Would you support these gun control measures? Why or why not?

3. What evidence does Carl T. Bogus offer that gun ownership is dangerous? How would David B. Kopel criticize this evidence? What evidence does Kopel offer that gun ownership provides security? How would Bogus criticize this? Which argument is closer to your own views? Why?

Chapter 4

1. According to James D. Wright and Joseph F. Sheley, juveniles carry guns for self-protection. What solution do Wright and Sheley propose? What solution does Roy Romer propose? Why do juveniles carry guns, in Romer's opinion?

2. The juvenile justice system was based on the idea that juveniles are too young to be fully responsible for their crimes. What is Rita Kramer's view of rehabilitation for juveniles? How would Alex Kotlowitz view the possibility of rehabilitation for juveniles? Do you feel that juveniles are more likely to be rehabilitated than adults? Why or why not?

3. In describing boot camps, Dennis E. Mack states that drill instructors may demand push-ups for any infraction of the rules. What is his view of the benefits of this sort of punishment? What does Frank Bentayou say about the dangers of arbitrary discipline?

Chapter 5

1. Stephen J. Adler and Wade Lambert argue that everyone breaks rules and laws at times. Do you agree with Sen. Daniel Patrick Moynihan that America's moral values are slipping? Do you feel that crime is the most important issue in your life? Explain your answer.

2. According to Michel McQueen, what role do the media play in creating fear of crime? How does Froma Harrop view the media's role? Do you think the media sensationalize crime?

3. What is your personal experience with police? How do you feel about police? Do you feel safer when you see police patrolling your neighborhood? Do you think that police brutality is a more widespread problem than is reported in the news? Why or why not?

Organizations to Contact

The editors have compiled the following list of organizations concerned with the issues debated in this book. The descriptions are derived from materials provided by the organizations. All have publications or information available for interested readers. The list was compiled on the date of publication of the present volume; names, addresses, and phone numbers may change. Be aware that many organizations take several weeks or longer to respond to inquiries, so allow as much time as possible.

American Civil Liberties Union (ACLU)
National Prison Project (NPP)
1875 Connecticut Ave. NW, Suite 410
Washington, DC 20009
(202) 234-4830
Fax (202) 234-4890

Formed in 1972, the project serves as a national resource center and litigates cases to strengthen and protect adult and juvenile offenders' Eighth Amendment rights. It publishes the quarterly *National Prison Project Journal* and the booklets *AIDS in Prisons: The Facts for Inmates and Officers* and *AIDS in Prison Bibliography*.

Campaign for an Effective Crime Policy
918 F St. NW, Suite 501
Washington, DC 20004
(202) 628-1903

Coordinated by the Sentencing Project, the campaign's purpose is to promote information, ideas, discussion, and debate about criminal justice policy and to advance change in sentencing policy toward alternative sentencing. The campaign's core document, available to the public, is *A Call for a Rational Debate on Crime and Punishment*.

Coalition to Stop Gun Violence
100 Maryland Ave. NE
Washington, DC 20002
(202) 544-7190
Fax (202) 544-7213

Formerly the National Coalition to Ban Handguns, the coalition lobbies at the local, state, and federal level to ban the sale of handguns and assault weapons to individuals and litigates cases against firearms makers. Upon request, the coalition sends legislative updates and statistics on gun violence.

Edna McConnell Clark Foundation
250 Park Ave.
New York, NY 10177
(212) 551-9100

Founded in 1974, this philanthropic group supports organizations that work to reduce unnecessary incarceration and to improve conditions in America's jails and prisons. The foundation publishes and distributes the research reports *Americans Behind Bars, Crime and Punishment—The Public's View, Punishing Criminals—The Public's View,* and the book *Overcrowded Time: Why Prisons Are So Crowded and What Can Be Done.*

Educational Fund to End Handgun Violence
Box 72
110 Maryland Ave. NE
Washington, DC 20002
(202) 544-7227

The fund is a nonprofit educational charity dedicated to ending gun violence. It initiates public education campaigns; acts as an information and research source for journalists, legislators, and the general public; provides expert legal assistance to victims and their attorneys; and publishes the newsletter *Firearms Litigation Reporter.*

Families Against Mandatory Minimums (FAMM)
1001 Pennsylvania Ave. NW, Suite 200S
Washington, DC 20005
(202) 457-5790

Founded in 1991, the organization seeks the repeal of laws that impose mandatory minimum sentences for offenses involving firearms and drugs. FAMM publicizes unjust applications of mandatory sentences and offers information on and analysis of mandatory sentences to legislators, the public, and the media. It publishes a biannual newsletter, *FAMM-gram.*

First Freedom Coalition
c/o Shaw, Pittman, Potts & Trowbridge
2300 N St. NW
Washington, DC 20037
(202) 663-8000

Founded by former justice officials of the Bush administration, this nonprofit group advocates and lobbies for reforms of the "revolving-door" criminal justice system that include increased mandatory prison sentences and the building of more prisons. Its publications include *The First Freedom Update* newsletter, intermittent *First Freedom Alerts,* and occasional papers.

Friends Outside National Organization
3031 Tisch Way, Suite 507
San Jose, CA 95128
(408) 985-8807
Fax (408) 985-8839

This nonprofit organization is dedicated to breaking the cycle of crime and delinquency by addressing the factors that cause violence—child and spousal abuse, dependency on the welfare system, and criminal lifestyle. It is particularly concerned with the high recidivism rate of ex-convicts and provides pre- and post-release assistance for offenders.

Handgun Control, Inc.
1225 Eye St. NW, Suite 1100
Washington, DC 20005
(202) 898-0792

A public citizens' lobby working for federal regulation of the manufacture, sale, and civilian possession of handguns and automatic weapons, the organization successfully promoted passage of the Brady Law, which mandates a five-day waiting period for the purchase of handguns. The lobby publishes the quarterly *Handgun Control—Washington Report* and the book *Guns Don't Die—People Do*, as well as legislative reports and pamphlets.

Independence Institute
14142 Denver West Pkwy., Suite 101
Golden, CO 80401
(303) 279-6536

The Independence Institute is a pro-free-market, pro-bill-of-rights think tank that supports gun ownership as a civil liberty. Its publications include books and booklets opposing gun control, such as *Children and Guns: Sensible Solutions*; *The Assault Weapon Panic: "Political Correctness" Takes Aim at the Constitution*; and *The Samurai, the Mountie and the Cowboy*.

National Center on Institutions and Alternatives (NCIA)
635 Slaters Ln., Suite G-100
Alexandria, VA 22314
(703) 684-0373

A nonprofit agency that promotes alternatives to prisons and mental hospitals, the center prepares alternative sentencing proposals in individual cases and prepares mitigative studies in death penalty cases. It also operates clinical programs for violent offenders and sex offenders. The NCIA publishes *Hobbling a Generation: Young African-American Males in Washington, D.C.'s Criminal Justice System*.

National Council on Crime and Delinquency (NCCD)
685 Market St., Suite 620
San Francisco, CA 94105
(415) 896-6223
Fax (415) 896-5109

The NCCD supports crime prevention programs aimed at strengthening families, reducing school dropout rates, and increasing employment opportunities for low-income youth. It publishes the quarterly journal *Crime and Delinquency*, the quarterly *FOCUS Research Briefs*, and semiannual policy papers, including *Reducing Crime in America: A Pragmatic Approach*.

National Crime Prevention Council (NCPC)
1700 K St. NW, 2nd Fl.
Washington, DC 20006-3817
(202) 466-6272

A private nonprofit organization, the mission of the NCPC is to prevent crime by helping individuals learn to reduce their risk of being a crime victim and by building crime-resistant communities. The council organizes the Take A Bite Out of Crime campaign and distributes crime prevention booklets, videos, and program kits.

National Institute of Justice (NIJ)
National Criminal Justice Reference Service (NCJRS)
Box 6000
Rockville, MD 20850
(301) 251-5500
(800) 851-3420

A component of the Office of Justice Programs of the U.S. Department of Justice, the NIJ supports research on crime, criminal behavior, and crime prevention. The National Criminal Justice Reference Service acts as a clearinghouse for criminal justice information for researchers and other interested individuals. It publishes and distributes reports and books, including reports of the Bureau of Justice Statistics.

National Rifle Association of America (NRA)
1600 Rhode Island Ave. NW
Washington, DC 20036
(202) 828-6000

An organization of hunters, gun collectors, and others interested in firearms, the NRA promotes hunting and firearm safety. The NRA's Political Victory Fund finances lobbying efforts against gun control and against crime at the local, state, and federal levels. The NRA publishes *American Rifleman* and *American Hunter* monthly.

Office of Juvenile Justice and Delinquency Prevention (OJJDP)
633 Indiana Ave. NW
Washington, DC 20531
(202) 307-0751

As the primary federal agency charged with monitoring and improving the juvenile justice system, OJJDP develops and funds programs on juvenile justice. Through its National Youth Gang Clearinghouse, OJJDP investigates and focuses public attention on the problem of youth gangs. The office publishes the *OJJDP Juvenile Justice Bulletin* periodically.

Second Amendment Foundation
12500 NE Tenth Pl.
Bellevue, WA 98005
(206) 454-7012

The foundation is dedicated to promoting a better understanding of "our Constitutional heritage to privately own and possess firearms." It maintains biographical archives and a library, compiles statistics, and publishes the *Journal on Firearms and Public Policy* periodically, the *Second Amendment Reporter* quarterly, *Women and Guns* monthly, and other monographs and pamphlets.

The Sentencing Project
918 F St. NW, Suite 501
Washington, DC 20004
(202) 628-0871
Fax (202) 628-1091

Established in 1986, the project promotes alternatives to incarceration and advocates programs to improve sentencing practices, particularly for indigent defendants. The project publishes briefing papers, technical assistance reports, major research reports, and policy reports. Its policy reports include *Young Black Men and the Criminal Justice System: A Growing National Problem* and *Americans Behind Bars*.

Violence Policy Center
1300 N St. NW
Washington, DC 20005
(202) 783-4071

The center is an educational foundation that conducts research on firearms violence, works to educate the public concerning the dangers of guns, and supports gun-control measures. The center's publications include *Cease Fire: A Comprehensive Strategy to Reduce Firearms Violence*.

Bibliography of Books

Jay S. Albanese — *Dealing with Delinquency: The Future of Juvenile Justice.* Chicago: Nelson-Hall, 1993.

Jay S. Albanese and Robert D. Pursley — *Crime in America: Some Existing and Emerging Issues.* Englewood Cliffs, NJ: Regents/Prentice-Hall, 1993.

James Austin and John Irwin — *Does Imprisonment Reduce Crime? A Critique of "Voodoo" Criminology.* San Francisco: National Council on Crime and Delinquency, 1993.

Gary S. Becker and William M. Landes — *Essays in the Economics of Crime and Punishment.* New York: Columbia University Press, 1974.

William J. Bennett — *The De-valuing of America: The Fight for Our Culture and Our Children.* New York: Summit Books, 1992.

Thomas J. Bernard — *The Cycle of Juvenile Justice.* New York: Oxford University Press, 1992.

George Cadwalader — *Castaways: The Penikese Island Experiment.* Chelsea, VT: Chelsea Green Publishing Co., 1988.

Dean J. Champion and G. Larry Mays — *Transferring Juveniles to Criminal Courts: Trends and Implications for Criminal Justice.* New York: Praeger, 1991.

Charles W. Colson — *Changed Hearts: The Solution to America's Crime Problem.* Washington, DC: Prison Fellowship Ministries, 1989.

Elliott Currie — *Reckoning: Drugs, Cities, and the American Future.* New York: Hill and Wang, 1993.

Deborah W. Denno — *Biology and Violence: From Birth to Adulthood.* Cambridge: Cambridge University Press, 1990.

Charles Derber — *Money, Murder, and the American Dream: Wilding from Wall Street to Main Street.* Boston: Faber and Faber, 1992.

John J. DiIulio Jr. — *No Escape: The Future of American Corrections.* New York: Basic Books, 1991.

John Doble — *Crime and Punishment: The Public's View.* New York: Public Agenda Foundation, 1987.

Charles Patrick Ewing — *Kids Who Kill.* Lexington, MA: Lexington Books, 1990.

Barry C. Feld — *Justice for Children: The Right to Counsel and the Juvenile Courts*. Boston: Northeastern University Press, 1993.

Mark S. Fleisher — *Warehousing Violence*. London: Sage Publications, 1989.

Ronald Barri Flowers — *The Adolescent Criminal: An Examination of Today's Juvenile Offender*. Jefferson, NC: McFarland & Co., 1990.

Ronald Barri Flowers — *Minorities and Criminality*. New York: Greenwood Press, 1988.

Diana R. Gordon — *The Justice Juggernaut: Fighting Street Crime, Controlling Citizens*. New Brunswick, NJ: Rutgers University Press, 1990.

David F. Greenberg — *Crime and Capitalism: Readings in Marxist Criminology*. Philadelphia: Temple University Press, 1993.

Stephen P. Halbrook — *That Every Man Be Armed*. Oakland, CA: Independent Institute, 1984.

Adele V. Harrell and George E. Peterson — *Drugs, Crime, and Social Isolation: Barriers to Urban Opportunity*. Washington, DC: Urban Institute Press, 1992.

Donald D. Hook — *Gun Control: The Continuing Debate*. Bellevue, WA: Second Amendment Foundation, 1992.

Gary Kleck — *Point Blank: Guns and Violence in America*. New York: A. de Gruyter, 1991.

Rita Kramer — *At a Tender Age*. New York: Henry Holt & Co., 1988.

Barry Krisberg and James F. Austin — *Reinventing Juvenile Justice*. Newbury Park, CA: Sage Publications, 1993.

Marc Mauer — *Young Black Men and the Criminal Justice System: A Growing National Problem*. Washington, DC: The Sentencing Project, 1990.

Jerome G. Miller — *Hobbling a Generation: Young African-American Males in Washington, D.C.'s Criminal Justice System*. Washington, DC: National Center on Institutions and Alternatives, 1992.

Jerome G. Miller — *Last One over the Wall: The Massachusetts Experiment in Closing Reform Schools*. Columbus: Ohio State University Press, 1991.

Lee Nisbet — *The Gun Control Debate: You Decide*. Buffalo: Prometheus Books, 1990.

Albert Reiss Jr. and Jeffrey A. Roth, eds.
Understanding and Preventing Violence. Washington, DC: National Academy Press, 1993.

Peter Reuter et al.
Money from Crime: A Study of the Economics of Drug Dealing in Washington, D.C. Washington, DC: RAND Corp., June 1990.

Irving A. Spergel, Ronald L. Chance, and G. David Curry
National Youth Gang Suppression and Intervention Program. Washington, DC: U.S. Department of Justice, Office of Juvenile Justice and Delinquency Prevention, 1991.

Josh Sugarmann
National Rifle Association: Money, Firepower and Fear. Washington, DC: National Press Books, 1992.

Michael Tonry, ed.
Crime and Justice: An Annual Review of Research series. Chicago: University of Chicago Press, c1979- .

Curtis R. Tucker Jr.
To Rebuild Is Not Enough: Final Report and Recommendations of the (California) Assembly Special Committee on the Los Angeles Crisis. Sacramento, CA: Assembly Publications Office, 1992.

U.S. Department of Health and Human Services
Youth Homicide: A Public Health Issue. Washington, DC: Government Printing Office, 1990.

James Q. Wilson and Richard J. Herrnstein
Crime and Human Nature. New York: Simon and Schuster, 1985.

Franklin E. Zimring
Gun Control. Washington, DC: U.S. Department of Justice, National Institute of Justice, 1988.

Index

281

282